CONTESTING PRECARITY IN JAPAN

CONTESTING PRECARITY IN JAPAN

The Rise of Nonregular Workers and the New Policy Dissensus

Saori Shibata

ILR PRESS

AN IMPRINT OF CORNELL UNIVERSITY PRESS   ITHACA AND LONDON

First published 2020 by Cornell University Press

Library of Congress Cataloging-in-Publication Data

Names: Shibata, Saori, 1973– author.
Title: Contesting precarity in Japan : the rise of nonregular workers and the new policy dissensus / Saori Shibata.
Description: Ithaca [New York] : ILR Press, an imprint of Cornell University Press, 2020. | Includes bibliographical references and index.
Identifiers: LCCN 2019044583 (print) | LCCN 2019044584 (ebook) | ISBN 9781501749926 (hardcover) | ISBN 9781501749933 (paperback) | ISBN 9781501749957 (pdf) | ISBN 9781501749940 (epub)
Subjects: LCSH: Precarious employment—Social aspects—Japan. | Labor policy—Japan. | Labor market—Japan. | Neoliberalism—Japan. | Japan—Economic conditions.
Classification: LCC HD5858.J3 S55 2020 (print) | LCC HD5858.J3 (ebook) | DDC 331.25/72—dc23
LC record available at https://lccn.loc.gov/2019044583
LC ebook record available at https://lccn.loc.gov/2019044584

Contents

Acknowledgments

This book benefited from the guidance, comments, support, and suggestions of many people throughout the research and writing process. Part of the research was conducted at the University of Birmingham, where Peter Burnham provided me with important advice, feedback, and oversight. Others who read and commented on the text as it developed, and to whom I am grateful, include Werner Bonefeld, Peter Kerr, Julie Gilson, Mark Beeson, Juanita Elias, Andre Broome, Len Seabrooke, Ben Clift, Kasia Cwiertka, Lindsay Black, Aya Ezawa, and Guita Winkel. Fran Benson provided important editorial encouragement as the book traveled through the publication process. I also thank the union and NPO activists who kindly agreed to be interviewed for this research, and who continue to impress me with their ongoing efforts to fight for precarious workers. I especially thank David Bailey, without whose support this book would not have been published. Finally, I also would like to thank my children, Itsuki and Masaki, who continue to make my life exciting—and who also instructed me to acknowledge them!

Abbreviations

ACW2	Action Center for Working Women
DPJ	Democratic Party of Japan
GDP	gross domestic product
HTS	Hankyu Travel Support
JA	Japan Agricultural Cooperative
JA-Zenchu	Central Union of Agricultural Cooperatives
LDP	Liberal Democratic Party of Japan
MHLW	Ministry of Health, Labor, and Welfare
NEETs	Not in education, employed, or in training
NPO	Nonprofit organization
SCAP	Supreme Commander for the Allied Powers
SME	Small and medium-size enterprise
TMG	Tokyo Metropolitan Government
TPP	Trans-Pacific Partnership
VoC	*Varieties of Capitalism*
WDL	Worker Dispatch Law
WUT	Women's Union Tokyo

CONTESTING PRECARITY IN JAPAN

Introduction

Japan, the third-largest economy in the world, appears increasingly unable to generate a sustainable standard of living for its population. Low pay, job insecurity, sluggish economic growth, unaffordable housing, excessive working hours, rising public debt, labor shortages, and declining fertility have each become a stubbornly persistent problem facing Japanese society. As a result, they have grown in prominence in the national debate, routinely troubling the country's politicians, media, and the wider public. This lingering malaise was initially summed up by the notion of a lost decade, which subsequently became two lost decades and is now nearing the end of a third lost decade (Botman, Danninger, and Schiff 2015). This contrasts starkly with the situation in the 1980s, when the Japanese model of capitalism—with its commitment to lifetime employment, stable industrial relations, and innovations such as Toyotism and just-in-time production—was widely considered to be the new face of high-growth, high-technology capitalism, generated by an inclusive approach to labor relations. The Japanese model had been widely considered a miracle of economic development, allowing Japan to recover from the defeat and devastation of the Second World War to become a leading economic power with the potential to rival the United States as the next global economic hegemon (for characteristic portrayals of Japan's economic miracle, see Friedman 1988; Johnson 1982; on Japan's anticipated hegemonic potential, see especially Arrighi 1994). The transition between these two remarkably different contexts is typically dated to the bursting of Japan's economic bubble in 1991.

This book traces the post-1991 transformation of the Japanese model and the unraveling of the institutions that until that point had appeared to constitute a mutually beneficial form of coordination between business, organized labor, and a developmental state. It charts the decline of Japan's postwar economic institutions and the subsequent emergence of a new and growing body of precarious, or nonregular,[1] workers. This echoes similar developments globally, where neoliberal reforms have resulted in the emergence of a new group of precarious labor, the "precariat" (Standing 2011). While the emergence of this new class of precarious workers represents a weakening of Japanese labor and a corresponding worsening of workers' standard of living, we can also witness the emergence of new forms of resistance, protest, and dissent associated with this new social group. Japan's growing class of nonregular workers are also adopting new ways to oppose and contest their precarious working and living conditions. As we shall see, this new disruptive potential has created significant problems for Japan's political and economic elite.

Since 1991 we have witnessed a process of creeping neoliberalization. Yet such efforts have been increasingly thwarted and obstructed by a social coalition built around opposition to precarity and the protection of precarious workers. Faced with this new wave of opposition, and in a context where at least a rhetorical commitment to social stability and inclusion remains in place, Japan's policymakers and business leaders have found themselves having to backtrack, resort to making concessions, or completely abandon their attempts to implement neoliberal reforms. It is this new contentious political economy of Japan, and especially the influence of this new group of nonregular workers within it, that this book sets out to uncover. Where previous contributions to research and the literature have tended either to lament the passing of Japan's era of social harmony and prosperity or to highlight the continuing distinctiveness of Japan's political economy, this book shows how Japan's political economy has changed, but not only in ways that represent the defeat of labor. Indeed, as we shall see, if anything the turbulence witnessed in Japan's political economy reflects precisely the inability to pacify Japan's new precarious working class.

The Rise of a Contentious Nonregular Workforce

Around the middle of the first decade of the 2000s, terms such as "working poor," "Net Café refugees," "NEETs [not in education, employed, or in training]," "McDonalds refugees," and "*haken*" (dispatch workers) began to appear with increasing frequency in newspapers and television news. These mentions were in reports of an apparently new form of in-work poverty growing in Japan. Nonregular workers especially were identified as a key group whose members were suffering from low wages and insecure employment, fitting a pattern that many had identified with the onset of the neoliberal reforms introduced across the global political economy, especially in the Global North.[2] Their problems include uncertain, short-term, and rapidly adjustable (or flexible) patterns of employment, low wages, and a lack of social benefits or other workers' entitlements (Vosko 2010; Harrod 2006).

As part of this growth in nonregular employment, Japan has also witnessed a growing number of protests, which have both sought to highlight the plight of Japan's precarious workers and attempted to oppose and resist the new conditions that they were experiencing. The global economic crisis, sparked by the subprime crisis of 2007 and associated in collective global memory with the collapse of Lehman Brothers in 2008, saw an acceleration of each of these trends. December 2008 saw the broadcast of a series of reports depicting homeless and newly unemployed workers queuing at a soup kitchen in Tokyo's Hibiya Park. Foreshadowing what would become common occupations of public squares in 2008, workers, activists, and trade unionists collectively undertook an occupation of this public space in Tokyo, protesting both the corporations that had caused the homelessness and impoverishment of their former employees and the government's apparent unwillingness to do anything to address the issue (on the wave of public space occupations that arose in the wake of the global economic crisis, see especially Tejerina et al. 2013; Flesher Fominaya and Cox 2013; Gerbaudo 2017). The occupation of Hibiya Park, known as *Hakenmura* (temporary camp for the unemployed and homeless), symbolized the social anxiety and fear rising in Japan at the time. It also prompted an ongoing public debate regarding the new working conditions at the center of Japan's changing model of capitalism.

The conditions under which nonregular workers are employed in Japan are systematically worse than those of regular workers. Nonregular workers earn, on average, around one-third of the salary of regular workers. As we shall see, nonregular workers have routinely experienced problems with the under- or nonpayment of wages. Nonregular work is often considerably more dangerous than that of regular work. This became particularly visible in the aftermath of the Fukushima disaster in 2011, with nonregular workers outnumbering regular workers in the Fukushima nuclear power plant 9,195 to 1,108, and low-paid contract workers speaking of hiding their injuries during the cleanup to avoid problems with their employers (Herod 2011).

The emergence of this new class of nonregular workers in Japan has been widely noted, but commentators have tended to underestimate the ability of this new social group to both mobilize and influence Japan's politics and economy. As Richard Watanabe states, unions' "efforts to organise non-regular and marginalised regular workers have been insufficient" (2015, 510). This, he claims, is in part the result of "regular workers' tacit approval of the deregulation of non-regular employment," which in turn has "undermined labour's power resources by increasing the number of unorganised non-regular workers" (2018, 3–4). Likewise, Jun Imai finds that "the significance of labor unions is declining" and that this can be understood in terms of the long-term practice of nonconfrontational unionism: "The background of this decline is the historical development of cooperative unionism that undermined their [unions'] militancy, the capability to fight against employers, for about fifty years" (2017, 102). This has tended to become a more general view within the political economy literature: that Japan's workers remain relatively passive and lack agency and the capacity to assert their interests vis-à-vis capital, and that therefore the move toward a growing proportion of nonregular workers within the Japanese labor market has gone relatively uncontested.

This lack of focus on the labor movement and its impact on politics in studies of the country's political economy is particularly notable, given growing concerns about increasing inequality and poverty in Japan (Chiavacci and Hommerich 2017; Shinoda 2008; Goto 2011). This rise in inequality is also linked to changing trends in the labor market. In particular, the impact of flexibilization and the casualization of labor are assumed to have been generated partly by the neoliberalization of the Japanese political economy and have become key points of concern among commentators (Tachibanaki 2006; Goto 2011; Miura 2012; Song 2014; Yun 2016). Furthermore, the post-2008 global economic crisis caused a serious recession in Japan and resulted in a dramatic increase in dismissals of temporary workers (Miura 2012; Song 2014; Imai 2011; Yun 2016; Shibata 2016) and a rise in economic insecurity and social tension (Miura 2008; Shinoda 2008; Miura 2012; Song 2014; Shibata 2016; Bailey and Shibata 2014 and 2017). Despite these trends, the existing literature has tended to focus on systemic levels of change and continuity in Japan's economy, rather than draw attention to the responses that have been witnessed by those workers and other individuals affected by these changes. Instead, the literature has typically focused on the form of the state and party system (Rosenbluth and Thies 2010; Schoppa 2011; Reed, McElwain, and Shimizu 2011); corporate governance (Aguilera and Jackson 2010; Ahmadjian 2012; Witt and Redding 2009); the coordinated market economy; and the capitalist class and/or elite-level officials and institutions, including corporate managers or state officials (Culpepper 2011; Hatch 2010; Rosenbluth and Thies 2010).

Insufficient attention has been paid to workers' agency and contestation. When considering global) restructuring, much of the literature tends to view workers as powerless (Cumbers, Nativel, and Routledge 2008, 369). There have been studies on the Japanese labor market, including employment relations (Imai 2011; Rebick 2005), nonregular workers (Fu 2011), impacts of change in the labor market on the welfare system (Miura 2012), the segmented nature of Japan's youth labor market (Brinton 2011), the dualization of the Japanese labor market (Yun

2016), comparisons between labor market reform in Korea and Japan (Song 2014), and between Japan and Italy (Watanabe 2014). This literature presents accounts of the transformation of the Japanese labor market, including liberalization, deregulation and dualization and the increasing number of nonregular workers and the resulting inequality in the workplace. These studies enrich our knowledge of labor and the challenges workers face. However, at times they tend to depict Japan's workers as excessively passive and as a result consider Japan's socioeconomic model as relatively static or stable (Ahmadjian 2012; Sako 2006; Thelen and Kume 2003 and 2006; Rosenbluth and Thies 2010, 174, Witt 2006; Anchordoguy 2005, 3; Dore 2000; Estévez-Abe 2008, 16). What are missing are an account that considers the scope for agency that has been witnessed by Japan's new group of precarious nonregular workers and an understanding of the way in which this has contributed to the instability of Japan's socioeconomic model.

An important element in the process of Japan's restructuring has therefore been overlooked. The study of workers' agency and contestation in response to the restructuring of workplace production is needed to help understand contemporary changes in Japanese capitalism. According to Jeffrey Harrod, power relations in the workplace have a tendency to produce a shared consciousness between unprotected workers with the potential to resist in the context of global restructuring (2006, 59–60). In Japan, new unions have emerged to represent unprotected workers and oppose social injustice and exploitation by corporate elites. Individual labor disputes over issues such as unpaid wages, retirement benefits, and disadvantageous changes to working conditions have increased dramatically since the early 1990s (Fackler 2008; Bailey and Shibata 2014; Shibata 2016; Shinoda 2008, 150; Miura 2008, 168). Similarly, government agencies that regulate labor matters have received a growing number of complaints (Shinoda 2008, 150). These developments increasingly demand our attention. Thus, the Japanese political economy and labor market literatures tend to overlook the scope for (and exercise of) workers' agency and contestation. In response, this book investigates the way in which Japanese capitalism has undergone a process of restructuring, with a particular focus on the workplace and how changing socioeconomic structures have affected workers. It examines the new category of nonregular workers that has emerged as a result of recent changes to relations between capital and labor in Japan. Finally, it explores the way in which workers have responded and contributed to the construction of the Japanese political economy, as well as how the country's model of capitalism has been transformed as a result.

Japan has witnessed the emergence of a new form of labor activism over the past twenty years. Drawing on an analysis of over 4,000 reports of acts of mobilization conducted by workers, trade unions, and other proworker organizations in the period 1980–2017 and presenting the results of qualitative research into a number of concrete campaigns and policy cases, this book highlights the changing instances of contestation conducted by changing forms of labor and the responses that contestation has produced among Japan's political and economic elite. This includes the results of a series of interviews with trade union activists and members of nonprofit campaigning organizations, as well as official documents published by both the government and trade unions and reports from the high-quality Japanese-language news media (especially *Asahi Shinbun*). The book presents a more vibrant form of worker agency than what is commonly depicted. Instances of innovative social mobilization—especially that conducted by Japan's growing population of precarious, nonregular workers—have demonstrated a capacity to contest and disrupt the aims of both firms and successive governments in their efforts to deregulate Japan's labor market, worsen the working conditions of Japanese labor, and liberalize (or neoliberalize) Japan's model of capitalism. It is only through a consideration of this growing presence of nonregular labor and its capacity to mobilize, oppose, and resist, the book claims, that we can understand both Japan's prolonged period of stagnation and the tense, difficult, and often unsuccessful efforts to adopt a new model of economic growth.

Political Economy, Neoliberalism, and Precarious Labor

The trends outlined above form part of a wider set of processes that have been studied within the comparative and critical political economy literatures. In presenting the case of Japan, this book seeks to contribute to a number of these debates. In doing so, it aims both to draw on some of the key insights within the political economy literature and highlight the contribution to knowledge that an analysis of the Japanese case can provide.

The comparative political economy literature has tended to focus on the institutional, social, and political conditions that contribute to the broader socioeconomic frameworks within which national economies are located. This is often contrasted with the discipline of economics, which has tended to focus on a more abstract notion of the economy, reduced to a set of market relations entered into by equally abstract economic actors—each of whom is presumed to be governed by a standard set of nonreal assumptions. These assumptions include the existence of utility-maximizing agents, perfect competition, rational decision making, and so on (for some of the best current literature on the standard economics literature and the peculiar assumptions that go into the consideration of these nonreal economic relations, see Shaikh 2016; Watson 2018). In contrast, the comparative political economy literature focuses on broader institutional and social conditions that tend to distinguish between different national economies in specific concrete contexts, with a particular focus on the differences that these conditions make in terms of socioeconomic outcomes. This might include aspects such as trade union density, welfare state provisions, the degree of intervention and support offered to firms by the state, the role of different types of political parties, the impact of voter preferences, trade relations and policies, the break-down between different types of production in specific national economies, the location of global value chains, and different degrees of social inequality, among many other considerations. For constructivist political economists, moreover, the framework of ideas about each of these aspects of the political economy are both constitutive and therefore central to an understanding of how each aspect operates, and these economists focus on the way in which particular social norms and shared understandings inform the policy paradigms that prevail in particular political economies at particular times (for a relevant discussion, see Clift 2014).

Central to debates within the recent comparative political economy literature has been a consideration of the degree to which global economic integration has precluded the possibility of different policy and socioeconomic alternatives. In the 1990s, and in the context of heightened concern about the process of globalization, much of the political economy literature turned to the question of state capacity. This included an interest in the possibility of interventionist economic policies, scope for fiscal policy discretion and redistributive welfare policies, and the extent to which trade unions could continue to assert the interests of national labor movements in an increasingly globalized economy. Especially after the publication of Peter Hall and David Soskice's seminal *Varieties of Capitalism* (VoC) in 2001, the debates began to focus on what were considered to be two alternative models of political economy. The choice facing state managers, according to the VoC perspective, was between a coordinated model of capitalism in which economic agents typically entered into negotiated relations with one another, and a liberal market economy in which socioeconomic interaction was governed by more impersonal market forces (for similar approaches that adopted different models, see Coates 2005; Amable 2003; Boyer 2000). Since the onset of the global economic crisis in 2008, however, the VoC literature has become less prominent in the comparative political economy literature. This has occurred alongside a reconsideration of alternative growth models, accompanied by renewed interest in questions of whether national economic models are driven by debt, wages, or profit, and which models are likely to be most successful (Baccaro and Pontusson 2016).

In terms of its relevance for the current study, the comparative political economy literature offers a number of important insights into the types of pressures that are exerted on national economies, including that of Japan. Alternative national political economies are assumed to be relatively autonomous in the sense that they are able to adopt alternative configurations of key political economic attributes (welfare provisions, industrial relations, corporatist policymaking arrangements, and so on), but the literature also recognizes that national economies must be competitive in the global political economy, which creates pressure on them to conform to global standards of efficiency and productivity (which in turns limits the capacity for national divergence). It is this question of the interaction between national traditions and policy options, on the one hand, and global pressures to compete in terms of productivity and economic competitiveness, on the other hand, that may be central to the concern of the comparative political economy literature. In particular, it is the role of global economic integration and the heightened pressure that this has put on national economic competitiveness that are a key concern of this book. In this sense, the book aims, among other things, to explore the pressures exerted by global economic competition on the policy options and alternative political economic models available to economic actors within Japan and to consider the degree to which global economic pressures have (or have not) ruled out the possibility of social compromise—which once underpinned, albeit in an imperfect form, the Japanese model of capitalism.

In contrast to the comparative political economy literature considered above, contributions to the critical political economy literature have tended to focus more on the pressures of global economic integration and the corresponding attempt by economic and political elites to harness these (and other) pressures to sharpen social inequality and the power and role of corporate business interests (Davies and Ryner 2006). In doing so, critical political economy scholars have tended to view these trends as part of a general process of neoliberalization (Bruff 2011, 2014; Bruff and Horn 2012; Tansel 2018; Crouch 2001). In doing so, moreover, the critical political economy literature has highlighted a number of key processes that constitute the period of neoliberal capitalism. This includes processes of depoliticization and dedemocratization that have sought to silence and exclude exponents of alternatives to neoliberal socioeconomic models (Dönmez 2019), a heightened role for private-sector actors and business (Hathaway 2018), less generous welfare provisions and increased conditionality placed on the receipt of welfare measures (Belfrage and Ryner 2009), an attempt to disarticulate and undermine the role of organized labor and trade unions (Jackson 2016; Upchurch, Taylor, and Mathers 2009), a welcoming of open trade relations as a way to consolidate the role of the market (De Ville and Orbie 2014), and the promotion of an entrepreneurialism of the self as part of a more general process of reducing government responsibility for individual well-being (Kiersey 2009). Recent contributions to the critical political economy literature have also sought to highlight the role of protest and resistance as a way to contest these trends in contemporary neoliberal capitalism (Bailey et al. 2018).

The critical political economy literature, therefore, provides a number of important insights of relevance to the present study. It conceptualizes the global economic pressures and trends that are systematically influencing national political economies, including that of Japan, as part of a concrete political project in which efforts are made to systematically disempower organized labor and simultaneously re-empower corporate business interests. Thus, this literature directs our attention to the political processes through which such efforts are pursued in the Japanese context, alongside a consideration of the ways in which these efforts are resisted and contested.

In addition to the comparative and critical political economy literatures, the industrial relations literature makes an important contribution to our understanding of the decline of organized labor, the emergence of a new precarious working class, and the modes of organization and contestation that this new precariat might be capable of forming (for some key recent contributions, see especially Gumbrell-McCormick and Hyman 2013; Moody 2017; Ikeler 2018). Two key trends have been noted in the industrial relations literature, both of which are typically considered to be central to the neoliberalization of contemporary global capitalism. First, we see a systematic (albeit to different degrees in different contexts) decline in the proportion of workers who are members of trade unions, producing a general incremental downward trajectory of union density across the advanced industrial democracies. This is typically considered to be a result of changing working practices associated with the move toward a predominantly service sector–based economy in post-Fordism. It also results from the political attack on trade unions associated with the neoliberal period, a fragmentation of production processes that has resulted in a more heterogeneous workforce, and the reduced capacity for trade union influence in a globally integrated economy (Daniels and McIlroy 2009; MacDonald 2014). Second, alongside this trend, and in part in response to it, a number of commentators have begun to view new and innovative forms of workplace organizing—often in a form fused with the more independent and noninstitutionalized actions and practices of social movements—as the most likely route for reinvigorating the agency of labor. This is often referred to as social movement unionism, a phrase that describes a process whereby either workers organizing outside of trade unions adopt the methods of social movements or trade unions seek to invigorate themselves by rejecting traditional trade union practices and instead replicating those of alternative social movements (Ibsen and Tapia 2017; Mathers, Upchurch, and Taylor 2018). In considering the changing forms of mobilization of labor in Japan, therefore, this book seeks to contribute to these ongoing debates in the industrial relations literature, focusing especially on the capacity for Japan's new precarious workers to organize collectively and assert their collective interest. Thus, the study promises to contribute to knowledge beyond the Japanese case and to enhance our understanding both of the scope for labor agency within the contemporary context and its likely effect.

The Political Economy of Japan: Existing Accounts

Existing accounts that consider and conceptualize the political economy of Japan have tended to engage with one or several of the discussions outlined above. The political economy of Japan has often been of wider interest (beyond that of the national case alone) to those concerned with questions of national political economy models. It is of relevance to those who question the degree to which we see a global convergence on a neoliberal model, stripped of democratic choice, welfare policy options, or institutions through which to coordinate and regulate market outcomes (for a discussion, see Shibata 2017). In this existing literature, we can identify three key claims: First, those adopting a VoC approach argue that Japan's coordinated market economy has important internal mechanisms that ensure continuity along the institutional path of coordination and negotiated economic outcomes (Vogel 2006). Second, those who are more skeptical about the degree to which the Japanese model remains globally distinct—especially those adopting a regulation theory approach (described below)—perceive a decline in the degree of coordination, including a process whereby the power of labor in the Japanese model is increasingly diminished (Lechevalier 2014a, b, and c). Third, contributions to the industrial relations literature on Japan have sought to show the difficulties facing organized labor in Japan's political economy and in so doing have highlighted the weakness (and corresponding docility) that characterizes Japanese labor (R. Watanabe 2018).

While each of these claims provides important insights into Japan's contemporary political economy, they nevertheless fail to present a convincing account of recent changes and empirical developments. Rather than the continuity of Japan's coordinated model, we instead witness a process of disorganization. Likewise, whereas the regulation theory accounts view a marginalization or weakening of labor in the Japanese model, we instead witness changing forms and expressions of social conflict, in which the changing role of Japanese labor has been central.

Japan's Coordinated Market Economy

The VoC literature rests on the central claim that economies can be divided between those that coordinate economic relations through the market (liberal market economies) and those that rely more on negotiated outcomes between organized interests (coordinated market economies). This division, in turn, has implications for how a range of economic processes are organized, including industrial relations; training and education; corporate governance; interfirm relations; and the hiring, firing, and management of employees (Hall and Soskice 2001). For VoC scholars, Japan has typically been considered a key example of a coordinated market economy and indeed remains so (see, for instance, the categorization of Japan in Hope and Soskice 2016). Those adopting such a perspective have therefore tended to highlight the fact that Japan's traditionally coordinated model has adapted and adjusted to global economic pressures in ways that represent a continuation of the coordinated market economy model (albeit often in an adapted form). Indeed, rather than depicting a process of institutional stasis, the more nuanced contributions to the VoC literature have tended to see Japan's socioeconomic model as undergoing a process of neoliberal change, but one in which this adaptation is influenced by (and as a result in part retains) elements of Japan's historically coordinated model. As Steven Vogel, one of the key VoC scholars on Japan, observes, "the existing institutions of Japanese capitalism are shaping their own transformation" (2006, 4).

As a result of the ongoing role of institutions of coordination in Japan's political economy, VoC scholars claim, Japan continues to rely on negotiated outcomes in seeking to adapt to the pressures emerging from changes to the global economy. This includes cooperative relations among *Nikkeiren* (the Japan Federation of Employers' Association), the Japanese government, and Japanese organized labor in seeking to regulate labor markets in a way that would be acceptable to Japanese labor organizations (Vogel 2006, 56–57). Likewise, Vogel highlights the role of the Ministry of Health, Labor, and Welfare in pursuing economic reforms that would preserve employment (ibid., 82). In this way, we see while Japan's coordinated market economy might be experiencing pressures for (neoliberal) reform, the pressures are mediated by institutions of coordination that have enabled the continuation of negotiated outcomes between affected parties.

Similarly, Marie Anchordoguy argues that the Japanese model retains much of its preexisting commitment to communities (in what she refers to as a "communitarian" model of capitalism), highlighting changes to institutions such as the *yokonarabi* arrangement—whereby the idea of companies operating as communities is instituted as a principle governing relationships between firms (2005, 3, 13). Thus, despite attempts to introduce market-oriented reforms, we see the continuation of practices such as "convoy systems" (in which "stronger banks shore up weaker ones") and of an education system that aims to enhance "conformity and egalitarianism" (ibid.). This moderation of market liberalization can also be witnessed, according to Anchordoguy, in the reforms of the computer industry. Here we see that growing competition led firms to introduce cost-cutting measures and to move toward the unprecedented construction of new buyer-supplier relations between firms outside of *keiretsu* networks (ibid., 144). However, this occurred alongside attempts by the Japanese state to promote the continuation of community and stability, which were typically viewed as being under threat from markets, competition, and foreign firms (ibid., 76). As a result, the introduction of market-oriented reforms has been slow and incremental (ibid., 229–32).

More recent studies have found similar results. For instance, John Buchanan, Dominic Chai, and Simon Deakin (2018) describe how hedge fund activism has little impact on the corporate governance of Japan's coordinated economy, in stark contrast to the effect it had on the liberal economy of the United States. Michael Witt and coauthors (2018) consider Japan to be the most highly coordinated of the sixty-one major economies that they studied. Dirk Hofäker and colleagues (2016) show how the continuing influence of Japanese firms' commitment to lifelong learning has minimized the proportion of involuntary retirements (especially in terms of global comparisons) and thereby had an impact on national pension policy.

The VoC account of Japan's political economy therefore emphasizes the continued role for its traditional institutions of coordination. These, it is claimed, have affected the way in which Japan has adapted to a number of the challenges posed to political economy outcomes at the national level, especially during the move toward a global neoliberal political economy. Thus, Japan retains a number of important institutional features that differentiate it from more liberal market economies (such as the United States and United Kingdom), which have more wholeheartedly moved toward a neoliberal model of capitalism. While not disputing the relative national distinctiveness of Japan's socioeconomic model, this book takes issue with the (sometimes implied) claim within these VoC accounts that Japan's national political economy has successfully avoided neoliberal reforms or processes of neoliberalization. Indeed, as we shall see in chapter 1, the unraveling of Japan's institutions of market coordination cannot be refuted. Across a range of socioeconomic relations and processes, Japan has experienced a systematic erosion, dismantling, and/or abandonment of key socioeconomic practices and institutions that has produced a thorough disarticulation of the classical Japanese model. Therefore, in contrast to the accounts of VoC scholars, we have seen a disorganization of Japan's political economy.

Declining Coordination, Marginalizing Labor

A second body of literature covering the political economy of Japan has adopted a regulation theory account. Regulation theory attempts to consider the institutional forms that enable a temporary and partial resolution of the problems and tensions that are intrinsic to capitalist relations of production. Thus, regulation theory follows the VoC approach in considering particular institutional formations that mark different national political economies. However, regulation theory is far less sanguine than VoC accounts about the possibility of creating sustainable forms of social cooperation, compromise, and stability. As a result, regulation theory accounts of Japan's political economy have tended in recent years to highlight the decline of Japan's classic institutions of coordination and the way in which they have eroded (see, for instance, Lechevalier 2014b).

Sébastien Lechevalier, one of the key contributors to regulation theory in terms of Japan's political economy, presents one of the most thorough analyses of the transition of Japan's model of capitalism (2014b). Thus, for Lechevalier, Japan has undergone a process in which the classic model of Japanese capitalism (in particular, the institutions that contributed to its earlier coordination) has been systematically dismantled "by the implementation, in a progressive and non-linear fashion, of neo-liberal reforms since the beginning of the 1980s" (2014a, 157). This includes especially a decline in the coherence of the *keiretsu* integrated ownership systems that were oriented around central main banks, increased fluidity of subcontracting relations, a severe decline in the *Shuntou* system of coordinated wage negotiations, and a decline in the role of government industrial policy. We especially see a decline in the role of the Ministry of International Trade and Industry, which was earlier a key institution in Japan's "developmental state" model (Lechevalier 2014c, 77–78).

Other scholars adopting a regulation theory approach have come to similar conclusions. For instance, Toshio Yamada and Yasuo Hirano (2012) refer to recent changes to the classic Japanese mode of regulation. This was once referred to as companyism, due to the central role of companies in forming compromises with both employees (through lifelong employment security) and between firms and banks (the so-called main bank system). As Yamada and Hirano show, the increased role of financialization and short-term foreign stock holders has undermined the compromise between firms and banks, in turn prompting a rapid liberalization of the labor market and the creation of a considerable proportion of nonregular employees. This, they claim, has resulted in a "dysfunction of companyist regulation" [that] has resulted in many problems (ibid., 28). Likewise, Hiroyasu Uemura, who also adopts a regulation theory approach, highlights the way in which "the companyist mode of *régulation* has been continuously eroded so that is has become dysfunctional" (2012, 125). This includes a heightened role for stock market–focused foreign investors, heightened economic inequality, and a growth in nonregular work and labor market insecurity (ibid., 17).

The overall picture presented in the regulation theory literature on Japan is that of a process of decline of the classic Japanese companyist mode of regulation. In its place, we see a disintegration of the mechanisms of coordination and a corresponding inability to generate a new, stable mode of accumulation and growth. There is much to agree with here. Indeed, as we shall see, this book also adopts some of the key insights of regulation theory to understand and contextualize the recent developments in the Japanese model of capitalism. Yet the regulation theory accounts have also been reluctant to consider the active role of labor in their analysis of Japan's economic transformation. Central to many of these accounts is a straightforward decline in the power of labor, and in some instances labor is considered relatively inconsequential. According to Uemura, since 2002 we have seen that the "institutionalized wage coordination mechanism almost broke down due to the declining bargaining power of trade unions" (2012, 120). While organized labor is considered to have been weakened, moreover, it is also considered to have little capacity to act even if it were not in such an impotent state. As Lechevalier puts it, "even if unions such as *Rengo* [the Japanese Trade Union Confederation] bear a part of the responsibility, the main issue concerns the wage policies of firms . . . [are] backed up by neo-liberal-inspired recommendations" (2014c, 83). When acts of workers' resistance are considered, they take a remarkably moderate form: "It would certainly be exaggerated to conclude that we are seeing a return to class struggle. . . . More modestly, we may speak of a return of the social question, as witnessed by numerous articles and reports on poor workers or homeless people" (Lechevalier 2014e, 94).

In discussing the potential for social change, and especially the likelihood of constructing an alternative mode of regulation, regulation theory appears to neglect the role of labor, which is particularly surprising given its Marxist origins. Uemura, for instance, hopes only for some unspecified "new social consensus among the Japanese people" (2012, 127). In contrast, Yamada and Hirano, highlight the importance of political will. In doing so, however, they neither highlight the role of labor nor consider whether labor might currently play an active role in the processes under consideration: "The most important thing that is needed to create a demand-and-supply system in these fields is political will on the parts of both the central and the local governments. Along with political will, highly active non-profitable organizations or associations are also required. In this respect, it is essential that Japan not only develops institutions and movements (party politics centered on policies, a non-expensive election system, etc.) that will help to adapt political will to the social needs but also to facilitate the creation of various associations and their networks that will be in the forefront of the new economic *régulation*" (Yamada and Hirano 2012, 29).

It is the claim of this book that it is precisely to the neglected role of labor, and especially its continuing capacity for disruption, that we should look to understand the ways in which social change, or a new mode of economic regulation, might begin to come about in contemporary Japanese capitalism.

The Industrial Relations of Japan: An Absent Role for Labor

A number of recent studies of the industrial relations of Japan have highlighted the declining role of organized labor. This is often associated directly with the rise of the proportion of nonregular workers in Japan's labor market and a number of obstacles that stand in the way of efforts to organize this new group of workers collectively. For instance, Richard Watanabe (2018) describes the way in which both regular and nonregular workers have faced an increasingly liberalized labor market since the 1990s. This, it is claimed, has reduced the power resources of labor in Japan, which itself both contributes to and is being consolidated by a process of declining union density. As Watanabe shows, despite efforts to recruit workers, an inability to adopt a coherent industrial strategy, as well as divisions between different groups of workers, has contributed to an inability to rejuvenate the established unions, especially the *Rengo* (see also R. Watanabe 2015). Similar findings have been identified by other industrial relations scholars. For instance, Imai shows how "the significance of labor unions is declining," a trend that is in large part the result of an earlier decision to adopt a long-term cooperative approach toward employers (2017, 103). In addition, employees are considered conflict averse: "Regular members of a firm began to see organizing and/or participating in labor disputes through labor unions illegitimate since these activities may disturb firms' productivity" (ibid., 103).

In contrast to this prevalent account of Japanese industrial relations, the present book sets out to identify nascent forms of mobilization, opposition, and resistance conducted by workers (especially nonregular workers) in Japan. In doing so, it builds on recent attempts in the critical political economy literature to shift the focus of analysis away from a consideration of ways in which labor is dominated and subordinated under neoliberalism and to a consideration of the different (often "subterranean," nascent, relatively underdeveloped, or less "visible") ways that labor has found to disrupt contemporary patterns of domination (Huke, Bailey, and Clua-Losada 2015). This draws on the so-called Copernican revolution introduced by autonomist Marxism, according to which it is always labor (not capital), and especially labor's capacity for refusal, that drives the development of capitalism. From this perspective, we should instead seek to understand not the silence, defeat, or disappearance of organized labor, but rather the different and changing form and role of workers in contemporary capitalism at any particular moment. It is to such an analysis that this book now turns.

The Approach of This Book: Regulation Theory and Class Conflict

The approach adopted in this book combines the insights of regulation theory with a heightened focus on class conflict and the disruptive capacity of labor in Japan. In doing so, it considers the specificities of the Japanese model of capitalism and how these have changed, all in keeping with the regulation theory approach to political economy. Yet it also argues that regulation theory has paid too little attention to the role of workers' agency, and especially the ineluctable propensity for contestation, resistance, and disruption that characterizes the nature of labor in capitalism. In this sense, the approach presented combines the insights of regulation theory regarding the role of institutional formations in temporarily stabilizing particular modes of capital accumulation with the claims advanced by autonomist Marxism that working class agency is always and unavoidably central to the instability experienced by any particular mode of accumulation.

Regulation theory is particularly appropriate for the present study due to its attempt to consider the national specificities of particular modes of capital accumulation in a form that acknowledges the possibility for temporary (and partial) stability at particular moments in capitalism. At the same time, regulation theory acknowledges a central underlying drive toward major capitalist crises that is inherent in the socioeconomic system and ensures that this stability eventually gives way to instability, crisis, and change (Boyer 2018). Given both that Japan's model of capitalism has been widely considered in terms of the degree to which it differs from a "standard" liberal or Anglo-Saxon model of cutthroat capitalism and that Japan's model of capitalism has experienced considerable pressures for change over the past three decades, regulation theory is a particularly useful approach to use in considering these developments.

Regulation theory attempts to explain "the emergence, reproduction, and crisis of different capitalist regimes through linking micro- and macro-level factors and processes" (Bohle and Greskovits 2009, 357). In contrast to the VoC approach, regulation theory adopts the insights of Marxist political economy in refusing to accept that capitalism should be considered a rational system able to achieve a self-sustaining equilibrium. Instead, capitalism is considered prone to crises and therefore subject to instability and tendencies that undermine the sustainability of any particular mode of regulation (Jessop and Sum 2006, 215–16; Baccaro and Howell 2011, 525).

Central to regulation theory is the observation that the tensions and contradictions that characterize capitalism can be temporarily stabilized as a result of institutions' producing a degree of social cohesion. Thus, a mode of regulation is a set of mediations that can counteract the distortions created by the accumulation of capital to generate temporary social cohesion within each nation (Aglietta 1998, 44). This mode of regulation emerges from a class compromise and consists of an institutional framework as well as policies, norms, and modes of behavior that coordinate temporary stability and growth—a so-called regime of accumulation, which results in macroeconomic growth based on institutional settlements (Neilson 2012, 162; Boyer and Saillard 2002; Boyer, Uemura, and Isogai 2012a). Social cohesion functions as a mediatory mechanism that can moderate tensions between individuals and society and helps regulate the capitalist system. The overall context changes "along with the collective interests that are activated by the interaction of the various wills within the mediation mechanisms" (Aglietta 1998, 51). Therefore, mechanisms of mediation help shape a particular mode of regulation, including through institutionalized rules and compromises that manage social tension and guide the accumulation of capital in the direction of social progress and cohesion (ibid.).

However, this social cohesion is a temporary phenomenon, as any particular mode of regulation ultimately wanes (Aglietta 1998, 44). As Robert Boyer puts it, "the contradictions inherent in accumulation manifest themselves by the endogenous destabilization of any accumulation regime: this implies a major crisis, when the viability of the institutional architecture that shapes the *régulation* mode, i.e. the adjustment processes that drive accumulation are at stake" (2018, 285–286). From this perspective, therefore, the study of capitalism requires analyzing the development and transformation of nationally specific regimes of accumulation and modes of regulation and understanding the changing processes and patterns of behavior in times of crisis (Aglietta 1998, 44).

In drawing on regulation theory, this book analyzes changes in the Japanese model of capitalism as they have occurred over time, paying particular attention to the way in which social and class conflict is moderated (or not) through the institutions that constitute Japan's changing mode of regulation.

Contributors to the development of regulation theory have identified five key socioeconomic institutions that should be studied to understand a particular mode of regulation: the national economy's insertion in the international regime, the monetary and financial regime, the form of competition, the form of the state, and the wage-labor nexus (Boyer and Saillard 2002; Boyer and Yamada 2000). Each of these is discussed briefly below.

First, in discussing the national economy's insertion in the international regime, regulation theory refers to a set of principles and decision-making procedures whereby institutions seek to manage the relationship between the national and the international economies (Nadel 2002, 33–34). This includes the level of globalization, the relationship to the world market, and the international division of labor (Aglietta 1998, 53). Second, money serves as the fundamental institution in any market economy (Aglietta 1998, 46). The monetary and financial regime attempts to generate cohesion and stability in terms of the allocation of capital, connecting economic units and compensating for shortfalls and oversupply between economic agents (Boyer and Saillard 2002, 39). In doing so, moreover, the monetary and financial regime regulates conflicts over the allocation of capital, especially between finance and industry and between financial institutions (Nabeshima 2000, 104). Third, the form of competition refers to interfirm relations (Hollard 2002, 101). This includes relationships between firms at different stages of the production process, coordination between producers, and relations both between finance and industry and between buyers and sellers in the market (ibid., 101–5). It might also include a degree of coordination between firms and other institutions, enabling a smoothing of the production process.

Fourth, in considering the form of the state, regulation theory refers to the different ways in which public authorities are linked to national economies, including in terms of providing overall shape to and coordination among the other types of institutions (such as interfirm relations, insertion within the international market) (Boyer and Saillard 2002, 38–41). The particular form adopted by any one state—neoclassical or minimal, Keynesian or demand management, social democratic, developmental, and so on—therefore represents a particular type of coordination between the market and the public, capital and labor, financial institutions and firms, and the economy and politics. Fifth and finally, the wage-labor nexus refers to "the process of socialisation of production activity under capitalism" (Boyer 2000, 73) and the reproduction of a wage-earning class. Due to the inherently conflict-prone nature of the wage relationship, moreover, regulation theory considers it necessary for some mechanism to be put in place to stabilize this relationship (Boyer 2000, 73–74; Aglietta 1998, 47).

Regulation theory is therefore concerned with the mode of regulation that accompanies any one particular mode of accumulation. This mode of regulation consists of an interlinked configuration of the five institutionas listed above. Any particular mode of regulation is considered in terms of its ability to produce a temporary stabilization of the tensions and conflicts that constitute capitalism and the process of capital accumulation. Nevertheless, these tensions and conflicts are considered overwhelming in the longer term, eventually resulting in crisis tendencies that unsettle and destabilize the mode of regulation to such an extent that it is rendered unsustainable and eventually replaced (if possible) with an alternative mode of regulation.

While regulation theory views instability as central to capitalism and any particular mode of regulation, it has nevertheless been accused by its critics of overstating the potential for stability (Durand and Légé 2013; Vidal 2012). Those who adopt a more conflict-focused conceptualization of capitalism do not expect social conflict to be absent or contained even in the short term. For similar reasons, critics have also tended to consider regulation theory to be relatively uninterested in patterns of class conflict and social tension. While the theory proclaims the importance of social and political struggles, therefore, it often appears relatively uninterested in the struggles themselves and more interested in the mode of regulation that contains and mediates them (Juego 2011). Moreover, regulation theory has been accused of assuming too great a degree of control on the part of capital, thereby replacing a Marxist theory of class conflict with a theory of class domination (Clarke 1988, 10). In this sense, regulation theory risks becoming a "process without a subject" (Bonefeld and Holloway 1991, 63).

The relatively conflict-free nature of regulation theory is particularly problematic from the perspective of autonomist Marxist approaches. Indeed, those influenced by Mario Tronti and the Italian Operaismo movement of the 1960s and 1970s reversed traditional Marxist analysis, replacing accounts that prioritized the domination of capital over labor with an account that highlighted the problems caused by labor for capital (Tronti 1964; for an overview of Operaismo and autonomist Marxism, see Wright 2002; for a more recent application, see Huke, Bailey, and Clua-Losada 2015).

Those who adopt a more conventional Marxist account also tend to ground their analysis in processes of class struggle (Burnham 2006, 188). According to such accounts, capital grows by extracting surplus value from labor, which in turn requires the state to intervene to ensure the successful reproduction of the social circuit of capital and its integration within international regimes (Burnham 2001, 104, and 2006, 188). Although capitalism is a system of class domination, it is also open to workers' protests (Burnham 2006, 188). Thus, one of the key methods of capitalist expansion is to divide and stratify workers while capturing the benefits of their cooperation in the process of production. This creates a central contradiction, as the process of cooperation brings workers together, but capitalism also requires their division and separation to ensure their continued domination and maintain the authority of capital over labor (Lebowitz 2003, 88). Capitalists and workers therefore exist in an unavoidably contentious relationship marked by daily struggles over issues such as the speed and intensity of the labor process, labor conditions, and workers' rights (Harvey 2006, 32). Thus, instead of considering whether resistance and contestation exist, we need to consider the different types and forms of resistance that exist in any particular mode of accumulation.

In building on these insights, therefore, this book adopts a regulation theory approach in considering the changing institutional forms that have characterized Japan's changing model of capitalism since the end of the Second World War. In doing so, it foregrounds the different forms of resistance and contestation, especially those used by labor, and the destabilizing effect that they have had. Such an account is best placed to highlight the ongoing problems and tensions that Japan's contemporary socioeconomic model faces.

The book proceeds as follows. Chapter 1 provides an overview of the key changes that have been witnessed in Japan's political economy throughout the postwar period. Deploying a regulation theory approach, it shows how Japan has experienced a process of neoliberalization since its economic bubble burst in 1991, with one of the key effects being the emergence of a new and growing group of precarious nonregular workers. The coordination between firms, workers, and institutions that enabled stability in employment relations from the end of the Second World War to the 1980s has been replaced by a trend toward neoliberalization, deregulation, and a lack of coordination. Chapter 2 provides an account of the changing nature of Japan's labor and social movements as they developed during the same period. Chapter 3 draws on an original data set of protest events in Japan to highlight the key trends in Japan's labor movement as they have developed in the form of social conflict and protest. Precarious workers have become increasingly mobilized, contributing to an increased frequency of protests and a greater proclivity toward more confrontational forms of protest activity. Chapter 4 provides an account of the way Japan's newly recomposed working class has begun to challenge the experience of precarity in the workplace, which is having a significant effect on the actions and practices of firms in Japan's economy. This chapter focuses especially on temp agency workers, new organizations that have arisen to represent women workers, and the attempt to mobilize dispatch workers in the auto industry. Chapter 5 shows how a similar process of contestation has occurred between nonregular Japanese workers and the policies of the state, focusing especially on reforms in the areas of pensions, agriculture, and fiscal policy. Chapter 6 returns to one of the key questions raised by regulation theory— the extent to which a new mode of regulation can be seen in Japan. Japanese state managers have largely failed in their attempts to install a successful mode of regulation, in part due to the social tension generated by Japan's newly recomposed working class. Finally, the book concludes with some reflections on the trajectory of capitalism in Japan and the role of its precarious workers in that process.

FROM COORDINATED TO DISORGANIZED CAPITALISM IN JAPAN

The Japanese economy was devastated by the Second World War. In the war's immediate aftermath, the period 1945–1951, the country's political economy was controlled by the occupation government. While far behind other countries with advanced economies such as the United States and the United Kingdom, Japan had unprecedented levels of economic growth (around 10 percent average gross domestic product [GDP] growth per year throughout the 1950s and 1960s), which attracted considerable international attention. Concepts referring to Japanese ways of doing business—including just-in-time production, *keiretsu* (closely knit business networks), *kaizen* (continuous and incremental improvement), and teamwork—each became popular buzzwords among international corporate elites.

In the 1970s, Japan experienced a slowing of GDP growth, although it maintained a growth rate of over 3 percent per year until the late 1980s. Efforts to maintain a sustained level of growth during the 1980s resulted in a "bubble economy," with asset prices rising rapidly. This bubble burst in 1991, which was a pivotal point in the country's postwar economic history and, as we shall see, led to a number of changes to Japan's mode of regulation. This chapter describes the key changes that occurred throughout this process. It highlights the way in which each of the five institutions that are typically considered in regulation theory accounts underwent important changes, producing a disorganization of Japan's political economy.

The chapter argues that changes to each of the five institutions—the mode of insertion in the international economy, the form of competition, the monetary and financial regime, the form of the state, and the form adopted by the wage-labor nexus—combined to produce pressures for increased economic competition. Changes to any one of the key institutions in Japan's mode of regulation had effects—often mutually reinforcing—on each of the other institutions. One of the key consequences of these developments was the demise of long-term labor market security, which had been a feature of the postwar model in Japan. The institutional mix that had previously produced a degree of consensus over time mutated into a regime characterized by heightened instability, an absence of coordination and collaboration, the exclusion of organized labor, and intensified exploitation. Table 1.1 summarizes these changes, highlighting how different developments occurred and institutional dynamics shifted during the broad time periods described. While the dividing line between each of these periods is not always clear-cut, demarcating them as shown allows us to capture some of the key broad trends and changes that occurred over time. The Japanese model of capitalism has become increasingly disorganized, resulting in heightened anxiety and insecurity among workers.

Japan's Insertion in the International Market

In terms of its relationship to the international market, the Japanese economy has been transformed over the past fifty years from a protected and insulated market to a more open and liberalized one that is integrated into the competitive international market. This process of increasing openness to the international economy has resulted in mutually reinforcing pressures to liberalize other aspects of the Japanese political economy. The process of internationalization has had implications in terms of the form of the state (less protectionist) and an increased inflow of foreign capital (which has altered the monetary and financial regime and the form of competition in Japan)—all of which has heightened the overall pressure of market competition across the country's political economy.

Japan's rapid economic growth in the 1960s through the 1980s was widely heralded as a successful model of development. However, this growth was also largely associated with trade surpluses, prompting criticism from and moves toward protectionist measures in both the United States and Europe. This in turn incentivized Japanese firms to relocate production in the United States and Europe to circumvent protectionist barriers to trade, and as a result the firms increasingly used locally produced input materials. Japan's industrial bases therefore underwent what many considered to be a process of "hollowing out," in

TABLE 1.1 Transformation of Japanese capitalism from coordination to disorganization

	INSERTION IN THE INTERNATIONAL MARKET	FORM OF COMPETITION	MONETARY AND FINANCIAL REGIME	FORM OF THE STATE	WAGE-LABOR NEXUS
1980s: coordinated capitalism	Economic expansion Development of production in international markets Pressure from the United States	*Keiretsu* Parent firms subcontracting interfirm relations Bank-based financing Cross-shareholding	Main bank system Adequate capital for corporations Introduction of financial deregulation Enhanced risk taking by banks and firms	Developmental state Support for main bank system and *keiretsu* networks Welfare through work Welfare-tax mix (preferential tax treatment)	Capital-labor compromise Co-opted labor Long-term employment relations
1990s: crises, deregulation, and liberalization	Increased globalization Hollowing out of Japanese production bases abroad Pressure from the United States Trade liberalization Foreign firms enter Japanese market	Tight *keiretsu* networks undermined to some degree Hollowing out Divisions between competitive and weak subcontracting small and medium-size enterprises (SMEs) Enhanced level of Anglo-Saxon style corporate governance	Burst bubble, economy and banking crises Asian financial crisis Decreased influence of main bank system Weakening bank-based financing Increased search for finance outside of Japan as a result of nonperforming loans' problem Increase of foreign shares	Introduction of deregulation and liberalization Selective policies that favor capital Inability to provide uniform regulation with the market Preferential treatment prompted by new electoral system in 1994	Undermined long-term employment relations Foreign firms' and shareholders' influence on capital-labor relations Gradual increase of nonregular workers Stratification of the working class
Early 2000s: acceleration of neoliberalization, undermining of social cohesion and increasing social inequality	Integration of Japanese economy into Asian markets	Development of regional supply networks in Asia Polarization among subcontracting SMEs SME bankruptcies Development of mergers and acquisitions Undermined level of *keiretsu* networks and cross-shareholding Anglo-Saxon corporate governance	Increase of foreign investors, shares, and ownership Deregulation in bank-based financing system Undermined relations between banks and firms Shift to direct finance system	Introduction of deregulation and liberalization in finance, business, and labor areas Accelerating neoliberalization by Prime Minister Junichiro Koizumi's structural reforms Establishment of Council on Economic and Fiscal Policy Establishment of bank-regulatory institutions Reduction in social welfare Meager welfare state exposed by employment insecurity	Decline in the number of permanent employees Flexibilization and individualization of labor Increased unemployment rate Increased income disparities and inequality Intensifying commodification of labor

(continued)

TABLE 1.1 (continued)

	INSERTION IN THE INTERNATIONAL MARKET	FORM OF COMPETITION	MONETARY AND FINANCIAL REGIME	FORM OF THE STATE	WAGE-LABOR NEXUS
Late 2000s: disorganized model of capitalism	Development of production and sales in Asia Increased level of dependency on Asian markets Growth of competitive Chinese market	Corporate governance (government emphasis on shareholders) Increased competition Further business difficulties among SMEs	Global financial crisis Increase in public debt due to the stimulus package Bank loans to SMEs navigated by the state Reregulation of the financial market	Succession of cabinet reshuffles Shift in political leadership from the Liberal Democratic Party of Japan to the Democratic Party of Japan	Undermined employment security Decreased labor shares Increased dismissals Impoverishment of the working class
2010s: disorganized model of capitalism	Further liberalization of trade Reduced level of protectionism in the agricultural sector Heightened competition within East Asia, especially China	Polarization between competitive and uncompetitive firms Increased pressure to compete with China and Southeast Asia with regard to labor costs Further weakening of keiretsu ties in Japan	Growth in shareholder influence and increase in dividend payments	Abenomics and austerity challenging the welfare regime Dismantling of social security brought about by more universalistic tax system (increase of sales tax) Inability of state elites to reconstruct coherent alternative growth model Fiscal austerity (increased sales tax rate)	The highest rate of nonregular workers A new way of dismissing workers (zero hour contracts, bullying, imposing extremely harsh working conditions, and terminating contracts of new graduates after six-month probation periods)

which production was increasingly moved outside of Japan and to the country where sales would take place. This process of hollowing out reached its peak in 1995, prompting concerns over its impact on both production and employment in Japan (Schaede 2007, 82 and 96; Bailey and Sugden 2007, 136). It should be noted, however, that the potentially detrimental effect of these developments was in part mitigated during the 1980s as a result of state provisions such as subsidies, publicly funded research and development, and government supervision of declining industries, and thus in that period the state took on a coordinating role despite the impact of internationalization (Witt 2006, 88–89).

Alongside pressure to relocate to the United States and Europe, firms based in Japan faced difficulties as a result of declining growth in the 1980s, especially after the bubble burst in 1991. This prompted a shift in the orientation of both investment and exports toward international markets, particularly in Asia (Yamada and Hirano 2012, 15). As a result of these efforts to increase access to international markets, Japan faced pressure from other advanced economies to "lower trade barriers, relax capital controls, and reduce anti-competitive regulation" (Vogel 2006, 33). The opening up of trade also allowed foreign firms to enter the Japanese market, thereby challenging the close *keiretsu* networks.

The combined effect of increased trade liberalization and the so-called hollowing out of Japan through a process of relocating production abroad resulted in increased competition between firms as established supply chains and relations between firms were increasingly disturbed by competitive pressures, especially to reduce costs. This in turn had an especially negative effect on less competitive small and medium-size enterprises (SMEs), as well as an indirect effect on Japanese labor—as firms were forced to exert greater discipline in the workplace in an attempt to respond to the heightened market competition that they faced (Isogai, Ebizuka, and Uemura 2000, 51).

Further efforts were made by Japanese firms to expand into foreign markets during the 1990s and 2000s. One of the consequences of the bursting of Japan's economic bubble in 1991 was a sharp rise in the number of nonperforming loans.[1] The decline in consumer and investor confidence that occurred as a result of this financial instability in turn produced what many considered to be a domestic underconsumption problem. As a result, firms (supported by the Japanese government) put more emphasis on attempting to increase exports to Asian markets. Initially, this led to increased trade with Southeast Asia, bit after the 1997–1998 Asian financial crisis focus switched again, this time toward China (Calder 2003, 609). At the same time, China's growth, especially in manufacturing, put further competitive pressure on Japanese firms (Mouer and Kawanishi 2005, 105).

These changing trade relations and growing internationalization can be seen in terms of Japan's trade statistics. Exports to China accounted for 5.0 percent of

Japan's total exports in 1995, rising to 13.5 percent in 2005 and 17.5 percent in 2015 (Ministry of Finance 2019). Similarly, exports to Asia increased from 43.5 percent of Japan's total exports in 1995 to 48.4 percent in 2005 and 53.3 percent in 2015 (ibid.).

This trend in internationalization advanced further in the wake of the 2007–2008 global financial crisis. This included an increase in Japanese corporations' production and sales overseas, rising exports from overseas production bases, and increased purchases of more locally manufactured parts and components (Ministry of Economy, Trade, and Industry 2011, 96–100). Perhaps one of the most noteworthy aspects of this growing internationalization can be seen in the 2017 decision by the government of Prime Minister Shinzō Abe to join the Trans-Pacific Partnership. This represented a significant further liberalization of the Japanese agricultural sector, which had long been considered overly protected (especially by Japan's trading partners). The strong opposition from the Japan Agricultural Cooperative—the country's agricultural cooperative organization, itself politically important as a source of support for the LDP—also highlights the degree to which this represented a significant change in the Japanese model (Choi and Oh 2017).

Japanese firms continued to increase production and sales in Asia throughout the 2010s. The number of Japanese overseas affiliates in Asia increased from fewer than 2,000 in 1990 to more than 6,000 in 2010. In the period 2000–2015, over 90 percent of new Japanese overseas affiliates were based in Asia (Hirano and Yamada 2018, 436 and 444–47). This led to both a rise in production by Japanese firms based in Asia and an increase in procurement from local firms based there. These trends illustrate how Japanese firms continued to seek cheaper goods and workers in Asia, thereby increasing competition between Japanese domestic firms and other Asian firms. Yasuo Hirano and Toshio Yamada argue that this indicates a decreased competitiveness and reduced exports on the part of firms based in Japan. This has occurred alongside an improvement in the financial situation of Japanese overseas affiliates. Thus, we see a "decoupling of Japanese firms from the Japanese economy," with improved performance of Japanese multinational corporations occurring largely outside of Japan (ibid., 444). This has enabled Japanese firms to improve their performance without at the same time increasing domestic economic growth. Heightened pressure from international competition has also produced a downward pressure on wages in Japan, as the domestic economy's insertion in the world economy creates ongoing pressure to compete and be cost-effective.

Most obviously, the rise of China has had a considerable impact on Japan's position in the world economy. This includes a further expansion of trade with and investment in China during the 2010s, with exports to China reaching a record high of 14.9 trillion yen in 2017—making China second only to the United States in terms of Japanese export destinations (Ministry of Economy, Trade, and Industry 2018, 3). A large proportion of the Japanese companies based in China are manufacturing companies, which have increased both their sales and their profits due to the increased demand related to the Chinese domestic market and its increasing trade (ibid.). While Japan benefits from the expansion of its trade and investment relations with China, Japan's export competitiveness has gradually been reduced. Hirano and Yamada claim that the share of Japanese exports as a proportion of total world exports declined by almost half, from 9.5 percent in 1995 to 4.9 percent in 2011 (2018, 438). This is especially evident in terms of the export of machinery—a key focus for Japan—with such exports as a proportion of global machinery exports decreasing from 15.2 percent in 1995 to 8.5 percent in 2011 (ibid.). This contrasts with China, which has seen a sharp rise in its exports of machinery (Obashi and Kimura 2016, 7). In terms of trade within East Asia, a key trend is that both China and South Korea had a growth of about 50 percent in exports of machinery in the period 2007–2013, while Japan's machinery exports were stagnant (ibid., 20).

In sum, therefore, changes to the integration of Japan in the international economy have produced a consistent process of liberalization and internationalization. This includes both the move of production overseas and an increase in trade. Moreover, the result of these developments has been to increase domestic competition—in turn putting indirect pressure on workers in Japan—as firms struggle to compete. We can see Japan's declining wage share, a growing wage gap between workers with high and those with low skills, and increased pressure on rural economies—all of which have resulted from changes in the way that Japan's economy is located in the international market (Ministry of Health, Labor, and Welfare [MHLW] 2008, 169–72). These changes have had a mutually reinforcing effect on the other key institutions identified by regulation theory.

Monetary and Financial Regime

As noted in the overview of regulation theory above in this chapter, monetary and financial regimes are considered crucial to any mode of regulation. This is because money is "the primordial social link in market economies," serving as the fundamental institution in any market economy (Aglietta 1998, 46). As many commentators have observed, the post-Fordist mode of capital accumulation has been widely associated with a growing and increasingly central role for finance, including the heightened liquidity of capital markets and an upsurge in the role of investment funds (Aglietta and Rebérioux 2006). This process of financialization has occurred in Japan, with the initial postwar model being transformed since the bubble burst in 1991. Moreover, these changes have in turn produced a more general increase in the susceptibility of the Japanese political economy to the pressures exerted by the need to be competitive in the global market economy (Guttmann 2002, 62).

Three pillars were central to the classic mode of regulation that emerged in Japan during the postwar period: a regulated financial market that was overseen by the interventionist Bank of Japan operating in coordination with the Ministry of Finance, a financial system (based on main banks) that represented the key route through which corporations could gain access to finance, and a related system of corporate governance in which main banks monitored the use and investment of the finances to which they provided access. This system therefore depended on the role of what is commonly referred to as the main bank, meaning the key bank integrated in and central to the funding of each network of firms (*keiretsu*). The relatively regulated and monitored nature of finance in the classic model in turn ensured that Japan's high levels of growth up until the 1970s could be achieved with a degree of stability, including stable interfirm and employment relations (Nabeshima 2000, 105–11; Tohyama 2000; Rosenbluth and Thies 2010).

The declining growth that was experienced in Japan in the 1980s produced a number of outcomes that began the unraveling of this monetary and financial regime. Large firms sought to reduce their costs by searching for cheaper funds. At the same time, Prime Minister Yasuhiro Nakasone implemented a program of financial deregulation that was prompted in part by the need to increase access to financial markets to finance growing levels of public debt (Lechevalier 2014e, 101). In addition, the Bank of Japan sought to stimulate growth through loose monetary policy. These developments prompted the larger firms to increase their reliance on alternative sources of finance, including through the stock market (Tohyama 2000, 79). There were two effects of this move toward alternative sources of finance: First, the role of main banks declined, as the relationship between firms and the banks eroded. Second, the increased financial stimulus, implemented at the same time as the monitoring role of the main banks was in decline, resulted in heightened (and nonproductive) speculation, fueling the bubble economy of the mid- to late 1980s that would eventually burst in 1991 (Nabeshima 2000, 113–14).

That bursting prompted a further increase in the role of international finance in Japan's economy. Nonperforming loans became a particular problem, prompting an increased search for finance outside of Japan. This had the additional effect of increasing the role of foreign actors in Japan's financial market and thereby further undoing the main bank system of finance that been central to the classic model of Japanese capitalism. In turn, the heightened role of foreign capital increased the frequency of foreign takeovers, which was exacerbated by the declining value of the yen (Uemura 2000; Schaede 2007). As a result, the foreign share of banking assets increased, especially in foreign exchange trading, private banking, loan syndication, and foreign currency deposits (Katz 2003, 186–87).

The 2000s witnessed the further disarticulation of Japan's postwar financial regime, although the difficulties that this created—especially for SMEs unable to gain access to sufficient sources of funding—prompted a slight reversal of liberalization, as demonstrated by the 2002 instruction of the government of Prime Minister Junichiro Koizumi to banks to provide loans to firms facing such a problem (Hoshi and Kashyap 2010, 403 and 404). This prompted the adoption in 2009 of the SME Financing Facilitation Act, although notably this did little to ease the heightened competition (especially the indirect pressure that this created in the labor market) that the process of financial liberalization had created in the Japanese economy (Gotoh and Sinclair 2018, 1045).

These trends increased after the global financial crisis. Investments in securities (stocks and bonds) increased by over 120 percent from 2012 to 2017 (Ministry of Finance 2017), strengthening the influence of shareholders in firms during the course of the Abe administration. As a result, earnings were increasingly distributed to shareholders rather than workers, with dividends increasing by nearly 160 percent from 2012 to 2017 and internal reserves growing by nearly 390 percent during the same period (ibid.). This has further consolidated the neoliberalization of the monetary and financial regime in the 2010s.

In sum, Japan's monetary and financial regime has undergone a process of internationalization and liberalization since the 1980s. This was largely driven by the need to identify alternative sources of financing in the context of low growth and a concomitant need to cut costs. While the initial move toward financialization fueled the economic bubble of the 1980s, the bursting of that bubble in 1991 prompted a further round of liberalization, particularly as a result of the problems created by nonperforming loans. This in turn has increased the role of more footloose, speculative, and foreign capital, further increasing pressure on firms to focus on costs rather than the maintenance of existing networks and supply chains. The impact of financial liberalization can also be seen in terms of consolidating a more general process of liberalization across Japan's mode of regulation—with the pressures for competition that have been engendered in turn making themselves felt on the regulation of firms (as the main bank system has been undermined) and the wage-labor nexus (as pressure for competition has resulted in a more disciplinary approach toward the labor market, as we shall see below).

The Form of Competition in the Japanese Model

In referring to the form of competition within a particular mode of regulation, regulation theory highlights the importance of considering the nature of inter-firm relations. This refers to the way in which firms relate to each other and the degree to which this is a competitive or a negotiated and/or coordinated type of relationship (Hollard 2002, 101). In the case of Japan, during the period of the classic postwar model, the relationship between firms took on a particularly novel form of cooperation that was widely remarked on. This consisted of cross-shareholding (which was referred to as "horizontal *keiretsu*") and a subcontractor system (known as "vertical *keiretsu*").

Under the system of cross-shareholding, the Bank of Japan and the Ministry of International Trade and Industry encouraged banks to buy shares in companies in key industries. As a result, by the 1960s some 65–70 percent of the shares of large companies were held by allied firms. These networks were typically organized around a single main bank. This relationship was sometimes termed "alliance capitalism," since it generated a degree of cooperation between firms and enabled firms to sacrifice the short-term maximization of profit in pursuit of longer-term goals (Anchordoguy 2005, 47–49; Witt 2006, 85–87).

The subcontractor system became increasingly common during the 1970s and 1980s. This took the form of stable subcontracting relationships between supplier and buying firms that allowed larger (buyer) firms to externalize labor-intensive production and gave subcontracting firms a stable supply relationship with the buyer firm. This was considered a key mechanism for limiting unemployment, as supplier firms could be confident that their goods would be bought on a steady basis (Isogai, Ebizuka, and Uemura 2000, 35–36).

During the 1980s the *keiretsu* system became increasingly strained. Larger firms such as Toyota, Canon, and Panasonic became profitable enough to finance their own investments through retained earnings. Under pressure from slower growth, firms also began to seek cheaper sources of credit from outside of the main bank system, including from overseas. As a result, the reliance on the main banks and the *keiretsu* networks were weakened (Anchordoguy 2005, 50; Lechevalier 2014c, 77; Rosenbluth and Thies 2010, 82).

Supply chains also began to change, especially during the 1990s as firms looked to Asia to obtain raw materials, resources, and cheaper labor. The possibility of hiring low-paid workers in China also incentivized Japanese corporations to move their production overseas, resulting in the breakup of supply chains as many subcontractors were unable to make the move overseas (M. Suzuki et al. 2010, 530; Bailey and Sugden 2007, 135).

At the same time, the influence of foreign capital was growing, and opinion leaders in Japan increasingly believed that corporations should be made more accountable to shareholders, especially to combat corporate mismanagement (Vogel 2006, 91). As a result, the government introduced what was known as the statutory auditor system in 1994, expanding shareholders' rights and making it easier to file shareholder suits (ibid., 92).

In addition to these developments, the 2000s witnessed a growing trend of mergers and acquisitions among manufacturing corporations seeking to increase their competitiveness and expand sales into East Asia (MHLW 2009, 185). This also included further growth in the role of foreign capital, including takeovers by foreign firms, more foreign-owned shares, and a corresponding increase in the need for firms to be respondent to shorter-term profit concerns (Rosenbluth and Thies 2010, 131; Hongo 2010).

We continue to witness the polarization of firms—between competitive "winners" and uncompetitive "losers"—in Japan in the 2010s. Hirano and Yamada argue that wage differentials between multinational and domestic firms diverged since the devaluation of the yen after the 2008 crisis. This decline of the value of the yen benefited large export-focused corporations such as Toyota, Nissan, Hitachi, and Nippon Telegraph and Telephone (NTT), enabling them to increase wages considerably. In contrast, firms that focused on domestic markets could not match these increases (Hirano and Yamada 2018, 448–49).

Japan has also continued to experience further integration of its market into international markets. As noted above, Japanese manufacturing firms established many subsidiaries in China starting in the 1990s. These firms increasingly assemble components to make goods in China and export them to Japan, the United States, and Europe. In the 2010s, these Japanese firms began to move factories from China to Southeast Asia to further reduce labor costs (Hirakawa et al. 2016, vi). The pursuit of cheaper labor in Southeast Asia by Japanese multinational firms continues to create competition and pressure on Japanese domestic manufacturers. Thus, we see a combination of overseas production in pursuit of cheaper labor, especially in China and now Southeast Asia, together with the hiring of cheaper nonregular workers in Japan's domestic labor market. These processes of neoliberalization have undermined the close ties between *keiretsu* firms.

In sum, since the 1980s we have seen a steady erosion of the relatively cooperative interfirm relations that were established in Japan in the 1960s and 1970s. The main bank system has also eroded as firms have become increasingly unwilling to restrict their supply of credit to a single domestic bank. And the subcontractor system has been eroded by firms becoming international and pursuing cheaper costs of production. In turn, the move toward a greater role for foreign capital has contributed to a shift in management culture, resulting in particular in a greater focus on meeting shareholder demands and corporate governance oriented around the shareholder—and this brings with it a greater concern for short-term profit considerations. One of the consequences of these trends has been a growing divide between larger firms (which are more able to adapt to the heightened pressure to be competitive and use shareholder-based corporate governance) and SMEs (which struggle to adapt) (Lechevalier 2014d, 65–68). This has further reinforced the breakup of integrated networks of firms that had been central to the Japanese form of competition.

The Form of the State

Regulation theory considers the form that the state adopts to be one of the central features of any particular mode of regulation (Boyer and Saillard 2002; Aglietta 1998). Under the classic postwar mode of regulation, the Japanese state has typically been viewed as a developmental state, especially one built around a "symbiotic relationship between government and business" (Walter 2005, 406). While the direct welfare provision allocated by the Japanese state never reached the levels of generosity associated with social democratic or corporatist welfare states such as Sweden and Germany, the classic postwar Japanese model did include considerable welfare provisions—albeit typically allocated through the firm and family. But both of these methods of welfare provision were supported indirectly by the Japanese state, especially through the state's role in underpinning the interfirm relations and employment practices that led to highly stable employment practices, as well as state support for rural policies that underpinned many wider family support networks. Thus, as Margarita Estévez-Abe sums up, the role of the state under the classic Japanese model includes the provision of "public works, subsidies to rural families, market-restricting regulations, and employment protections," all of which act as mechanisms to protect the livelihood of citizens" (2008, 3).

As we have seen in each of the other institutions that make up the Japanese mode of regulation, the form of the state also went through a series of considerable changes from the 1980s to the present. In particular, there were moves to further reduce welfare generosity, reduce the role of public enterprise, facilitate the introduction of increased market competition (especially through measures designed to support the dismantling of the *keiretsu*), and facilitate the liberalization of the labor market. Over this period, therefore, there was a move from a consensus-oriented development state toward a form of state that favors capital over labor and that has sought to increase the degree of market competition in product, financial, and labor markets. These trends echo many of the neoliberal

TABLE 1.2   Major policies and reforms, 1980s–2010s

	NEOLIBERAL REFORMS	MAIN EFFECT
1980s	1982 Abolition of free medical care for the elderly	Welfare retrenchment
	1983 Employment insurance reforms	Welfare retrenchment
	1984 Reduction of state subsidies in employment insurance	Welfare retrenchment
	1985 Pension reform	Welfare retrenchment
	1987 Worker Dispatch Law (WDL)	Labor market liberalization
	1987 Designated work system	Labor market liberalization
	1987 Variable workweek system	Labor market liberalization
1990s	1993 Labor Standard Law	Labor market liberalization
	1994 Statutory audit system	Procompetition reform
	1996 Council for Regulatory Reform	Probusiness, procompetition reform
	1997 Amendment to the WDL	Labor market liberalization
	1999 Reduction in farmers' pension benefits	Welfare retrenchment
2000s	2003 Amendment to the WDL	Labor market liberalization
	2000 Employment Labor Insurance Law	Heightened precarity for nonregular workers
	2001 Council on Economic and Fiscal Policy	Probusiness reform
2010s	2012 Amendment to the WDL	Labor market liberalization
	2013 Trans-Pacific Partnership task force	Trade liberalization
	2015 Amendment to the WDL	Labor market liberalization
	2015 Macroeconomic slide	Welfare retrenchment

reforms witnessed globally during the same period. Even when attempts have been made to reverse this trend—especially following the 2009 election, when the Democratic Party of Japan (DPJ) came to power—these efforts have been both muddled and poorly implemented, leading to both policy failures and reversals. The Japanese state form has therefore undergone an important transformation, in a neoliberal direction, between the 1990s and the end of the 2010s (see table 1.2 for a summary).

The introduction of neoliberal reforms to the Japanese state had already begun by the 1980s. In a context of declining growth, the governing Liberal Democratic Party of Japan (LDP) came to view welfare policies as burdensome and introduced a number of austerity measures. This included the abolition of free medical care for the elderly; raising the pension eligibility age from sixty to sixty-five; and cutting benefits in health care, pensions, children's allowance, and unemployment— all during the 1980s (Estévez-Abe 2008; Miura 2012; Park and Ide 2014). The 1980s also witnessed initial attempts to liberalize the labor market (although these were to accelerate considerably after the bursting of the bubble in 1991). For example, the government introduced legislation to permit the so-called designated work system (*sairyo rodo seido*) in 1987, providing employers with the discretion to demand that white-collar employees work according to flexible working times, and the variable workweek system (*henkei rodo jikan seido*), which increased the amount of unpaid overtime that employers could demand of employees. The share of firms using the latter system increased from 7 percent in 1989 to 53 percent in 2000 (Mouer and Kawanishi 2005, 11–15).

The 1990s witnessed additional moves by the Japanese state to liberalize the trade and financial sectors, as well as supporting the deregulation of the labor market and implementing further welfare reforms. These moves were largely with the support of business associations such as *Nikkeiren* (Japan Federation of Employers' Association), and in spite of opposition from organized labor (Miura 2008, 164–65). The moves culminated in the adoption of a key piece of legislation in 1999—an important amendment to the Worker Dispatch Law—that greatly extended firms' ability to hire nonregular workers (including temporary agency workers) by allowing them to employ a greater share of such workers and to keep them for a longer time. This consolidated the growing divide between regular and nonregular workers, with labor market flexibilization policies increasingly serving to widen the gap between the two groups in terms of both working conditions and pay (M. Suzuki et al. 2010, 532; Vogel 2006, 81; Mouer and Kawanishi 2005, 114–15; Yun 2010).

The increased tendency for the government to form alliances with capital was also increasingly evident during the 1990s and the 2000s. This could be seen, for instance, with the creation of the Council for Regulatory Reform in 1996, which was set up in an attempt to promote market deregulation and decentralization. It included no representatives from labor, and a majority of its members were representatives of large corporations and advocates of neoliberal reforms (Miura 2008, 164–65). The new Council on Economic and Fiscal Policy was set up in 2001 to monitor the monopolized power of planning budgets by the Ministry of Finance and facilitate the exercise of the prime minister's leadership; it reflected the opinions of neoliberal, private-sector experts on economic and policy formation (Kang 2010, 579). This council, under the strong control and leadership of the prime minister, exclusively favors business leaders and their opinions, with a focus on reducing costs, achieving employment flexibility, and maintaining economic competitiveness in global markets (M. Suzuki et al. 2010, 531–32). Likewise, the Koizumi administration excluded labor in forming its Labor Policy Council, which met without labor union representatives (R. Watanabe 2012, 40).

The 2000s saw further efforts by the Japanese government to increase internationalization through trade policies and financial deregulation (Schaede and Grimes 2003, 3). This added to ongoing pressure that led to the breakup of the *keiretsu* (Vogel 2006, 33). These neoliberal reforms were consolidated by the

Koizumi government, with efforts to reduce public works (and thereby lower public debt) (Rebick 2005, 102–3; M. Suzuki et al. 2010, 530). Other policies further widened the growing gap between regular and nonregular workers. For instance, the Employment Labor Insurance Law of 2000 improved unemployment benefits for regular workers while reducing the employment security of nonregular workers (Vogel 2006, 82).

In 2009 the DPJ took power with the expectation that it would reverse the trend of rising inequality. To move toward that goal, on entering office the DPJ adopted a fiscal stimulus package that included support for SMEs, tax deductions, the enhancement of regional and local development, the establishment of a safety net for employment, and a troubled asset recovery program to support financial institutions and the auto industries. While this activity produced a recovery in exports and household consumption, that was only temporary (largely driven by the temporary tax deduction), and in the longer term the public debt increased (Ninomiya 2012, 38–39). In addition, the DPJ government underwent a series of policy U-turns, resulting in a confused and incoherent policy program that was largely unsuccessful in terms of achieving its desired policy goals (Shibata 2016, 513–16).

These moves toward the neoliberalization of the Japanese state were largely extended by the Abe government. There were two additional amendments to the Worker Dispatch Law, extending the length of time that employers could hire temporary agency workers; the liberalization of the agricultural sector; trade liberalization; a sales tax hike' and pensions reforms that sought to reduce pensions by 2.5 percent (MHLW 2015b; *Asahi Shinbun* 2015x).

This formed part of what has been named Abenomics—is a package of economic reforms adopted under the Abe administration. Abenomics seeks to revamp Japan's economy through what have been presented as "three arrows," meaning three types of reforms or policy measures. The first type of measure took the form of expansionary monetary policy, including quantitative easing as a way to increase the money supply to prompt investment and therefore economic growth. The second type is the fiscal stimulus, which intended to stimulate the economy, especially by increasing public spending (in particular on infrastructure) and aggregate demand and employment. The third type' included a range of structural reforms, most of which were liberalization measures in areas such as agriculture, trade, and the labor market, and all of which were intended to produce the conditions needed for longer-term productivity gains and therefore sustainable economic growth. Abenomics thus consisted of policy measures and reforms that combined short-term measures designed to prompt growth and longer-term structural reforms designed to produce a shift toward a more neoliberal model of economic activity.

The Wage–Labor Nexus

Regulation theory considers the way in which the capital-labor relationship is managed. This consideration focuses particularly on the form taken by wage labor and therefore measures put in place to reduce the potential conflict between workers and employers. This is considered a central aspect of any mode of regulation. In the case of Japan, by far the biggest change that we have seen over the past four decades has been the dramatic rise in the role of nonregular workers in the Japanese labor market. Indeed, during the 1970s and 1980s, the mechanisms that were in place to ensure Japan's system of high employment stability—including long-term employment, a seniority wage system, high-quality job training, and job security—were admired all over the world. These have each been undermined as part of the wider changes to the Japanese mode of regulation that we have been considering in this chapter.

Measures were introduced as early as 1987 in an attempt to increase flexibility in the Japanese labor market. Such efforts became more earnest after the 1997–1998 Asian financial crisis, following which many firms sought to reduce labor costs by dismissing employees, breaking links with subcontractors, regulating overtime work, and laying off nonregular workers (Mouer and Kawanishi 2005, 106). This represented a transformation of Japan's model of labor adjustment, which had previously adopted the practice of transferring employees between fellow firms in a *keiretsu*. In a context where these networks were in decline, however, this became less possible (Rebick 2005, 41). As a result, the unemployment rate began to increase rapidly in the late 1990s, particularly in the manufacturing sector—which lost almost three million jobs in the period 1992–2001, 55 percent of which were lost in the first four years after the Asian financial crisis (Rebick 2005, 91 and 97). This drop was exacerbated by the shift of investment to other Asian countries, especially China, prompted by the high labor costs in Japan (ibid., 97).

As we have seen, one of the key pieces of legislation enabling the expansion of nonregular workers in the Japanese labor market was the 1999 amendment to the Worker Dispatch Law. This resulted in a steady increase in the proportion of nonregular workers in the Japanese labor force, from around 19 percent in 1990 to 24 percent in 1999 and nearly 40 percent in 2015. This liberalization process gave employers the opportunity to employ nonregular workers with flexible contracts.

The 1990s also saw a weakening of Japanese organized labor. This especially manifested itself in trade unions' declining ability (or willingness) to push for wage increases. Many unions in particular sought to protect job security rather than make wage demands. In addition, public-sector unions accepted the argument that low wage demands were in the national interest. As a result, a number of these unions agreed not to seek an increase in the basic wage—a principle known as "Base Zero" (Weathers 2008, 179; Rebick 2005, 82). Instead, increased payments (when they occurred) were enacted through bonuses, on the ground that these increased expenses were more easy for firms to manage (Weathers 2008, 179). Despite these attempts by the unions to reach a compromise under adverse economic conditions, however, between 1995 and 2000 economic growth slowed further, prompting employers to seek to weaken the influence of unions (ibid., 180).

The growing internationalization of the Japanese economy also created increased pressure on Japanese firms to compete. This in turn resulted in a further destabilization of the wage-labor nexus, as firms sought to reduce labor costs (Uni 2000, 68). This trend was accelerated by the Koizumi reforms and the attempt to reduce public enterprises and public support for the regions (M. Suzuki et al. 2010, 530). Moreover, in 2003 an additional amendment was made to the Worker Dispatch Law. This resulted in an increase in the most precarious form of employment—day labor (*hiyatoi*)[2]—during the 2000s (ibid., 532). These trends were exacerbated further following the global economic crisis, during which 790,000 nonregular workers were dismissed in the wake of declining production, and in a context in which firms preferred to avoid dismissing core regular workers (MHLW 2010, 155–58). We also see a rise in the number of workers on "free shift" or "zero hour" contracts—which do not specify working conditions, days, or hours or monthly payment, and which require workers to be available on demand without any guarantee of work.[3]

As a result of a combination of processes, therefore, the role of nonregular workers in the Japanese labor market has grown dramatically. In 2015, these workers made up 37.4 percent of the total workforce (Ministry of Internal Affairs and Communications 2019). In 2016 regular workers earned an average annual salary of 4.87 million yen, compared with 1.72 million yen for nonregular workers (National Tax Agency 2016). Nonregular workers' pensions are also much lower than those of regular workers. Nonregular workers have limited opportunities for in-house training, which further contributes to their lower income level and limits their opportunities to become regular workers (Cabinet Office 2009, 204). The increase in the proportion of nonregular workers in the Japanese labor market therefore represents a clear move to reduce the cost of labor and contain wage growth.

Finally, alongside the increased precarity created by the rise in nonregular jobs, we have witnessed an increasing number of instances where employers indirectly encourage employees to leave jobs voluntarily. Following the global financial crisis, and in response to public criticism of widespread dismissals, employees have been encouraged or coerced to "voluntarily" leave employment. For instance, employers have been known to bully employees or impose extremely harsh working conditions in an attempt to encourage them to resign and thereby avoid the potential legal risks associated with dismissals.[4] Similarly, new graduates have been dismissed at the end of their six-month probationary period.[5] Corporate elites are thus seeking innovative ways of directly and indirectly forcing workers to leave to avoid legal and industrial disputes, as well as public criticism.

The Japanese model of capitalism has been fundamentally transformed since the late 1980s. In each of the five institutions identified by regulation theory—insertion in the international market, monetary and financial regime, the form of competition, the form of the state, and the wage-labor nexus—there have been many substantial changes. A common trend is clear: whereas the classic Japan model represented an attempt to control and mediate the potential for instability, tension, and class conflict, the changes that we have seen have resulted in a disorganization of each of these earlier mechanisms of coordination. The internationalization of the Japanese economy has undone many of the compromises that were in place, heightening competition and reducing the degree of coordination between firms. The monetary and financial regime has seen the injection of foreign capital with a greater focus on short-term profit. Interfirm relations have moved away from both horizontal and vertical *keiretsu*. The state has become increasingly neoliberal. And in the wage-labor nexus we see a dramatic rise in the proportion of nonregular workers in the Japanese labor market. Each of these changes was prompted by the experience of declining growth in the 1980s and the more dramatic bursting of the bubble in 1991, and each change had a mutually reinforcing effect on the others.

Following Wolfgang Streeck's description of recent changes to the German economy (2009), we can consider the changes to Japan's model of capitalism outlined above to be a process of disorganization. As table 1.1 summarizes, the result of this disorganization has been a decline in the scope for social compromise and a corresponding increase in the degree of social conflict and division. Growing divides exist between more and less competitive firms, employers and employees, and regular and nonregular workers. Supply networks that had been established and consolidated have been dismantled. A state form that once sought to produce consensus has moved increasingly to represent business and exclude labor. In doing so, moreover, the Japanese state has moved from being a development state to one that focuses predominantly on increasing the pressure to compete. Institutions of collective wage bargaining have become redundant. The long-term security that was previously provided by firms (with the support of the government) has been steadily dismantled. The institutional mix that previously achieved a certain degree of consensus has been weakened and become unable to produce a similar level of coordination and consensus. In sum, political and economic institutions in contemporary Japan have become increasingly characterized by heightened instability, an absence of coordination and collaboration, the exclusion of organized labor, and the pursuit of intensified exploitation. It is in this context, in which Japan's model of capitalism is being disorganized, that we turn next to consider the scope for labor resistance and agency. First, in chapter 2, we consider the way Japan's labor movement has developed over time. Then, and in the remainder of the book, we examine the key instances of resistance and protest that have accompanied these changes to Japan's political economy, the effect they have had, and the resulting disorganization of Japan's contemporary socioeconomic model.

ORGANIZED LABOR AND
SOCIAL CONFLICT IN JAPAN

Japan has typically been portrayed as a national economy with harmonious labor relations, in which strikes are absent and confrontation is avoided by those trade unions that do exist (on this common, yet partly misleading, portrayal of Japanese industrial relations, see, for instance, Chalmers 1982). While such a picture of industrial harmony has always been limited in the degree to which it corresponds to the reality of Japanese class relations, it has become increasingly outdated over the past thirty years. To understand the contemporary circumstances facing Japanese labor (in both its organized and disorganized forms), and therefore to advance our attempt to assess the nature of class struggle and class tensions in Japan, we need first to explore the historical experience of trade unions. This includes a concern for both firm-based unions (usually referred to as "enterprise unions") and unions not linked to a specific firm ("community unions"), as each type has developed over time in Japan. This chapter therefore presents a historical overview of the development of the Japanese labor movement throughout the postwar period. With some exceptions, workers in Japan have been predominantly organized in unions that have had a commitment to a relatively nonconfrontational approach toward industrial relations. This organization has come to be challenged in more recent years, however, since the classic model of Japanese labor relations has faced increasing strain as part of the wider changes to the Japanese model of capitalism.

Alongside this historical overview of organized labor, this chapter also considers the development of other (non-labor) social movements. This includes those movements that have emerged to promote the interests of social groups whose interests overlap with those of labor but who might not immediately identify themselves as part of the labor movement, such as the homeless, unemployed, and students.

The trajectory of social conflict in Japan during the past thirty years has seen a move away from the classic model of social compromise. Various types of social conflict—both inside and outside of the workplace, and involving either workers or those less typically identified with organized labor—have become increasingly common.

From Militant Unions to Cooperative Enterprise Unionism

Japan's industrial relations witnessed an outbreak of widespread and disruptive acts of labor militancy in 1945–1947. Union membership rose from almost nothing to around five million workers. The new Supreme Commander for the Allied Powers (SCAP) introduced three labor laws that entitled workers to join unions, bargain, and take part in strike activity. These new labor rights, combined with conditions of deprivation, hunger, and dramatically rising inflation, resulted in rapid unionization and widespread industrial unrest during these first two postwar years (Jeong and Aguilera 2008, 115). Newly radicalized and organized workers took part in a series of high-profile and largely successful pay-related disputes, with over 150,000 workers participating in more than 250 incidents of "production control"—in which factories were taken over and managed by workers (Gordon 1985, 331–32).

In an attempt to regain control over Japanese society following this outbreak of worker militancy, SCAP responded by constructing a system of labor relations that was to last for much of the immediate postwar period and coincide with a period of sustained economic growth.

As part of these efforts to restabilize Japanese industrial relations, both the Japanese government and SCAP, with the support of the *Nikkeiren* (Japan Federation of Employers' Association), sought to put in place a number of measures that would reduce the power of Japanese labor, and especially the trade unions and other organizations that sought to represent it. Central to this process was a concerted effort to ensure that trade unions would be led by moderates (especially not communists) and aligned with the firms that employed their members (through the introduction of the enterprise unions mentioned above).

The government of Prime Minister Shigeru Yoshida (1946–1952) introduced a number of employment laws to further this goal of moderating Japanese labor. In 1948, the left-wing public employees' unions were tackled through the introduction of legislation that prevented workers in public enterprises from striking. This prohibition was also extended to civil servants. The initial postwar labor legislation was further revised in 1949, with the specific goal of reducing the possibility that communist-backed organizations could claim official trade union rights. Twelve thousand labor activists were dismissed as part of the "red purges" that accompanied the outbreak of the Korean War. To ensure that trade unions would take the form of enterprise unions (rather than industry-wide industrial unions), the Yoshida government, in collaboration with SCAP and *Nikkeiren*, sought to bring down the most important of the industrial unions, *Densan* (the Conference of Electricity Unions). To achieve this goal, *Nippatsu* (the national electricity supply company) was divided into nine regional enterprises, thereby disaggregating the industry, and *Densan* was similarly disaggregated (Jeong and Aguilera 2008, 117–18).

Having seen the outburst of labor militancy in the early postwar period successfully constrained, trade unionism in Japan increasingly developed by forming enterprise unions. This trend was largely based on a social compromise according to which workers and their unions would limit wage demands, in exchange for a high level of employment security (so-called lifelong employment). These enterprise union-based employment relations continued to expand throughout the 1960s and 1970s (Imai 2017, 91).

While industrial unions obviously did not disappear overnight, following the defeat of *Densan* in a prolonged industrial dispute of 1952 there were only glimpses of these alternatives to enterprise unionism. Confrontations led by more left-leaning and industry-wide trade unions, often with the support of *Sohyo* (General Council of Trade Unions of Japan), continued throughout the 1950s. However, most of these ended in defeat, eventually contributing to the demise of union types except for the enterprise unions. Therefore, the Japanese labor movement witnessed an eradication of industrial unions and a move toward more cooperative union leaders and enterprise unions, a process that was complete by the 1970s (Jeong and Aguilera 2008, 118–19).

As a result of these developments, enterprise unions became increasingly common and by the time of the 1970s they were by far the predominant form of trade union. Membership in enterprise unions is not based on industry or profession in the same way that it commonly is in the West (Ōhki 1998, 215). Instead, both white- and blue-collar employees are typically members of the same enterprise union, although the attachment of the enterprise union to a particular firm also routinely has the effect of excluding temporary workers from union membership (Shinoda 2008, 149; Jeong and Aguilera 2008, 114). As a result of this exclusion, moreover, enterprise unions have commonly been reported to "ignore the problems of temporary employees and the unemployed, and instead concentrate on activities exclusively to the benefit of permanent employees" (Ōhki 1998, 218; see also 220).

An additional consequence of the direct connection between enterprise unions and the firms to which they were attached was an alignment of interests between the two. Indeed, this was the main underlying reason for the initial opposition of SCAP and the Japanese government to industrial unions, which were expected to spread solidarity beyond the level of the firm and thereby increase the degree of collective bargaining strength and the militancy of workers. Once workers were collectivized in a particular firm only, their capacity to enter into disputes with "their" firm was diminished, as actions that would harm the firm would also directly affect the well-being of the workers. As a result, enterprise unions have generally adopted a policy of cooperating with management (Odaka 1999, 146; Nishinarita 1998, 197). Thus, labor activities are generally confined within the company and tend to be controlled by firms' values (Ōhki 1998, 217). This had contributed to the tradition of relatively harmonious relations between unions and management that is widely remarked on and became characteristic of postwar Japan, especially in comparison with other advanced industrial democracies (Odaka 1999, 146).

While the foregoing provides an account of the way Japan's unusually harmonious postwar industrial relations were constructed, we should recognize that the absence of open conflict does not represent the absence of exploitation or domination. Indeed, as John Holloway (1987) put it, in commenting on the opening of a new Nissan factory in the United Kingdom in 1986, it is merely a different style of domination by capital over labor—one in which relations of domination are disguised by the construction of consensus-based forms of capital-labor relations.

The potential for consensus-based industrial relations to limit the bargaining power of labor became more apparent once Japan entered a period of heightened economic strain. This was made especially visible in the light of the oil crisis of 1973 and the subsequent period of slower economic growth. In these conditions, "consensus" came to mean that enterprise unions would endorse the interests of the firm (which were interpreted in terms of the need to limit wage growth to survive the economic slowdown), with union officials and firm managers adopting remarkably similar functions (Tabata 1997, 85–86; Ōhki 1998, 221). Therefore, enterprise unions increasingly came to perform as another layer in the structure of labor management, acting in a way that was clearly supportive of firms' managers (Ōhki 1998, 221).

In sum, by the 1970s organized labor in Japan was almost entirely based on enterprise unions. In enterprise union systems, unions were typically associated with large firms, adopted a cooperative attitude toward "their" firms, and constructed a social compromise according to which wage growth would be limited in exchange for a high level of employment security. This form of enterprise unionism functioned to a degree while productivity and the economy were growing (enabling workers to acquire increased income as a result of higher levels of productivity). However, once productivity began to decline, and especially after 1991, the changes to Japan's labor market would highlight the limited capacity of enterprise unions to represent the interests of Japan's workers.

Key Unions and Their Role in Japan's Labor Movement

In addition to enterprise unions, however, *Sohyo*, under the influence of the Japan Socialist Party, continued to organize predominantly within the public sector. *Sohyo* adopted a more left-wing stance toward trade union organizing, having a more doctrinaire approach that was not always in keeping with the sentiments of public-sector workers. In strongly opposing the absence of these workers' right to strike, moreover, *Sohyo* entered into a number of disputes—for instance, with Japan National Railways—that would eventually lead to its further marginalization (R. Watanabe 2012, 29).

As *Sohyo* went into decline, it was gradually replaced by a new trade union federation, *Rengo* (the Japanese Trade Union Confederation), which included both private-sector and public-sector unions. The ability of *Rengo* to attract a broad range of unions was a source of strength. Yet it also meant that groups in *Rengo*—the internationally competitive export-oriented industries and the public-sector unions and those private-sector ones that were based in protected industries—had conflicting interests. The groups' contrasting positions would undermine the political influence of *Rengo* (R. Watanabe 2012, 29). *Rengo* has also been marked by a division between trade unions from firms of different sizes. In particular, a small number of large trade unions (representing some of the largest firms in Japan) have tended to dominate the organization, to the detriment of those unions based in small and medium-size firms (Ōhki 1998, 221–22).

While *Rengo* organizes the majority of enterprise unions based mainly at private-sector corporations, a majority of leftist unions—which considered *Sohyo* to be moderating its stance in the face of its decline, but which also opposed the probusiness stance of *Rengo*—formed *Zenroren* (the National Confederation of Trade Unions) (A. Suzuki 2008, 516). Most of *Zenroren*'s members are public workers' unions, including two of its largest members: *Jichiroren* (National Federation of Prefectural and Municipal Workers' Unions), a union representing local government officers, and *Zenkyo* (All Japan Federation of Teachers' Union.

In addition to *Rengo* and *Zenroren*, a third trade union federation, whose members are unions that disagree with the stances of the other two main federations, was also created in 1989. This is *Zenrokyo* (the National Trade Unions Council), which consists of roughly 300,000 workers under its branches across Japan. *Zenrokyo* includes a variety of unions, such as the postal workers' unions' association, cleaners' unions' association, and local community unions that are organized at the regional level.

These three federations came to form the three main national centers of union associations in Japan from 1989 onward. In terms of political affiliation, *Rengo* tends to support the main opposition parties that contest the electoral dominance of the Liberal Democratic Party of Japan. This includes support for the Democratic Party of Japan (before it split into a number of splinter parties in 2017). *Zenrokyo* loosely supports the Social Democratic Party, whereas *Zenroren* is inclined to support Communist Party of Japan,[1] although each of the federations are officially independent from any political parties.

Union membership has been consistently declining since the early 1990s (as in other developed economies), falling to about 18 percent in 2009 in Japan (A. Suzuki 2008, 493; Shinoda 2008, 150). Likewise, the numbers of unions and union members belonging to *Rengo* has been gradually decreasing (see figures 2.1 and 2.2). While *Rengo* has the largest number of member unions (mainly enterprise unions), the declining ability of those unions to pose a significant challenge to the authority of firms in a context of lower levels of economic growth in the period after 1991, alongside the growing proportion of nonregular workers (which unions in *Rengo* have struggled to represent), has led to a pattern of declining membership (and therefore declining influence). Indeed, on many occasions enterprise unions (which form the large majority of *Rengo*'s unions) have willingly acquiesced to the claim by firms that they need to cut costs and restructure to survive the economic downturn (Imai 2017, 90; A. Suzuki 2008, 494). This experience of decline, in turn, has led in more recent years to *Rengo*'s unions seeking ways to revitalize themselves, especially through alternative recruitment methods that seek to focus on nonregular workers. However, this strategy has faced considerable difficulties.

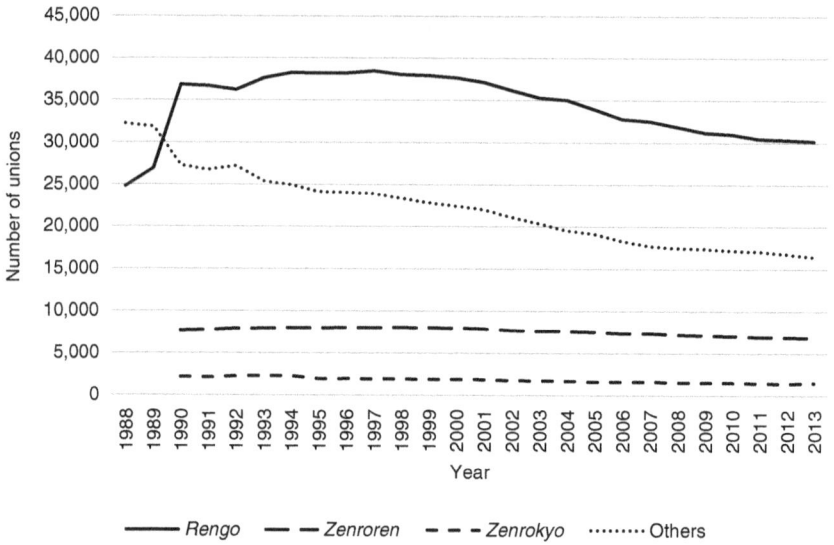

FIGURE 2.1. Number of unions, by union association, 1989–2013

Source: Labor Union Basic Survey: historical data (e-Stat).

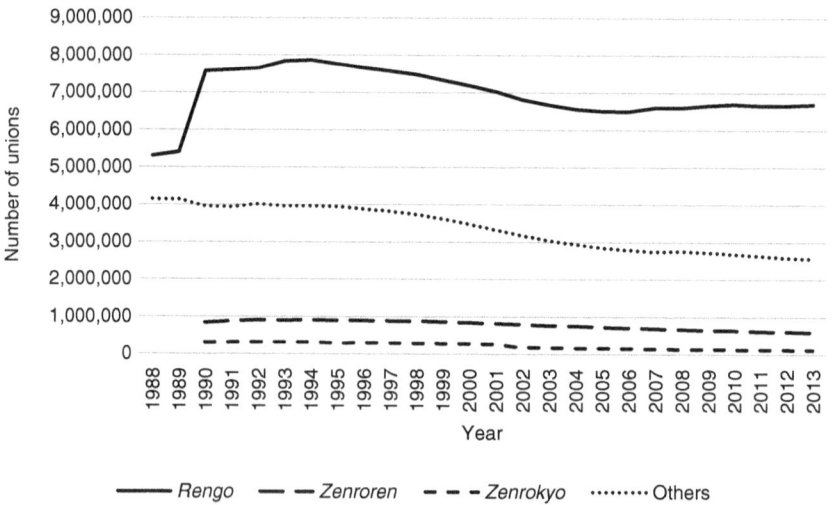

FIGURE 2.2. Number of union members, by union association, 1989–2013

Source: Labor Union Basic Survey: historical data (e-Stat).

The Emergence of Community Unions and Unions for Women

In addition to the major unions and union federations discussed above, in the past four decades of a number of more innovative types of trade unions have emerged in Japan. These types include especially community unions. As noted above, these organize around place, rather than industry, craft, or firm. The types also include a number of women-only unions, which seek to address what they consider to be the gender-blind practices of the more mainstream unions.

Community unions were first created in the early 1980s. They were typically set up by left-wing labor leaders who were seeking to recruit part-time workers (Weathers 2010, 68). Organizing in a particular place, and often in alliance with community-based and/or nonunion organizations, community unions sought to incorporate both regular and nonregular workers. However, community unions have tended to attract those whom the mainstream *Rengo* enterprise unions have largely failed to represent.[2] This includes especially nonregular and foreign workers (A. Suzuki 2008). Thus, the growth of community unions since their emergence in the early 1980s also reflects the changing nature of Japan's labor market (Kinoshita 2007, 149–53; Weathers 2010, 69). Available data suggest that union membership rates among nonregular workers have steadily increased, especially since the 1990s—in part facilitated by the creation of new community unions.

The majority of community unions were originally organized by regional labor councils affiliated with *Sohyo* (A. Suzuki 2008, 502). These councils sought to engage in a number of activities designed to improve the conditions of workers who were typically underrepresented by the larger, and more common, enterprise unions. This included nonregular workers and those who were based in smaller firms that had no enterprise unions. Organizing and recruitment methods included staging regional rallies or demonstrations, submitting policy proposals to local governments on issues that would improve the lot of workers, promoting the unionization of unorganized workers, and supporting councils' member unions when they were involved in labor disputes. In addition, some councils supported nonregular workers and workers in small firms (who in addition to often being excluded from enterprise unions, were frequently not unionized and experienced poor working conditions) (A. Suzuki 2008, 502–3). Due to their focus, community unions have tended to be relatively small organizations, with a higher proportion of women and foreign members than the more mainstream unions have (women and foreign workers combined make up the largest proportion of community unions' membership, around 40 percent) (ibid., 500). Reflecting changes in the Japanese labor market, the numbers of regional labor councils have grown steadily, increasing from seven in the mid-1980s to fifty in 1989 and ninety in 2009. Total membership in community unions had grown to around 17,000 by 2005 (A. Suzuki 2008, 504; Fukui 2005, 23).

As the number of community unions began to grow, attempts were made to coordinate their activities. The Community Union Nationwide Network was established in 1990 by sixty community unions that collectively represented 10,000 members. This network allowed the community unions to be loosely connected (A. Suzuki 2008, 504; Fukui 2005, 26). In addition, the Japan Community Union Federation was established as a national center for regional community unions in 2003.

As a result of some of these successes, a number of commentators have come to see community unions as holding an important potential to revitalize the labor movement in Japan, especially through their focus on the newer category of non-regular workers that is increasing in importance in Japan's labor market (Kazama 2007; Kinoshita 2007; Fukui 2005). However, the new group of community unions face a number of significant obstacles. In particular, the high turnover in employment of nonregular workers creates substantial obstacles to their recruitment, as workers without fixed employment have tended to have less motivation to join a union. The financial resources available to community unions have also been limited, in part as a result of recruiting lower-income workers with correspondingly low membership fees (Fukui 2005, 25; A. Suzuki 2008, 500).

In addition to community unions, another new development in Japan's labor movement has been the emergence of women-only unions, including *Onna Kumiai* (the Women's Labor Union), Jyosei Union Tokyo (Women's Union Tokyo), and Nanohana Union in Tokyo. These began to emerge in the 1980s, largely underpinned by an attempt by their founding members to "avoid the domination of male-dominated organizations and to raise women's consciousness" (Weathers 2010, 73). In particular, female labor activists came to view the mainstream (male-led) unions as insufficiently focused on issues of gender, including the gender pay gap, sexual harassment, the perpetuation of gender stereotypes, and internal union hierarchies that privilege male union leaders (Zacharias-Walsh 2016, 37).

New Social Movements

In addition to considering the development of Japan's labor movement, we can also consider the way in which other forms of social movements have developed during this period. While social movements and labor movements have tended to have different goals and their memberships have often had different demographic characteristics, nevertheless the scope for cross-fertilization between labor movements and social movements has been widely noted (Johnston 1994). In particular, methods of organizing and campaigning have often been transferred between the two, as lesson learning and the diffusion of strategies occur between different social, protest, and labor movements (Tarrow 2010). We focus here especially on the new social movements that are typically considered to have developed in the 1970s as an outcome of the New Left protest movements of the 1960s—including peace, environmentalist, and antinuclear movements (for a discussion of these developments in Europe, see Kriesi et al. 1995). Indeed, for a number of years these new social movements have been considered to be central to the processes of social conflict in contemporary advanced industrial democracies, and thus their impact on the wider terrain of labor movements is particularly worthy of consideration (Inglehart 1997).

In contrast to much of the rest of the Global North, however, in Japan the influence of the New Left, and especially its subsequent inspiration for a 1970s wave of new social movements, was considerably muted. While radical student movements emerged in Japan in the 1960s, focused especially on protest against the security treaty with the United States, the extent of the defeat of these movements (in part due to violent sectarian infighting) meant that they had much less lasting influence in Japan than in other countries (Cassegård 2014).

The new social movements that emerged during the 1970s and 1980s in Japan tended to focus on nuclear energy, environmentalism, and ethnic discrimination. Moreover, in the context of Japan's growing economy, concern for related problems, such as pollution and the failure of both national and local governments to deal properly with this growing issue, increasingly came to the fore (Funabashi 2011).

In the late 1990s and early 2000s a new wave of protest movements emerged in Japan. This in part reflected wider societal disillusionment with Japan's socioeconomic model and the neoliberal attempts that were being made to return to economic growth. While these movements were largely made up of youth groups, despondency over the earlier failures of the student movements of the 1960s and 1970s resulted in students adopting a "nonsect" strategy that sought to appeal to people outside of university campuses. One of the key methods of protest adopted during this time was a series of "sound demos" (or raves), whose participants were largely youth or precarious workers protesting against globalization, privatization, and war (Cassegård 2014; Hayashi and McKnight 2005).

Partly in an attempt to avoid the marginalization experienced by the earlier more doctrinaire and militant Marxist student movements, the sound demos increasingly adopted a street party–style of protest. This involved a conscious effort to "mobilize the political potential" of attendees "by reintroducing the elements of the pleasure principle of mass culture into ideologized political protest," including through the use of DJ sound trucks, dance, and cosplay clothing (Mōri 2005, 17). Likewise, some of the groups (such as Chance, which contributed to the antiwar movements of the early 2000s) deliberately distanced themselves from old leftist politics by refusing to use the term "demonstrations," instead referring to "Peace Walk" or "Walk" (ibid., 20). Youth movements of the late 1990s and early 2000s were typically made up of people with a less strongly leftist political agenda or identity who had less experience of political activism and sought to downplay ideology and theory in favor of the pursuit of pleasure through sources such as music and dance (Henk et al. 2010, 5; Cassegård 2014, 56).

Increasingly, new groups of people with different political agendas began to attend these sound demos (Hayashi and McKnight 2005, 94; Mōri 2005). As a result, young people, young part-time workers, and people opposed to Japan's long working hours—many of whom had little experience with political activism—increasingly joined the sound demos in Hibiya Park in Tokyo, as well as the subsequent series of street demonstrations and parties that accompanied the start of the Iraq War in 2003. These events also included criticism of the lifestyle associated with Japan's classic postwar socioeconomic model, especially that of the so-called salary man (whose lifestyle was becoming increasingly unattainable in the context of rising patterns of nonregular employment) (Cassegård 2014, 184). While the appeal to a newer generation of politicized youth had certain advantages, there were a number of limitations as well. Most notably, the predominant role of the internet in organizing protest events, along with the lack of substantive connections between participants, often led to a lack of lasting movements or networks that could be sustained between individual events (Mōri 2005, 17–19).

A final social movement to consider here is the homeless movement. Such a movement emerged in Tokyo in the early 1990s, in part driven by the rise in homelessness resulting from the changes to Japan's economic model at the time. This movement was led by a coalition of committed activists seeking to address the issue of homelessness, especially in areas where day laborers were concentrated (Hasegawa 2006, 83). In seeking to bring attention to the issue of homelessness, activists and homeless people enacted "sit-ins, hunger strikes, blockades, and a number of unregistered rallies and demonstrations" (ibid., 93).

The focus on housing in Tokyo also meant that the homeless movement direct confronted the Tokyo Metropolitan Government (TMG). Initial tactics by activists included patrolling, providing soup kitchens, and helping people fill out applications for welfare benefits. Each of these initiatives was relatively successful, contributing to the growth of the movement. However, initial growth was reversed by the actions of the TMG in the late 1990s, when police prevented the activities of the homeless movements (Hasegawa 2006, 101–102 and 139). This in turn prompted many homeless activists to adopt a less confrontational, more institutionalized, approach. Thus, activist leaders abandoned their initial goal of establishing self-sustenance support centers and instead entered into direct negotiations with government officials in a way that excluded the homeless from participating in the discussions (ibid., 138).

Not all of the homeless movements took the institutional route. *Moyai*—a nonprofit campaign group formed by Yuasa Makoto and Tsuyoshi Inaba, two grassroots activists who had been involved in the homeless movements in Tokyo in the 1990s—continued with a more grassroots-focused approach in the early 2000s. This included efforts to provide support for precarious youth and homeless people. In particular, attention was directed toward the increase in the number of so-called net café refugees, who tend to be homeless young people who work as temporary nonregular workers or day laborers and who use internet cafés as a cheap source of shelter. *Moyai*'s activities focused on seeking to provide housing for homeless people and vocalizing opposition toward, as well as highlighting the existence of, youth poverty, low pay, and homelessness.

Recent Trends

A number of recent trends can be seen in Japan's labor movement. In particular, we continue to witness efforts to represent nonregular workers in a number of different ways. These efforts often face a range of obstacles, which has arguably limited their impact. The traditional round of wage demands (*Shuntō*, or "spring offensive") was effectively ended in 2002 when the *Rengo* unions agreed not to make a wage claim (ostensibly due to the existence of deflation in the Japanese economy), but there have been a number of efforts to revive the initiative. In particular, in 2001 the *Paato Kyoutou Kaigi* (Part-Time Workers' Joint Struggle Council), set up by a coalition of unions belonging to *Rengo*, attempted to launch a collective wage bargaining initiative for part-time workers only. This reflects a broader concern in *Rengo* that membership decline and the changing nature of the Japanese labor market both imply that mainstream unions must reach out to nonregular workers if they are to remain viable and sustainable. This can be seen, for instance, in the case of *UA Zensen* (an association of enterprise unions in the service sector), whose membership grew by 50 percent between 2006 and 2016, largely as a result of recruiting nonregular workers[3] (Keizer 2019, 239). The number of *Rengo* unions reporting that they were acting on behalf of nonregular workers has also increased.[4] Similarly, the decline in union membership came to a halt in 2007, largely due to the increased recruitment of nonregular workers (Kalleberg and Hewison 2015, 26).

Despite these apparent successes by mainstream *Rengo*-group unions in their recruitment and representation of nonregular workers, there have been a number of obstacles to these initiatives. Unions have been less than wholehearted in their pursuit of nonregular workers' interests, largely on the ground that a conflict of interest is perceived between regular and nonregular workers. According to this view, if nonregular workers' conditions improved, that would have a detrimental effect on regular workers. As a result, most unions (whose majority of members remain regular workers) often offer only limited support for nonregular workers' initiatives. This can be seen in the collective wage bargaining initiative of the Part-Time Workers' Joint Struggle Council, which largely failed to have an impact on the firms with which it was seeking to negotiate (Weathers 2008, 185–91). In addition, the occasions on which unions such as *UI Zensen* have been successful have been largely limited to attempts to represent "upper tier" part-time workers (such as affluent housewives in prosperous urban areas). This is an outcome accredited by some to the continued failure to adopt a more confrontational approach toward employers, resulting in pay raises being awarded only in already prosperous areas—where employers are more inclined (and better able) to meet worker demands (ibid.).

One final development of significance to Japan's contemporary industrial relations is an increase in the frequency of individual workers' goings outside of the framework of trade unions. Each prefectural labor bureau has witnessed an increase in the number of disputes that non-unionized individual workers have entered into with their employers. This is partly due to the increase in a number of nonregular workers, who (as we have seen) tend to be considered difficult to represent and therefore also tend to be nonunionized and operate as individuals. In part as a response to this trend, some existing unions have begun to offer a shop-floor support system, whereby workers can access an individual support or consultation service—perhaps as one step toward unionization (Imai 2017, 98–99).

The labor movement in Japan historically has been oriented toward a nonconfrontational model of enterprise unions that moderated wage demands in exchange for long-term employment security. This form of enterprise unionism worked well when the economy was growing and productivity increasing, as it also resulted in an increase in wages. However, widening inequality since the 1990s and the exclusion of an increasing number of nonregular workers have led to Japan's labor movement experiencing a considerable loss of vitality. In particular, declining productivity and the rise of employment insecurity have tended to render the firm-level, nonconfrontational approach of enterprise unions largely ineffective.

It is in this context that we have seen various efforts to revive Japan's labor movement. While community unions have emerged in an effort to organize and recruit nonregular and atypical workers, unions in *Rengo* have also attempted to adjust their strategy to make themselves more appealing to nonregular workers. In the case of *Rengo*'s attempt to integrate nonregular workers, however, the instrumental nature of this strategy (driven largely by a desire to increase membership, without dealing with the apparent problem of conflicting interests between regular and nonregular worker members) has resulted in a somewhat halfhearted approach. Thus, if a revival of organized labor is to happen in Japan, it appears more likely that it will occur through community unions rather than *Rengo*. Instances of social conflict can also be observed through a study of social movements in Japan. While the militant and somewhat doctrinaire student movements of the 1960s were largely marginalized in Japanese society, since the 1990s we have seen less ideological networks forming around issues that speak directly to youth, including young nonregular workers. We might consider these more innovative forms of protest movements, therefore, to also have the potential to contribute to the revival of a movement representing nonregular workers in the workplace and Japan's labor market.

3

FROM PRECARITY TO CONTESTATION

Japan's transformation since the 1980s involved an increase in market competition, income insecurity, and the partial dismantling of the institutions of consensus-based capitalism. These changes also included the emergence of a new sector of the workforce: nonregular workers with low levels of job protection, low levels of loyalty to their employer, and no lifetime job guarantee—all of which were previously considered hallmarks of Japanese capitalism. Earlier studies have noted these trends but have tended to treat them as developments that have happened to individuals and workers in Japanese society. In contrast, this study seeks to consider the ways in which these changes have been contested, focusing especially on acts of resistance conducted by different types of workers in Japan.

This chapter explores the changing patterns of workers' resistance and protest that have occurred alongside, in opposition to, and as a response to the processes of neoliberalization that we discussed in chapter 1. This chapter presents the key findings of an analysis of protest events that involved compiling a catalog of over 4,000 reports in *Asahi Shinbun* (one of Japan's major national newspapers) from the 1980s to 2017 of protest events conducted by Japanese workers. The data set charts the type of actor, form of protest, and target of the protest for each reported event. These events are a sample taken from key periods in the transformation of Japan's political economy: 1986–1988 (to highlight trends before the bursting of the economic bubble), 1995–1998 (to provide an insight into patterns of protest during the initial wave of reforms introduced after the bursting of the bubble), 2000–2003 and 2005–2007 (to update trends as they occurred before the global financial crisis and during the reforming government of

Prime Minister Junichiro Koizumi), 2008–2009 (to provide insights into responses to the global crisis), and 2013–2014 and 2016–2017 (to highlight events in the administration of Prime Minister Shinzō Abe). A detailed discussion of the coding method and sampling rules of the research can be found in the appendix. The findings are used to consider the changing trends in worker-led protest throughout the period of neoliberalization. The results identify heightened contestation, with reported events undertaken increasingly by precarious and nonregular workers using different methods of protest. Later chapters will consider the effect of these changing patterns of resistance, highlighting the way they have rendered problematic the progress toward neoliberalization, especially as attempted by the Abe government.

The Rise of Labor Activism in Times of Change

The key event that prompted the transformation of Japan's mode of regulation was the bursting of the economic bubble in 1991. It is perhaps unsurprising, therefore, that we can also identify a clear change in both the frequency and form of protest events before versus after 1991. The frequency of protests rose dramatically from the 1980s to the 1990s (see table 3.1). It then declined in the first half of the 2000s but rose again to a peak of around ten times the level of the 1980s in the immediate aftermath of the global financial crisis and the beginning of the current Abe government, before declining again in the 2016–2017 period to an annual average frequency of 629 worker-led protest events (compared with an annual average of 90 events per year in the 1980s period).

These figures certainly suggest that the more stability-oriented mode of regulation in existence before the bursting of Japan's economic bubble and the subsequent process of disorganization described in the chapters 1 and 2 gave rise to an increase in worker-led acts of protest. These changing patterns can also be seen if we consider the types of actors protesting throughout this period. By charting the different types of protest activity, we can see the changing forms of protest during the study period. This is important because it allows us to consider the degrees to which protest events are more or less confrontational and challenge

TABLE 3.1 Average annual number of protest events, 1986–2017

PERIOD	1986–1988	1995–1998	2000–2007	2008–2009	2013–2017
Number of events	90	690	420	1,007	629

Source: Author's data set.

the status quo (and how) and therefore provides an indication of the likely impact that particular types of protest events will have on the social compromise in place at any one time. Figure 3.1 therefore presents details of the main types of agents undertaking the different protest events reported for each period. The organizations leading the majority of the more frequent protest events of the 1990s were the two major national trade union organizations, *Rengo* and *Zenroren*. In contrast, from 2008 onward the role of both *Rengo* and especially *Zenroren* declined, with protests led by nonregular workers and nonprofit organizations (NPOs)[1] and citizens' groups increasing in frequency. It appears, therefore, that in addition to an increasing frequency of acts of protest and dissent, Japan's political economy also saw a rise in the role of nonregular workers in conducting acts of dissent, especially from the mid-2000s onward. This reflects the changing form of Japan's model of capitalism, with new patterns of exploitation apparently giving rise to new agents of dissent.

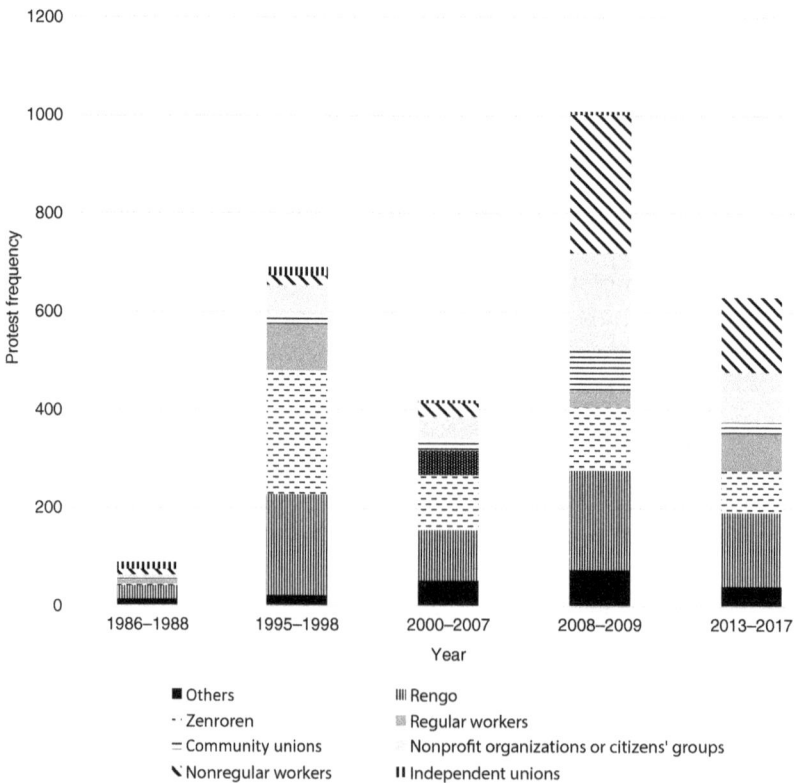

FIGURE 3.1.   Protest frequency, by type of agent, 1986–2017

Source: Author's data set.

To make this trend clearer, figure 3.2 compares the proportion of events conducted before to 2008 with those conducted in 2008–2017. As we can see, the role of the two main trade union federations declines (especially that of *Zenroren*), while the role of nonregular workers increases, as does that of the NPOs and citizens' groups.

The increased frequency of protests conducted by nonregular workers, rising dramatically in 2008–2009, was directly linked to both the experience of insecure, precarious employment and the sharp rise in dismissals that occurred following the global financial crisis. Many of the protest events conducted during this period by nonregular workers were directly in opposition to firms' dismissing nonregular workers. For instance, Nissan Diesel, which dismissed about 200 workers at the end of December 2008, faced a collective lawsuit from its nonregular workers (*Asahi Shinbun* 2008c). Likewise, dispatch workers[2] at Isuzu Motors in Kanagawa formed a union and mounted a legal challenge against the company after it announced the dismissal of 960 nonregular workers (*Asahi Shinbun* 2008f). Nonregular workers at Canon Oita formed a union and demanded job protection and their right to stay in their dormitories (the majority of nonregular workers live in company-provided accommodations) after the firm announced its plan to reduce the number of nonregular workers by over 1,000 in 2008 (*Asahi*

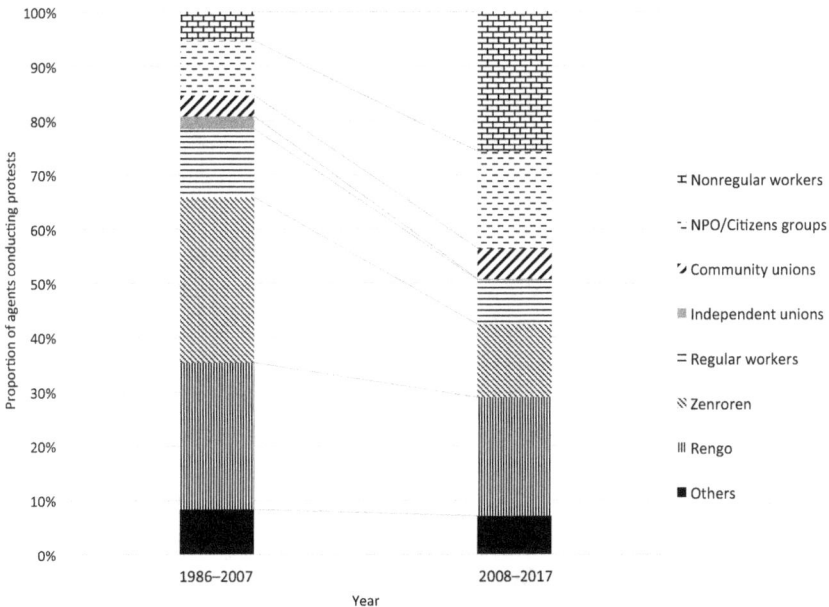

FIGURE 3.2.   Agents conducting protests as a proportion of total, 1986–2017

Source: Author's data set.

Shinbun 2008h). The grievances motivating many of these protests were also clearly visible in the language used by the protesting nonregular workers. For instance, one worker who had lost his job at Canon Oita noted that "we as contract workers live in the company's dormitory—losing jobs directly means losing our place to live" (quoted in *Asahi Shinbun* 2008e, author's translation). Other protestors who had also lost their jobs at Canon Oita exclaimed: "It is toward the end of the year—what do you think about people who lost their jobs and houses? . . . Are they [Canon Oita] telling us that we should die? They say that they have nothing to do with this dismissal since the temp agent is our employer" (quoted in ibid., author's translation).

The increased frequency with which protest events conducted by NPOs and citizens' groups occurred also reflected the changes affecting Japan's political economy. Community unions represent workers in a geographical region, in contrast to enterprise unions that are typically based in a specific firm. This alternative format of organizing adopted by community unions has also tended to be more appropriate for representing workers who had been underrepresented by the enterprise unions, especially women (A. Suzuki 2008, 500). For instance, the *Tokyo Kanrishoku* Union (Tokyo Managers' Union) and the Women's Union Tokyo both became increasingly active from the mid-1990s onward.[3] These developments also reflected the particular issues that women increasingly experienced as nonregular workers. As one union activist, Momoyo Kamo, then president of *Zenkoku* Union, explained, "part-time female workers have consistently faced an unstable employment status. For instance, female employees have typically been unable to acquire paid holidays, and they are not eligible for membership in enterprise unions. Thus, when their employment contracts are not renewed there has been no place for them to get support, and no institutions to represent part-time workers or negotiate with their employers."[4]

The changing patterns of protest events in Japan following the global financial crisis can also be observed if we consider the key actors divided into two types: Japan's traditional types of workers and workers' organizations (*Rengo, Zenroren*, and regular workers), versus the newer emerging types of workers and workers' organizations that appear to have come into existence as part of the neoliberalization of Japan's political economy (community unions, NPOs and citizens' groups, nonregular workers, students, homeless workers, and the unemployed). Figure 3.3 shows the proportion of all protest events carried out by the two groups in the study period. The traditional categories of workers and organizations were responsible for a large majority of the protests carried out in the 1980s and 1990s, but this trend was reversed in the wake of the global financial crisis, after which there was a small rise in the proportion of events carried out by the traditional categories in the 2010s. By the end of the period, therefore, the emerging group

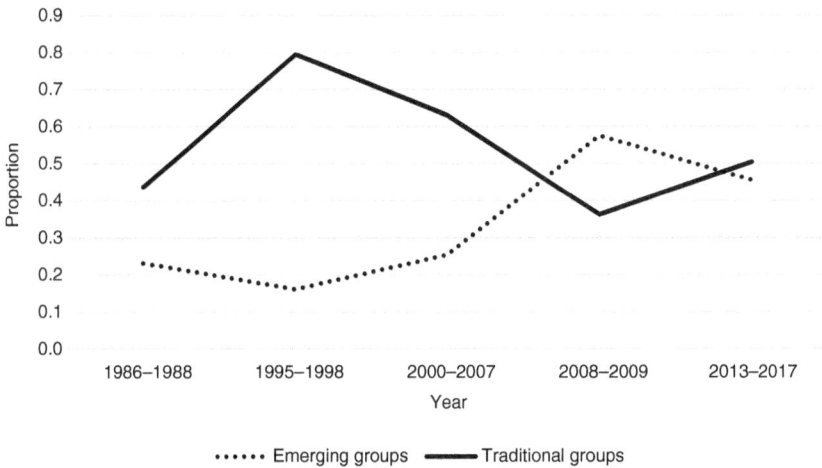

FIGURE 3.3. Proportion of protests conducted by traditional and emerging groups, 1986–2017

Source: Author's data set.

roughly equaled the more traditional actors in Japan's labor movement, at least in terms of the frequency with which they carried out protest events.

We can also witness changes in the types of actions conducted during the study period. Figure 3.4 divides the protest events into six different types: nondisruptive claims (petitions, letter-writing campaigns, meetings, and so on), May Day events (which form part of the institutionalized process through which workers' demands have typically been made in the classic Japanese model of capitalism), dissemination of workers' rights (through acts such as leafleting, providing consultation events, providing advice by phone, and other ways of informing workers of their legal rights), collective wage bargaining (whereby unions submit wage claims and subsequently enter into negotiations with firms), industrial and legal disputes, and nonroutine protest events (those which fall outside of the "standard" protests that accompany May Day).

Perhaps the most striking way protest events changed over the post-1991 period is the initial increase in protest activity immediately after the bursting of Japan's economic bubble is the increase in May Day protest events. In this sense, we might consider the responses and protests of the 1990s to have largely been conducted in one of the more conventional channels through which workers' interests and demands had typically been articulated in Japan's classic model of capitalism before 1991. This pattern of protest event types changed in the 2000s and 2010s. First, we can see a decline in the number of May Day events during 2000–2007, when the average annual number of all events also declined. However,

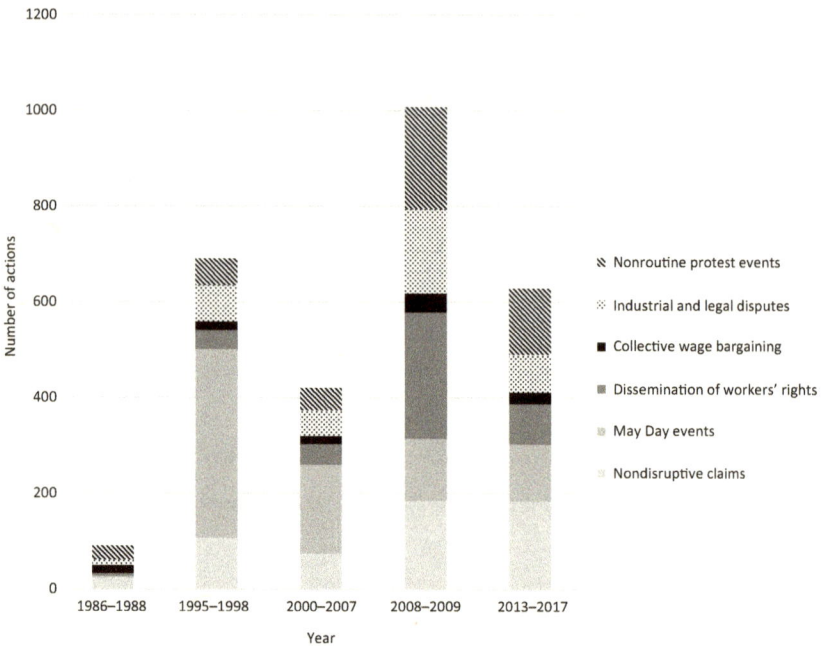

FIGURE 3.4.   Protest frequency, by type of action, 1986–2017

Source: Author's data set.

the crisis period of 2008–2009 saw the rise of other forms of protest—especially nonroutine protest, industrial and legal disputes, and events designed to disseminate workers' rights. This move away from standard forms of protest such as the May Day events and toward new forms of protest (especially reflected by the growth in nonroutine protest) therefore represents an important change in the way in which workers' interests have begun to be advanced in Japan's changing political economy. Indeed, while the total number of average annual protest events declined after 2008–2009, the types of protest activities remained constant—with a larger role for nonroutine protests and a smaller role for May Day events. Figure 3.5 makes this trend clearer still, by comparing the proportions of different types of events before 2008 and from 2008 onward. In comparing the 1980s with the post-1991 periods, we see both a rise in the number of protest events and a change in the identity of the actors and organizations conducting workers' protests, and in the form of those protests. Japan's political economy has generated new actors expressing dissent in different ways.

We can see these trends when we consider the rise of community unions. For example, in 2006 the *Freeter Zenpan Roudou Kumiai* (Unions for Casual Workers)

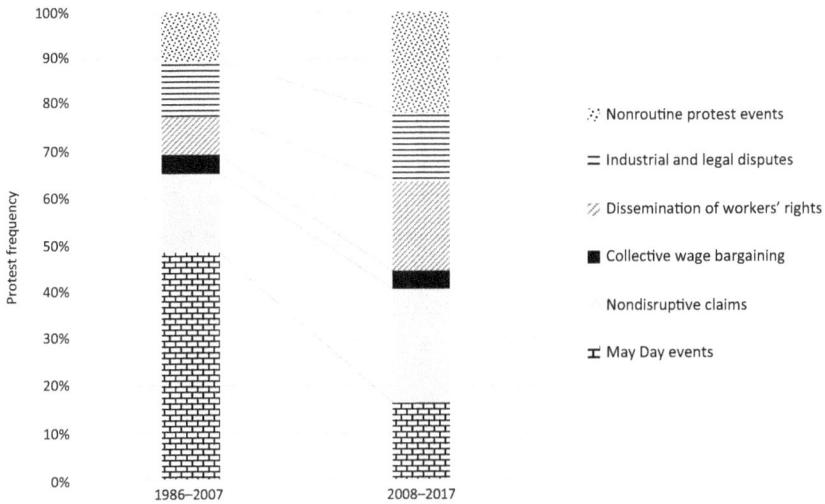

FIGURE 3.5. Proportion of protests, by type of action, 1986–2017

Source: Author's data set.

began to conduct events such as the May Day Rally for Freedom and Survival. This was an event organized separately from the traditional May Day events. A majority of the participants were younger workers, in particular nonregular workers and the unemployed. The events typically consist of actions conducted in the form of music, fashion, and criticism, similar to what we saw with regard to the sound demos discussed in chapter 2 and reflecting a similar intention to combine methods of social movements with trade union organizing. As one of the members of *Freeter Zenpan Roudou Kumiai* explained: "This May Day event is different from the annually held mainstream unions' May Day events, which are coordinated by national centers [unions' associations]. Our May Day basically allows anyone to participate however they want . . . and this may be one of the reasons that our event has been able to attract a large number of people."[5] In addition to the relatively open style of organizing, the demands made through this type of protest are also diverse and sometimes not related to work. These include broad issues such as social inequality, economic insecurity, poverty, nuclear plants, the nature of the contemporary social structure, discontent with the state and corporations, and problems facing precarious workers and the unemployed.

Another example of community unions emerging to promote the interests of nonregular workers is that of *Union Bochi Bochi*[6], an active and independent community union established in 2005 in Kyoto to represent all types of workers, including vulnerable and precarious workers and the unemployed. According to Mamoru Minami, one of the union's members: "We reach out, in particular, to workers and the unemployed who suffer from mental illness or discrimination due to gender identity disorder. Due to the diverse range of practices that have been used to force workers to leave their jobs—including by bullying and putting pressure on them, or by enforcing long working hours—many workers who come to this union have mental problems. They are often alienated and vulnerable, and not represented by other unions."[7]

Union Bochi Bochi therefore provides different types of support for people who are vulnerable, outside of traditional unions' activities. It creates spaces such as café-style meetings once a month where precarious and insecure people can gather and talk to each other in a relaxed environment. It also provides mental care by introducing those in need to doctors or by giving them an opportunity to exchange information with other union members about medication and medical support. As a result, *Union Bochi Bochi* has enlarged its networks to include doctors, lawyers, NPOs, and other unions so they can respond to the various needs of precarious workers.

We have also seen the ascendance of the role of NPOs and citizens' groups such as NPO *Moyai*, NPO *Attaka* Support (NPO Warm Support), NPO POSSE, and *Han Hinkon* Network (Antipoverty Network). These tend to provide advice and support for workers—in particular, nonregular workers who face extreme levels of anxiety, employment insecurity, and impoverishment. This includes giving advice on job opportunities for the unemployed and finding accommodation for the homeless. For example, the Antipoverty Network initiated antipoverty rallies, which led to the realization of the *Hakenmura* (tent city of the jobless over the New Year's period) event (discussed below).[8] It also includes antipoverty movements, which increasingly began to spring up during the 2000s. These movements were led by activists belonging to different institutions, such as citizens' groups for single mothers, NPOs that support homeless people, workers' groups, and groups for people with serious diseases.[9] As described by one such activist, Makoto Kawazoe, this also resulted in one of the most prominent episodes of resistance conducted in the aftermath of the global financial crisis: "These networks share a common concern: poverty in Japan. Their involvement has drawn attention to the working poor, net café refugees, and the illegal treatment of nonregular workers through media coverage. The NPO *Moyai* has encouraged activists to unite to support impoverished people; this led to the *Hakenmura* event."[10]

The *Hakenmura* event could be argued to have marked the beginning of a new labor movement in the 2000s. This witnessed the mobilization of thousands of impoverished workers and activists, who gathered to vocalize their opposition to the poverty associated with nonregular employment and the fallout from the global financial crisis.[11] These acts were largely coordinated horizontally among numerous unions and NPOs and contributed to the emergence of similar events organized by a group of activists and lawyers in different locations around the country.[12] This horizontal coordination reflected a further fusion of the methods of social movements with the more traditional repertoire of protest events conducted by organized labor, as theorists of social movement unionism have tended to advocate (Engeman 2015, 445). In addition, one of the consequences of the *Hakenmura* event was a subsequent move by the Tokyo Metropolitan Government to take on a number of the support roles that *Hakenmura* had provided, including providing temporary housing and job center services. To the extent that *Hakenmura* had identified a number of needs among people suffering from poverty in the wake of the 2008 global financial crisis and in the context of Japan's increasingly precarious labor market, we therefore witness alternative types of organizing leading directly to local government's taking on a new role in welfare provision (*Asahi Shinbun* 2014aa).[13]

Another example of the rising importance of NPOs and citizens' groups in Japan's changing political economy is that of the NPO POSSE, established by university students in Tokyo in 2006 to addresses rising youth unemployment. As Satoshi Ibaragi, one of the organizers of POSSE, notes:

> The unemployed, freeters,[14] other nonregular workers, and NEETs [not in education, employed, or in training] among the youth population were often criticized by state elites and members of the public under the Koizumi administration because many considered the problems surrounding youths to be their own fault. There was a perception or notion surrounding youths in general in the mid-2000s that young people are too lazy. This was given as the reason for why we see an increase of freeters—that they play games all of the time; that their brains are made of games![15]

Activists in POSSE have sought to change these perceptions, raising public awareness of the conditions faced by Japan's youth. One way this has been attempted is through the conducting of annual surveys of 3,000 young workers, unemployed workers, and students with part-time jobs to assess their situations and subsequently inform the public and trade unions about them. One of the key findings from these surveys was that young people were unaware that nonregular and/or part-time workers were protected by employment legislation, prompting POSSE to create a twenty-four-hour phone line and e-mail consultation service for people who faced problems in the workplace and were otherwise unable to access the union's support system. This also allowed POSSE to attempt to reverse the general sense among those who contact this service that their problems are their own responsibility and stem from their lack of ability, rather than interpreting them as social or labor problems.[16]

POSSE puts on events that seek to facilitate learning about labor-related issues in casual places such as in cafés, at music events, and in nightclubs, rather than in official and formal public facilities, to appeal to the younger generation. It also regularly holds a number of events that attempt to improve knowledge about workers' rights—including seminars, workshops, and cultural events—providing a space to discuss labor problems or distribute leaflets and handbooks that explain labor-related laws and regulations. Since 2008, more and more people have attended these events and asked for support. POSSE has therefore become more recognized publicly and attracted the attention of more workers. Its activists also provide a range of sources of support, including giving advice, information on available or relevant unions, and guidance on how to access the local labor standard inspection offices, as well as making people aware of local councils or lawyers. Other activities include the publication of journals that aim to politicize issues related to workplace problems and youth-focused employment problems.

The protest event analysis data also shows that newer (emerging) organizations and types of workers within Japan's political economy are more likely than some of the older (traditional) organizations to conduct more confrontational forms of protest—that is, nonroutine protests or industrial or legal disputes (see table 3.2). This highlights the way in which Japan is moving away from its more "harmonious" model of industrial relations. Japan's contemporary and changing model of capitalism is therefore characterized by the emergence of new actors, and they are more predisposed toward more confrontational forms of resistance.

Figures 3.6 and 3.7 illustrate these trends more clearly. Each figure displays the changing numbers of protests carried out by each of the two aggregated groups (emerging and traditional). The more confrontational forms of protest (nonroutine protest events and industrial legal disputes) make up a markedly larger share of the events conducted by the emerging actors, especially beginning in 2008–2009. In contrast, protest events conducted by the more traditional actors have included a much smaller proportion of confrontational events, although we do discern a

TABLE 3.2 Proportion of protests of a confrontational type, by emerging or traditional actors, 1988–2017

TYPE OF WORKERS AND ORGANIZATIONS	PROPORTION OF CONFRONTATIONAL PROTESTS
Emerging	0.45968
Traditional	0.18878

Source: Author's data set.

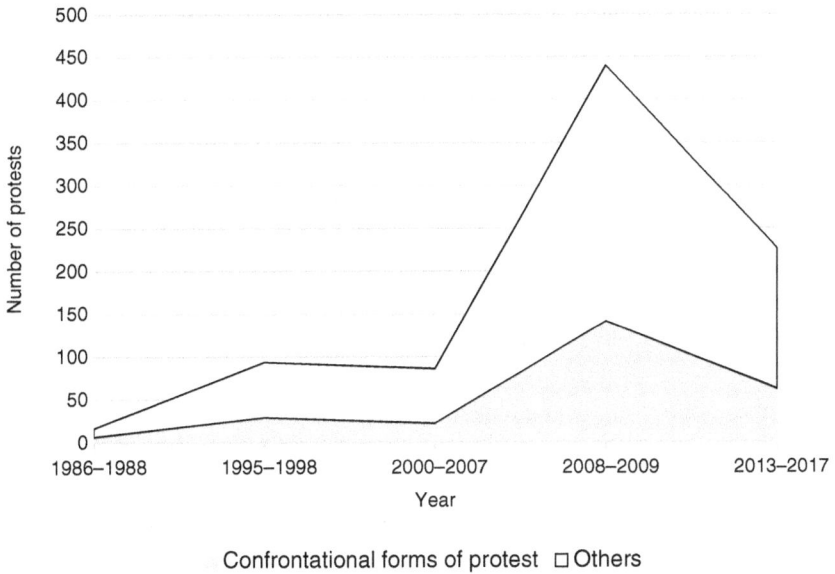

FIGURE 3.6. Numbers of protests conducted by emerging workers and workers' organizations, 1986–2017

Source: Author's data set.

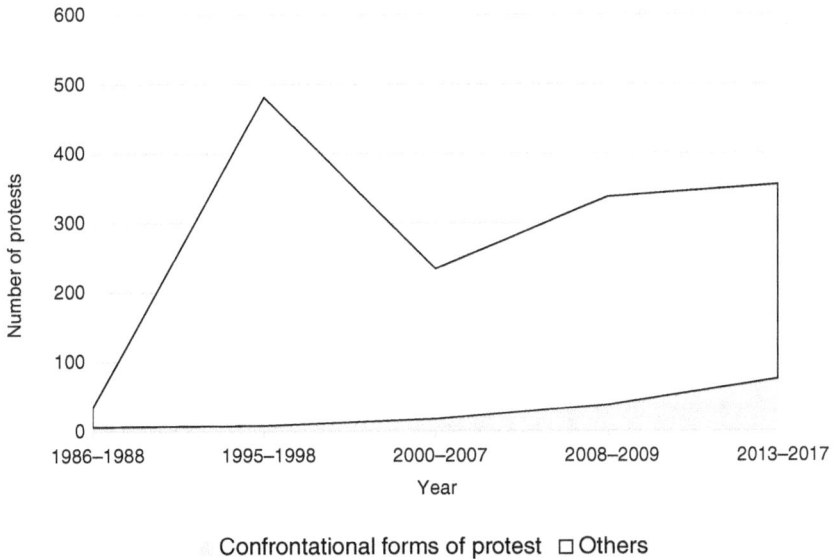

FIGURE 3.7. Numbers of protests conducted by traditional workers and workers' organizations, 1986–2017

Source: Author's data set.

rise in 2013–2017. This later increase in the adoption of more confrontational forms of protest by the more traditional actors also reflects a tendency for those actors to adopt some of the strategies and tactics of the emerging groups, in an attempt to avoid becoming outdated or failing to keep up with the changing nature of Japan's political economy. This desire among more traditional workers' organizations to keep up with the changing nature of class conflict in Japan can be seen, for instance, with *Rengo*'s decision in 2014 to stage protests simultaneously across forty-seven prefectures, involving 22,000 people who opposed to the proposed *zangyou dai zero houan* (Zero overtime payment bill). These events were jointly staged with May Day events, although they were conducted in a more confrontational and innovative manner than usual—including specific demands for the withdrawal of the proposed bill. In part this represented an attempt to put on large-scale events in response to the rise of smaller and more independent unions that had become more visible and increasingly begun to represent precarious workers. These changing activities also reflect an attempt by *Rengo* to avoid being left behind in terms of the workers that it represents.

To summarize the findings so far, during the 1980s the number of acts of contestation as recorded in the data presented here was relatively small, in part as a reflection of the ongoing commitment in the Japanese mode of regulation to some degree of social compromise. The protest events that did occur were most often institutionalized May Day events. These were typically organized by *Rengo* as part of a routine process of annual demonstrations, designed to raise awareness of contemporary labor-related problems in a relatively nonconfrontational, institutionalized manner and highlight broad public issues. Later a more contentious (and contested) model of capitalism arose, in which newer types of actors (most obviously, nonregular workers) have adopted newer and more confrontational means to express their interests.

In order to gain an insight into the forms of protest that comprise Japan's (contested) political economy, we can also consider the particular claims that have been made during the course of the study. By focusing on these claims, we are given an additional insight into the sources of tension, and therefore the nature of social conflict, in Japan's contested political economy. This answers a number of important questions: What claims did workers make? What were they resisting? What specific grievances underlay the patterns of protest events, and how have these changed over time? Figure 3.8 highlights the main changes to the types of claims made by workers during the period of the study.

As we can see, alongside changes in the types of actors and actions, Japan's political economy has also witnessed changes in the types of claims that workers have made through their different forms of mobilization. Four trends in particular stand out. First, the strong focus on pay claims during the 1980s declined

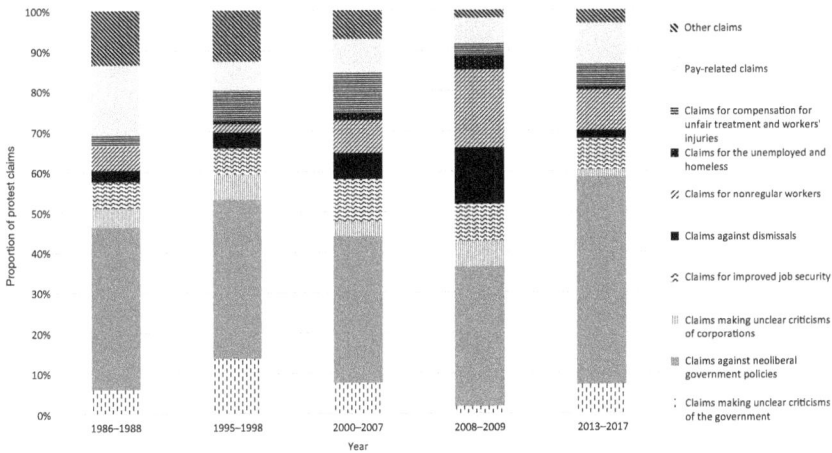

FIGURE 3.8. Protest events, by proportion of claims made, 1986–2017

Source: Author's data set.

significantly in the 1990s, reflecting a general move away from a standardized (ritual) *Shunto* system of coordinated wage negotiations (the spring offensive) in Japanese labor relations under the classic model of Japanese capitalism. Second, the proportion of claims placing demands on, or seeking a response from, the government declined from 53 percent in the 1990s to 36 percent in 2008–2009.

Third, this decline in the proportion of government-focused claims reflected a considerable increase, especially during 2008–2009, of claims made in support of nonregular workers and in opposition to dismissals by firms, which rose from less than 6 percent in the 1990s to 33 percent in 2008–2009. Perhaps most notable of the protests during the latter period was the 2008 *Hakenmura* (tent city of jobless over the New Year's period), a movement against widespread dismissals across Japan that had nonregular workers and unions demanding that corporations maintain their contracts with nonregular workers and pay all unpaid wages.[17] In addition, corporations that dismissed large numbers of dispatch workers also faced a rise in the number of collective lawsuits. Protests that focused on making demands related to the conditions of nonregular workers also continued after 2008. For instance, in May 2014, nonregular workers in the fast-food industry conducted a street demonstration to demand fair pay and an increase in wages. As participants taking part in the protest event stated, "the wage is too low to live without doing overtime work . . . we do exactly the same as other regular workers, but our wage is completely different. Nonregular workers are holding the current Japanese economy together. Companies should guarantee our life" (quoted in Takahashi 2014, author's translation). Similarly, in March 2013, fifteen former dispatch workers who had been dismissed from Mazda *Bofu* factory collectively sued Mazda with support from community unions, seeking reinstatement of their employment as regular workers. The regional court ordered the company to offer thirteen of these workers a contract of regular employment.[18] One of the plaintiffs angrily stated: "I cannot stand the way Mazda dismissed temp workers and pushed us to a devastating point. After bringing this into court, my life is a struggle with poverty" (quoted in *Asahi Shinbun*, 2013m, author's translation).

Finally, the 2013–2017 period, during the Abe government, saw a considerable revival in the proportion of claims or demands directed toward the government, which accounted for 59 percent of all claims. What is notable about this return to government-focused protest is the considerably greater opposition to the neoliberal direction of government policy, when we compare protests carried out during this period with those of the 1990s. Thus, the proportion of government-focused demands that were of a noneconomic nature declined from 26 percent in the 1990s to 12 percent under the Abe government.

Some of the noneconomic protests carried out in the 1990s focused on political issues or scandals of national interest, including opposition to the U.S. military base in Okinawa and the use of tax funds as part of one of the country's housing loan corporations' corruption scandal (*Jusen*). This is not to say that there was no opposition to the neoliberal direction of policy during the 1990s. Indeed, opposition was focused on such issues as the introduction of the *sairyou roudou sei* (designated work system) in 1997 and the amendment of the *henkei roudou seido* (variable workweek system) in the Labor Standard Law of 1998. In September 1998, for instance, two thousand people participated in a rally in Tokyo that severely criticized the government for its stance on labor market deregulation. As one union activist from *Zenroren* commented at the time, "the government has never fully engaged in debates surrounding problems of working conditions, but instead forcefully passed the bill [to amend the Labor Standard Law]. This is a betrayal of workers and citizens and undemocratic" (quoted in *Asahi Shinbun* 1998, author's translation). By the time the Abe government came to power, however, labor protest was focused considerably more directly on the neoliberal direction of policy, perhaps in part reflecting a move away from concerns about national issues and toward a focus on issues directly affecting workers in Japan. In other words, as Japan's political economy became more disorganized, organized labor became disinterested in issues of national concern and more focused on the promotion of its own interests, as we might expect.

The anti-neoliberal protests of the later period included opposition to the further flexibilization and deregulation of the labor market proposed under the set of economic reforms usually referred to as Abenomics (discussed in more detail in chapter 1). The protests also included opposition to a number of austerity policies, including a sales tax increase, pension reforms, and increased flexibility of the labor market (Bailey and Shibata 2017). For instance, the introduction of the Zero overtime payment bill prompted a round of protests by workers and unions in several cities across Japan. Similarly, a sit-in protest with 800 participants was held in front of Parliament in November 2014 to protest the proposed amendment of the Worker Dispatch Law (*Asahi Shinbun* 2014ab). Perhaps surprisingly, this protest was staged by the two largest national union federations, *Rengo* and *Zenroren*, thus highlighting the move by the more established trade unions to adopt innovative methods of protest in an attempt to avoid becoming outdated in Japan's changing political economy. Moreover, in spring 2014, 1,000 workers marched and rallied against Abenomics, claiming that the government's program was focused on improving the business environment and resulted in the intensified exploitation of ordinary workers (*Asahi Shinbun*, 2014o). In Fukuoka, 6,300 people rallied against inequality, seeking an increase in the minimum wage and demanding that the government make Abenomics more focused on the local economy and households (*Asahi Shinbun* 2014f). The Abe era therefore witnessed considerable opposition from Japan's changing labor movement to the neoliberal reforms of Abenomics.

The discussion of protest events in this chapter has highlighted a move away from the standard focus on pay-related claims by organized labor, as was seen under the classic Japanese model. In more recent years, worker-led protests increasingly focused on issues affecting nonregular workers. We also see a shift toward concern regarding heightened job dismissals (especially in the immediate aftermath of the global financial crisis), followed by a stronger focus on attacking the neoliberal direction of the Abe government. The increased tendency to protest in Japan's political economy, especially among the growing population of nonregular workers, was initially focused on challenging conditions in the workplace and subsequently moved to challenge specifically the neoliberal policies emanating from the Abe government. These trends will be considered in more detail below in this book, when we come to consider the different ways in which protest has destabilized and challenged the increasingly disorganized nature of Japan's neoliberalizing political economy.

The transformation of Japan's model of capitalism from a consensus-based to a neoliberal model has involved the construction of new socioeconomic institutions since the late 1980s. This shift has not been without opposition and resistance. The move toward a more unstable neoliberal model of capitalism has also been accompanied by the emergence of new workers and workers' organizations that have conducted greater numbers of protests, and these have shown a tendency to adopt more confrontational forms. This, we might conclude, represents a demonstration of the "potential and expression of the working-class power of 'refusal,' of its power to subvert capitalist domination" (Cleaver 1992, 129). This new and more confrontational activism involves the addressing of precarious nonregular workers' issues by community unions, NPOs, and citizens' groups. Discontent and class antagonism have therefore become more central contradictions and dilemmas in Japan's neoliberalizing model of capitalism.

Traditional enterprise unions have shown a limited ability to represent the newly flexibilized workforce of Japan, and other actors such as community unions, NPOs, and citizens' groups have sought to fill this gap. This has led to greater diversity in the types of acts of contestation being conducted in Japan. Some of these acts have adopted a form that we might consider to be a type of social movement unionism, in which unions encourage workers as well as the unemployed, students, and various nonregular workers to participate in acts of contestation (Waterman 1993). This includes acts designed to provide consultation and advice as well as temporary housing for nonregular workers, the unemployed, and the homeless.

This new form of activism also suggests that Japan's working class is reconfiguring itself, as those participating in precarious forms of labor and their supporters have developed a range of ways to resist the current round of socioeconomic reforms. Workers who experience rising levels of insecurity and impoverishment have simultaneously acknowledged the limits of traditional unions' ability to represent precarious labor. The emergence of new actors and the increasing role of nonregular workers in the labor market have, in turn, spurred traditional unions such as *Rengo* to support more proactive forms of protest.

Heightened social tension and class antagonism have therefore become part of the transformation of the Japanese model of capitalism. We might consider there to have been a partial recomposition of the working class in Japan. New unions such as *Freeter Zenpan Roudoukumiai* and *Union Bochi Bochi*, along with NPOs including POSSE and *Attaka* Support (both of which were established in the early or mid-2000s), have tended to adopt more flexible and inclusive approaches to interpreting individual problems and supporting precarious workers, youth, and the unemployed. As we shall see in chapter 4, this emergence of a more contentious Japanese working class has translated into a more antagonistic attitude toward business in Japan.

PRECARIOUS LABOR POWER AND JAPAN'S NEOLIBERALIZING FIRMS

The neoliberalization of Japan's political economy has therefore been accompanied by the emergence of a new group of nonregular workers with a greater willingness to mobilize in opposition to their experience of precarity. In particular, we have seen the development of more combative workers (and workers' organizations) who have sought to challenge their experiences directly in the workplace. In seeking to highlight and explore this newly mobilizing nonregular working class in Japan's political economy, this chapter presents four case studies documenting ways in which Japan's precarious workers have mobilized in opposition to Japanese employers, and some of the effects that the workers have had in doing so. The chapter therefore addresses a number of important questions: How do precarious workers contest exploitation in their workplace? To what extent do workers challenge domination and contest businesses? What are the outcomes of their acts of contestation?

Nonregular workers face working conditions characterized by precarity, lack of bargaining power, low wages, and a rapid turnover of employment. Nevertheless, these case studies illustrate a number of important ways in which, through collective action, nonregular workers in Japan have been able to impose a number of sanctions on employers and receive a range of important concessions. This has led to changes in corporate governance, better treatment of workers, the payment of unpaid wages, and improved employment security. In some cases, solidarity among precarious workers has led to the collapse of temporary employment agencies (temp agencies), clearly demonstrating that workers' acts of refusal can generate changes in employment practices.

In exploring different ways in which precarious workers have organized to challenge their experience of precarity in the workplace, the chapter seeks to contribute to a growing body of research highlighting different forms of agency enacted by precarious labor under conditions of neoliberalization (see also Preminger 2018; Ikeler 2018; Munck 2018; Woodcock 2017; Bailey et al. 2018; Moore 2018). As Kallberg and Hewison discuss (2015, 41), the experience of precarity has the potential to motivate workers who share conditions of anger, anomie, anxiety, and alienation to act collectively to pose a challenge to both employers and policymakers. The present chapter seeks to explore a number of instances in which we can witness the capacity of precarious workers to pose such a challenge. In doing so, it examines four particular ways in which precarious and nonregular workers in Japan have acted to challenge especially problematic practices by employers. These ways are efforts to organize against unlawful deductions from wages, a practice that had become common in a number of temp agencies such as Goodwill and Fullcast; challenges to the more general practice of temporary employment as also enacted by temp agencies (the *Tokyo Tobu* Union); instances of mobilization by female nonregular workers; and the creation of solidarity initiatives by dispatch workers, particularly those in the auto industry.

Each of the case studies discussed provides important insights into the means by which Japanese nonregular workers have been able to challenge the practices of their employers in the workplace. The focus in many of the case studies on efforts to organize workers recruited through temp agencies is especially important, given that it is the rapidly increasing use of such agencies that has driven the growth in numbers of nonregular workers in the Japanese labor market. Likewise, many of the cases discussed focus especially on newer community unions, which as we have seen have been particularly effective in providing an opportunity for nonregular workers to organize when the more standard enterprise unions appear unwilling to take up the workers' cause. Furthermore, the focus on female workers provides an important opportunity to consider ways in which gendered forms of nonregular employment have been contested in Japan. This is especially important given that the majority of nonregular workers are female. Finally, the focus on processes of contestation in Japan's auto industry highlights ways in which the large-scale dismissals that occurred as a result of the 2007–2008 financial crisis were contested.

Organizing against Unlawful Deductions from Wages: Goodwill and Fullcast

One of the key ways in which nonregular workers have risen in prominence in Japan's labor market has been through the increased rate of employment through temp agencies. Through a number of these agencies, including Goodwill, Fullcast, MyWork, and Emcrew, what are typically referred to in Japan as "dispatch workers" have become a common feature in Japan's workforce. These especially came to prominence in the aftermath of the global financial crisis due to their mass dismissals and outbreaks of protest against the treatment of dispatch workers by temp agencies. The number of temp agencies in Japan increased significantly after the 1991 bursting of Japan's economic bubble—from roughly 7,000 in the mid-1980s to 10,000 in 2000 and 75,000 in 2014 (Ministry of Health, Labor, and Welfare [MHLW] 2001 and 2016). As we shall see below, employment of dispatch workers by temp agencies brings with it a number of problems, but it has also led to a number of important responses by those workers and the organizations that have emerged to represent them.

The *Haken* Union and the Organization of Fullcast Workers

The *Haken* Union (Dispatch Workers' Union) has been one of the key agents supporting temp agency workers employed by one of Japan's major temp agencies, Fullcast. The creation of the union in 2005 reflected the increase in the number of temp workers and other nonregular workers that we have seen developing throughout the post-1991 period. The union's chair, Shuichiro Sekine, was initially alerted to the experience of temp workers in Japan as a result of the advice he was regularly providing through an emergency phone line that the union had set up for temp workers. In 2006, in an attempt to gain a better appreciation of the experience of temp workers and the challenges they faced, he decided to experience temp agency work at Goodwill himself.[1] He explained his experience in an interview conducted in July 2011 and in detail in his book, *Haken no Gyakusyu* (Counterattack by dispatch workers) (Sekine 2009). As Sekine recalled, during his time as a warehouse dispatch worker employed through a temp agency, staff members were required to pay for their own uniforms and work equipment, despite having low wages (848 yen [$7.50] per hour or 6,784 yen [$60] per day). One of the biggest hurdles to workplace organizing was the fact that work would change location on a daily basis, with the agency arranging the transportation to a particular workplace on each day. As a result, "the day laborers are sent from temp agency to temp agency and are often isolated and do not know anyone. They have no control over the type of work they do and face extreme levels of fatigue (both mental and physical)."[2]

In seeking to improve the working status and conditions of dispatch workers, Sekine held meetings with day laborers at *Haken* and collected information from those who had worked as dispatch day laborers with a range of temp agencies—including two of the largest ones, Goodwill and Fullcast.[3] As a result of these experiences, Sekine identified two key problems facing temp agency workers: superexploitative working conditions[4] and the common practice of what many employees felt were unlawful deductions of wages, often justified as "data management fees," which temp agencies claimed represented the cost of managing the information of registered workers.[5] Alongside these two key issues, Sekine also observed bullying from supervisors at the workplace, poor health and safety conditions, unpaid overtime work, and work placements in the construction sector (which is against Japan's labor market regulations) (Sekine 2009).

Similar conditions were observed for temp agency workers employed as office staff in the temp agencies themselves. As Sekine noted, "non-regular workers who work as office staff in temp agencies also experience long working hours and are responsible for the administrative tasks of managing day laborers. If non-regular workers who work for a temp agency cannot find enough day laborers, they have to work late without overtime payments until they find enough, or sometimes have to perform the work themselves. Those workers also said that they cannot go home for a week, and their wages are extremely low."[6] As a result of these experiences and observations, Sekine used his role in *Haken* to enable four non-regular workers to establish a new union—the Fullcast Union—with the aim of organizing dispatch workers hired through the temp agency Fullcast. This union was created in 2006 and affiliated with the *Haken* Union.[7] The new union for dispatch workers employed by Fullcast made a number of demands on the temp agency. For example, the union demanded an apology from Fullcast for failing to clarify the content of jobs that had been allocated to the temp agency, an increase in the minimum payment for dispatch workers, permanent contracts for a number of dispatch workers, transparent working rules, a review of the routine practice of long working hours and work in unsafe conditions, and payment of unpaid overtime (Sekine 2009).

Negotiations with Fullcast quickly led to the payment of unpaid overtime for the four original members. This was aided by the fact that Fullcast found itself in a weak legal position as a result of past unlawful practices. Following this success, the new union and Fullcast began four months of negotiations that eventually resulted in Fullcast making a small step toward improving dispatch workers' working conditions. In its new agreement with employees, Fullcast abolished the practice of illegally deducting fees from wages and agreed to delete information that it had been storing on the physical appearance of dispatch workers (on the ground that this represented a form of discrimination). The new agreement also guaranteed an end to the practice of requiring day laborers to meet before work started (additional time that Fullcast had refused to pay workers for) and guaranteed paid holidays for dispatch day laborers (Sekine 2009). Furthermore, the *Haken* Union successfully negotiated for day laborers who worked more than twenty-six days over two months to join the employment insurance program.

On the issue of employment insurance, the exclusion of dispatch workers from such programs had considerably contributed to their precarious conditions and economic insecurity. As a result, the *Haken* Union also agreed to lobby the MHLW, seeking to have the government contribute to employment insurance for day laborers. Despite attempts by the MHLW to avoid making a decision on this issue, media reporting gained in prominence throughout July 2007 and eventually led to the MHLW's announcement in August 2007 that welfare benefits would be extended to day laborers. This represented an important step for precarious workers.

Power of the Precarious: The Collapse of Goodwill

The initial successes of the *Haken* and Fullcast Unions in organizing dispatch workers in the Fullcast temp agency encouraged dispatch workers in other temp agencies to attempt similar initiatives. Thus, in March 2007 the *Haken* Union advised ten precarious workers from the Goodwill temp agency. This resulted in the creation of the Goodwill Union in March 2007. As had occurred with the Fullcast Union organizing, Sekine encouraged a number of labor activists and *Haken* Union members to sign up for work as dispatch workers at Goodwill. This allowed the activists to experience conditions at the temp agency. As had been the case with Fullcast, staff at Goodwill also routinely had deductions from their wages for a "data management fee" imposed by the agency. Through negotiations, the workers achieved similar goals to those reached by the Fullcast Union. Goodwill, which was aware of the abolition of illegal deductions from day laborers' wages at Fullcast, at first refused to conclude an agreement. However, in part due to the weak legal position that Goodwill found itself in, the agency eventually abolished the illegal deductions and agreed to return illegally withheld wages, albeit only to the seven original Goodwill Union members.[8]

This success at Goodwill (on top of the success achieved in organizing at Fullcast) allowed the *Haken* Union to mobilize more dispatch workers to organize to bring an end to the practice of unlawful deduction of wages that had become routine for many temp agencies. As Sekine recalls, "Goodwill Union and *Haken* Union used blog posts to encourage other day laborers to join their unions and claim their entitlement." Furthermore, the fact that dispatch workers routinely used the internet to search for job placements ensured that the news about the possibility of getting deducted wages spread quickly, with more than 100 workers signing up to claim such wages. In addition, a number of meetings that were organized by the *Haken* and Goodwill Unions to advise workers on how to engage in negotiations with employers resulted in another 150 workers joining the Goodwill Union.[9]

In contrast to what had been expected, however, rather than agree to pay the deducted wages to Goodwill Union's newly recruited workers, the agency refused to make the sort of payments that it had made with the first round of claimants. This was largely due to the increase in cost, as more workers came forward to reclaim their unpaid wages. In seeking to put further pressure on Goodwill, the *Haken* and Goodwill Unions informed the local labor standards inspection office in each area about the firm's illegal deductions from wages and unpaid overtime (Sekine 2009). In addition, the unions staged street demonstrations and rallies in front of the agency's headquarters, putting further pressure on the company. Publicity increased as a result of a company scandal that occurred at the same time: Comsun, a subsidiary company that recruited day laborers in the care and nursing sectors, was discovered to have made fraudulent claims for government fees. In seeking to appease public hostility, the chief executive of Goodwill held a press conference on June 8, 2007, at which (among other things) he promised to pay workers the deductions that had been made illegally and return the money owed to all claimants. In following up on this promise, however, Sekine was informed by Goodwill that it still did not intend to repay the deducted wages, and that the press conference had not constituted an official company announcement. In response, the Goodwill Union used publicity again to advance their members' interests, sending a public letter to Goodwill insisting once more that the deducted wages be paid. This time the response was more positive, with Goodwill, apparently eager to avoid any further public attention, agreeing to repay the money deducted over the past two years—the maximum required under the Labor Standard Law (Sekine 2009, 1354).

With Goodwill agreeing only to repay wages that had been deducted in the previous two years, the Goodwill Union set about trying to challenge this time limit. This initiative was aided by the decision of Fullcast to pay all deducted money, without any time limit. Twenty-six Goodwill Union members collectively sued Goodwill, demanding the return of all money illegally deducted from their wages—totaling 45,544,600 yen ($404,510) (Sekine 2009). Once the case got to court, moreover, details of the employment practices of Goodwill were further exposed, including the routine employment of harbor workers as dispatch workers, which had been banned by the Worker Dispatch Law, and the case of a day laborer who had been left disabled as a result of a workplace accident. This prompted the Tokyo Labor Standards Inspection Office to launch an investigation into illegal dispatch working conditions, eventually resulting in the MHLW announcing that it would suspend Goodwill's business operations for up to four months and a police investigation that led to the arrest of branch managers on June 3, 2008, and the cancellation of Goodwill's business operations on June 24 (Sekine 2009).

As these experiences of the *Haken* Union and its subsidiaries, the Fullcast and Goodwill Unions, show, precarious nonregular workers who are recruited through temp agencies have faced a number of challenges in the workplace. This includes unlawful deductions from wages, unlawful recruitment for work that is prohibited under national employment regulations, low pay, and long working hours. Such workers have also often found it difficult to organize collectively, as the nature of the employment by temp agencies is such that workplaces change on a daily basis and with minimal consultation of workers regarding the work to which they are assigned. As the accounts above also show, however, through a combination of innovative union activity—including recruitment efforts by labor activists willing to invest time and effort in studying the nature of the employment practices that precarious workers face, as well as the use of legal entitlements, publicity campaigns, and persistent negotiations—it has proven possible to extract a number of concessions from temp agencies. In the case of Goodwill, union activity was able to fundamentally challenge the malign operations of the agency. The cases outlined above therefore highlight the potential for publicity, legal entitlements, and union activity to result in a number of improvements for nonregular workers in Japan's new political economy. As we shall see in the case study that follows, nonregular workers have also been able to challenge the routine practice of employment by so-called zero-hour contracts by temp agencies, in this case through activity led by the *Tokyo Tobu* Union.

Challenging Temp Agencies: Zero-Hour Contract Workers and the *Tokyo Tobu* Union

Alongside the problem of unlawful deduction of wages, nonregular workers have also experienced the use of contracts with ultra short terms, often used for years on end. This creates a condition whereby workers have no employment security from day to day. Moreover, at times this also represents an unlawful contravention of Japanese employment regulations. While legal entitlements exist to prevent this kind of practice, nonregular workers are often unaware of these rights. One of the roles that unions have been able to play in this context is to support such workers in their attempt to uphold their employment rights. An example of contestation over the rights of nonregular workers and of an attempt to enforce them can be seen in the case of ten tour conductors who were employed by the Hankyu Travel Support (HTS) temp agency on ultra-flexible (or zero-hour) contracts, in some cases for up to ten years, and who were supported by the *Tokyo Tobu* Union in their efforts to improve their working conditions. The following discussion draws in part on an interview conducted with Ari Sugano, a chief secretary of the *Tokyo Tobu* Union.

The *Tokyo Tobu* Union was established in 1968, largely to represent factory workers. Unusually for a trade union in Japan, it was not formed as an enterprise union but rather represents workers in different workplaces and different sectors. It has forty-five branches in various workplaces and roughly 850 members, and it belongs to *Zenrokyo* (the National Trade Unions Council), one of the national trade union federations (discussed in chapter 2). Since 2005 more nonregular workers have joined the *Tokyo Tobu* Union, and they now make up the majority of its members—reflecting the increase in the number of nonregular workers in Japan's labor force.[10]

In January 2007, ten tour conductors formed the HTS Union as a branch of the *Tokyo Tobu* Union to demand appropriate employment status and adequate wages (NPO Houjin Rodo Soudan Center 2007c). The conductors were employed under the registered dispatch system, which allows temp agencies to pay staff members only on the days they are assigned to work at their client firms. In other words, the conductors were hired only for the length of time of each travel tour. This means that their employment contracts were of a highly flexible and short-term nature, with no guarantee of employment beyond the individual tour for which they were hired at any one time. Many of the tour conductors had been employed on these terms for several years, in some cases as long as ten years. Thus, this was a form of zero-hour contract, and they had jobs to those of regular workers, but without employment insurance or social insurance. This experience was made worse by harsh working conditions, including excessive overtime work and demands to meet the request of customers on the tours even if this was not included in the job description.[11]

In an attempt to respond to these poor working conditions, the *Tokyo Tobu* Union sought to enter into negotiations with HTS on behalf of the workers. When HTS refused, the union filed a complaint with the Tokyo Metropolitan Government Labor Relations Commission. In particular, the union highlighted the fact that the Labor Union Law forbids employers from treating union and nonunion members unequally, prohibits employers from intervening in unions' operations, and requires employers to respond to collective negotiation when asked to do so. On these grounds, the union requested that the commission support its attempt to enter into collective negotiations. Following this pressure from the union, the commission did agree to encourage HTS to enter into negotiations, which HTS eventually did.

In a series of ongoing negotiations, the *Tokyo Tobu* and HTS Unions made a number of demands as requested by their members. These demands included that members who worked more than twenty hours per week be entitled to join an employment insurance program, that those who had worked more than six months should be entitled to paid holidays, that any unpaid overtime from the past should be paid, and that overtime would be paid in the future (NPO Houjin Rodo Soudan Center 2007e).

The question of paid overtime for future work was a key sticking point in these negotiations. As a result, the *Tokyo Tobu* Union contacted the labor standards inspection office of Mita/Chyuou/Shinjyuku Ward, which informed the union that workers working more than eight hours per day were entitled to be paid overtime at 125 percent of the standard rate (NPO Houjin Rodo Soudan Center 2007b). Objecting to this regulation, however, were three employers' business groups in the tour conductors and travel industry (the Japan Travel Association and Japan Tour Conductor Service Association) and the national-level *Rengo* union organization for service tourism (Service Tourism Industrial Labor Union), each of which requested that the MHLW review the flexible working hours of tour conductors. However, the MHLW asserted that article 32 of the Labor Standard Law defines the legal working hours as eight hours per day, forty hours per week, and that anything over this amount therefore should be paid at an overtime rate (NPO Houjin Rodo Soudan Center 2007f and 2007d).

Following this decision by the MHLW, HTS became more accommodating during the ongoing negotiations. The agency agreed to increase daily payments by 1,000 yen ($9.20) and increase overtime payment for workers who worked early or late shifts. It also agreed to provide payment for other administrative work that tour conductors had previously done at home without pay (NPO Houjin Rodo Soudan Center 2007a).

In an attempt to extend these achievements, the HTS Union and its members set about trying to increase public awareness of their campaign. They made a number of attempts to gain publicity and public support, including through street protests and leafleting outside Tokyo Japan Railway station, where many tourists would arrive to begin their travels and tours. They also set up a stall to use as a base for leafleting at Ueno station, which was chosen because it was the starting and ending point for tour coaches (NPO Houjin Rodo Soudan Center 2007g). This also presented an opportunity for other community unions, female workers, and young workers who were facing similar problems as tour guides to join the street protest and encourage the public to sign a petition calling for better treatment for tour company workers. This was a clear attempt to use public support to increase the strength of the union in its negotiations with HTS. As Sugano put it, "these street protests and the leafleting attracted considerable attention and allowed us to inform the general public about the exploitative employment conditions operating in temp agencies' client firms, and that dispatch workers regularly experience."[12]

These efforts to raise public awareness were partly successful. A number of media outlets began reporting on the cases raised by the HTS Union, especially those related to the precarious working conditions of tour conductors. For instance, the national newspapers *Asahi Shinbun* and *Yomiuri Shinbun* both reported on the issue of unpaid overtime and the lack of social security faced by workers in the tour industry, as well as their lack of employment insurance and social insurance (NPO Houjin Rodo Soudan Center 2007g). Media attention made more visible the working conditions of dispatch tour guides, and dispatch workers more generally—conditions that normally were hidden from public view.

Growing public awareness also led to the issue of unpaid overtime and exploitative working conditions faced by dispatch tour conductors being discussed in the Diet (national parliament) by members of House of Representatives (NPO Houjin Rodo Soudan Center 2007h). In particular, Abe Sachiko, a member of the Social Democratic Party, argued that travel agencies and their temp agencies were not treating their employees adequately or legally. She asked the MHLW to tackle four travel agencies in particular, which she claimed had acted especially exploitatively toward their tour conductors.

One of the outcomes of this ongoing campaign of negotiations, legal claims, and public awareness raising was that HTS eventually agreed to let dispatch tour conductors join its employment insurance program. This guaranteed unemployment benefits for dispatch workers who lost their jobs. The agency also agreed to pay an overtime rate, pay unpaid holiday pay, and increase day wages. It refused, however, to change the payment rate for tour conductors required to work during holidays, which prompted the MHLW and the labor standards inspection office to intervene again by insisting on the need for appropriate payments to people who work overtime and on holidays (NPO Houjin Rodo Soudan Center 2007b and 2008a). On this point, however, HTS pointed to the noncompulsory nature of Labor Standard Inspection Office advice and refused to change its stance.[13]

This intransigence eventually resulted in a series of legal cases, brought by the *Tokyo Tobu* and HTS Unions on behalf of nine tour conductors due to unpaid overtime (NPO Houjin Rodo Soudan Center 2008b). In July 2008 the Tokyo District Court ruled that HTS must pay unpaid overtime and extra payments for work on holidays (NPO Houjin Rodo Soudan Center 2008c). This represented a significant victory for the rights of dispatch workers. In May 2010 the same court ruled against HTS again and demanded that the agency pay a dispatch tour conductor the appropriate amount of unpaid overtime and compensation (NPO Houjin Rodo Soudan Center 2010a). In September 2010, six other members of the *Tokyo Tobu* Union won their collective lawsuit and gained a favorable ruling by the Tokyo District Court against HTS. This ruling guaranteed a total of 22.8 million yen (around $200,000) in unpaid overtime over a period of two years for the six dispatch workers (NPO Houjin Rodo Soudan Center 2010b). Refusing to accept the ruling, HTS appealed to the Tokyo High Court and then to the Supreme Court (NPO Houjin Rodo Soudan Center 2011). Yet in January 2014, the Supreme Court ruled against HTS in all three collective lawsuits related to seven dispatch tour conductors. The court ordered HTS to pay a total of 27.5 million yen (about $245,000) (NPO Houjin Rodo Soudan Center 2014). In a further attempt to circumvent the ruling, however, HTS introduced an hourly wage system that threatened to reduce the income of dispatch tour conductors. This was done unilaterally and without union consultation, prompting further claims by the HTS Union that the wage changes amounted to a contravention of the requirements for collective bargaining, although on this claim the Tokyo High Court backed the employer rather than union, in a ruling in November 2018 (NPO Houjin Rodo Soudan Center 2018).

As we can see, there are considerable challenges facing unions that seek to organize nonregular dispatch workers, many of whom face intransigent employers, highly flexible terms of employment, and sometimes unlawful working conditions. As the experiences of the HTS Union workers shows, however, through a combination of the legal knowledge available to trade unions, public support for precarious workers, and ongoing negotiations, it has been possible to make a number of considerable improvements.

Nonregular Women Workers in Japan's New Workforce: Contesting Gendered Precarity

Although many women have been employed as nonregular workers, few cases of female workers' struggles have been reported. Women tend to be less willing than men to express their workplace grievances and more willing than men to avoid contention in the workplace (for a rare study of women workers organizing under conditions of neoliberalization in Japan, see Narisada 2010). Likewise, unions, unionism, and labor movements are often perceived as dominated by men. Similarly, labor activism is often gender-blind in the way that it is executed. As chair of *Moyai*, Tsuyoshi Inaba highlighted in his discussion of attempts to mobilize female workers and homeless women in the wake of the global financial crisis: "During the *Hakenmura* event [see chapter 3], temporary tents were set up for many homeless people to sleep in, which raised the challenge of how to accommodate the many female precarious workers."[14] Despite these challenges, a number of instances of successful workplace organizing by nonregular female workers can be observed in the context of Japan's changing political economy.

The Women's Union Tokyo

Perhaps one of the most prominent unions that has emerged to support precarious women workers is the Women's Union Tokyo (WUT). This is also one of the oldest and most active unions focused especially on organizing precariously employed female workers. It was set up in 1995 to improve female workers' rights and their position in the workplace, and it seeks to eliminate discrimination against women and achieve equal wages for male and female workers. It represents female workers on issues related to sexual harassment, dismissals due to family care responsibilities, and unequal payment and treatment.[15] As of August 2016, the union had advised workers on their rights in 7,668 cases. Frequently, mainstream, male-dominated and/or enterprise unions are reluctant to take up cases that are especially pertinent for women. This includes cases in which maternity leave is granted reluctantly or with an expectation that the woman will not return to work after taking her leave. It also includes instances of sexual harassment and cases where women experience pressure to resign from employers who seek to replace them with employees with no caring responsibilities (for a more in-depth discussion, see Zacharias-Walsh 2016).

Two cases illustrate well some of the activities that the WUT has been engaged in to advance women's rights in the workplace. In one recently reported case, a female worker (known only as "Miss K") working for a trading company faced persistent attempts by her employer to force her to leave her job after returning from a five-month maternity leave. This pressure increased when she announced that she was pregnant with her second child, eventually resulting in her losing her job as her department was closed. In supporting her in this case, the WUT first entered into negotiations with the employer on behalf of Miss K. Once this proved unsuccessful, support was garnered from the Tokyo Metropolitan Government Labor Relations Commission, again with the support of the WUT, eventually resulting in the company's being instructed to pay Miss K unpaid overtime and compensation for her treatment. As the case illustrates, therefore, women workers face considerable pressure in Japan, especially on having children, which necessitates the support of unions with a specific focus on supporting female workers (Women's Union Tokyo n.d.).

In a second case, the WUT supported another female worker, Ms. Y, who had worked as a sales representative for a travel agency for ten years, in her efforts to address ongoing sexual harassment. This harassment included persistent comments from male colleagues and supervisors, in which they would routinely suggest that she quit her job to become a mother, making comments such as, "Why not get married?" and "Why don't you think of marriage?" When the enterprise union that represented workers in Miss Y's workplace refused to take the harassment seriously, the WUT took up the case on her behalf and supported her in her demands to her employer. As a result, the company was forced to apologize, and Miss Y was able to keep her job, which had begun to look unlikely (Women's Union Tokyo, n.d.).

The WUT has also been supported by the Hataraku Jyoseino Zenkoku Sentar (Action Center for Working Women [ACW2]), which was established in January 2007 to provide opportunities for female workers to meet and discuss problems experienced in both the workplace and the home. The center also provided free phone consultations and workshops on issues related to work. According to Midori Ito, one of the founders of both the WUT and the ACW2, the center's aim "is to connect isolated individual female workers and unions, including Women's Union Tokyo, to help women reach out and empower themselves" (CGS Online 2007). Ito also said: "Schools have ceased teaching about unions and unionism, which makes it difficult for people to even find them. The center's activities create opportunities for women to think about work, discuss their problems, learn how to communicate, and how to become a consultant at the center" (quoted in Action Center for Working Women 2016, author's translation).

As each of these initiatives illustrate, female workers in Japan face specific challenges to which the more standard trade unions have been unable to adequately respond. As a result, women's unions such as the WUT take up women's cases to provide more substantial support, and in a way that takes account of the specific experiences of women in the Japanese workplace.

The *Cabacula* Union

In 2009, the community union *Freeter Zenpan Roudou Kumiai* (Unions for Casual Workers) began representing female nonregular workers who work in *cabacula*—bars or nightclubs where the majority of customers are men who pay to speak with, and be served by, female employees. In doing so the union created a new branch, the *Cabacula* Union, which would seek to organize those women workers (*Asahi Shinbun* 2009d). The *Cabacula* Union is one of the rare unions in Japan that represents precarious female workers in the *cabacula* business. Naoko Shimizu, then chair of the *Freeter Zenpan Rouso*, noted in an interview in 2011 that the large majority of women workers who were coming to the union for advice worked in the business. *Cabacula* workers routinely face a range of problems, including poverty, lack of employment insurance, and the social stigma associated with the type of work they do. In addition, deductions from wages are commonplace, often due to requirements to pay for workers' hair and makeup costs, dresses, absences, and being late for work. Other problems include sudden dismissals, bullying, and sexual harassment (*Cabacula* Union 2015). Furthermore, when *cabacula* workers require medical care, they are often ineligible for workers' compensation. When they cannot work or have to leave their jobs for medical reasons, they rarely receive unemployment benefits, and the gap in employment makes it harder for them to find other jobs (Hikita 2015). As Shimizu observed, "Women who work in the *cabacula* industry often face discrimination and tend to be socially ostracized for the nature of their work, which is viewed as selling sex. Female workers in this sector tend to be quiet about their workers' rights or entitlement as workers. . . . Therefore, these female workers tend to face unpaid wages, unreasonable dismissals, illegal fines—and this appears to be the practice in this industry: unpayment of salary of the month in which workers leave, and missing owners."[16] As a result of this large range of problems and the large number of requests for advice that the union was receiving, *Freeter Zenpan Rouso* decided to set up a new branch: the *Cabacula* Union.

Attempts to represent precarious female employees in the *cabacula* sector faced a number of considerable challenges. One of the most significant of these was the absence of an obvious interlocutor, as employment practices are not directly equivalent to those in workplaces such as factories, warehouses, or offices. While bar owners and managers are the obvious candidates to negotiate with, many failed to respond to requests. As Shimizu noted, "it is extremely difficult to identify who is responsible for employees or in charge of business operations in this industry. Many workers do not have employment contracts and do not know the identity of their employer. This setup allows employers to disappear if they close a shop; employees may be left with unpaid wages and no information about who is responsible. Thus for unions, pursuing such cases without sufficient information risks wasting a considerable amount of time and expense with little chance of success."[17]

Despite these challenges, the *Cabacula* Union has been able to make a number of advances. For instance, a pregnant twenty-nine-year-old woman who worked at one of the *cabacula* shops in Chiba told her supervisor in March 2015 that she was leaving to get married. After the supervisor refused to pay her wages for January and February 2015, she joined the *Cabacula* Union and pursued a claim for unpaid wages with the union's help. When the supervisor was approached by the union, he confirmed his refusal to pay. The shop manager told the woman that he needed to check whether she really worked there and said that the union representative should come back four days later. When the representative returned, however, the shop manager refused to talk, pay, or respond to the request for official negotiations. As a result, the police were invited to observe the discussion and listen to the claims made by the union. Despite an initial refusal to engage in any further discussion with the union, after persistent requests the shop manager agreed to pay the woman 100,000 yen ($900) in unpaid wages and 350,000 yen ($3,112) as compensation for unpaid overtime and illegal wage deductions (Hikita 2015). While this case highlights the difficulties faced by the *Cabacula* Union in seeking to reclaim unpaid wages, it also illustrates the roles that union support and persistence can play in achieving small successes that might otherwise not have been possible.

The *Cabacula* Union has also drawn on support from public authorities in initiating negotiations with difficult employers in similar attempts to uphold workers' entitlements. This includes receiving legal support from the Tokyo Metropolitan Government Labor Relations Commission, which acts as a third party and reviews potentially unfair labor practices. The commission listens to arguments on both sides and seeks a resolution for each case—sometimes by recommending reconciliation and sometimes by enforcing a legal order on employers (Tokyo Metropolitan Government Labor Relations Commission 2017). The commission also examines cases of dismissal or other unfair treatment and cases of refusal to investigate workers' grievances without adequate reason. It also can block employers' attempts to control or interfere in labor union operations and can intervene if a worker is treated unfairly after filing a complaint with the commission. The commission therefore seeks to guarantee "workers' rights to organize, negotiate and act collectively" (ibid.).

In describing the support of the commission, Naoko Shimizu recalled that "in many cases the commission put pressure on employers so that they would engage in negotiations."[18] Thus, small independent unions such as the *Cabacula* Union are able to draw on the support of public authorities in difficult cases.

In addition to drawing on support from public authorities and engaging in ongoing negotiations with unwilling employers, the *Cabacula* Union has used a range of publicity generating tactics. It regularly holds street protests and demonstrations in front of *cabacula* shops and distributes leaflets about unpaid wages and unreasonable business practices to pressure employers to negotiate. For instance, a street demonstration was held on March 26, 2010, to demand improvements to the working environment of *cabacula* workers, with the explicit aim of challenging efforts made by employers to keep the workers away from public attention (*Asahi Shinbun* 2010f; *Kihachi Logu* 2010). Similarly, the *Cabacula* Union has sought to provide regular advice to *cabacula* workers, offering a toll-free hotline to provide consultations on any problems faced by female precarious and impoverished workers in the sector.

While there are considerable challenges facing those who seek to organize *cabacula* workers in Japan, a number of important advances have been made. The creation of the *Cabacula* Union has provided women workers with an opportunity to seek advice and support, especially in tackling the many problems that they face in the workplace and in an industry that tends to be hidden from public view. In addition, the creation of a union has meant that access to support from public bodies is more readily available, especially through the Tokyo Metropolitan Government Labor Relations Commission.

Solidarity and the Fight of Dispatch Workers in the Auto Industry

Japan's auto industry faced widespread job losses in the aftermath of the global financial crisis of 2007–2008. This especially affected precarious or nonregular employees—including temporary workers and dispatch workers, who were hit particularly hard. This was due to the industry's increased use of short-term employment contracts as part of the neoliberalization of Japan's socioeconomic model that we considered in previous chapters. For instance, in November 2008, Mitsubishi Fuso announced that its Kawasaki factory would dismiss 500 nonregular workers by failing to renew temporary contracts in the light of reduced production requirements (*Asahi Shinbun* 2008c). Similarly, Nissan Diesel announced in 2008 that it would dismiss 200 dispatch workers out of its total 1,159 workers, due to a reduction in its production of medium-size trucks (ibid.). This was a pattern repeated across the sector: 3,000 temporary workers were dismissed at Toyota, 1,210 temporary workers at Honda, over 1,500 dispatch workers at Mazda, over 1,100 dispatch workers at Mitsubishi, 2,000 dispatch workers at Nissan, and 1,400 temporary workers at Isuzu (*Asahi Shinbun* 2008f and 2008g).

As this section will show, in the wake of these mass dismissals, auto industry workers mobilized in a number of ways in attempts to address their being rapidly pushed into unemployment, which often was also accompanied by becoming homelesss (as nonregular workers were routinely housed in employer-owned dormitories). Creative forms of contestation were adopted, often with the help of newer community unions with a specific focus on nonregular workers. Thus, this situation provides us with an opportunity to consider directly some of the newer forms of agency expressed by precarious workers in Japan's new political economy. What follows, therefore, is an attempt to highlight some of the more innovative forms of organizing by auto industry workers in the wake of the global financial crisis.

Mitsubishi Fuso and the Reinstatement of Dismissed Workers

One common way in which auto workers challenged dismissals was through Japan's legal system. Approximately seventy court cases were filed in an attempt by dispatch workers in the auto industry to challenge dismissals (*Syutoken Seinen* Union 2011). One particular case—that of Mitsubishi Fuso, which was challenged by the *Syutoken Seinen* Union—provides an illustrative example.

The union was established in December 2000 and was initially run by three full-time staff members, with voluntary help from members. Inspired by the WUT, the *Syutoken Seinen* Union was set up with the specific goal of focusing on young workers, who had typically been underrepresented.[19]

In the Mitsubishi Fuso case, two nonregular workers who had lost their jobs at the firm joined the *Syutoken Seinen* Union in an attempt to have the dismissals withdrawn and their right to stay in a company-provided dormitory reinstated (*Asahi Shinbun* 2008f). The campaign conducted by the union used a press conference and other announcements to gain considerable media attention and raise public awareness of the large numbers of dispatch workers being dismissed.[20] While the company refused to reinstate the two nonregular workers, adverse publicity led to its delaying the dismissal of twenty-eight temporary workers until their contracts had ended (rather than dismissing them with immediate effect, as had been the original intention) (*Asahi Shinbun* 2009a; *Syutoken Seinen* Union 2011). In addition, the case of the two nonregular workers was ultimately resolved through an undisclosed agreement with the company, and the workers themselves became labor activists and were involved with the *Hakenmura* protest camp.

The publicity related to the treatment of these nonregular workers provided an opportunity for further efforts by Mitsubishi Fuso employees to challenge what they considered to be unfair dismissals. For instance, Shigemitsu Suzuki brought a legal claim against the firm on the ground that he had been hired to work in the same way as those on permanent contracts between April 2005 and December 2012. According to the Worker Dispatch Law, he was therefore entitled to a permanent contract. Yet he had been unlawfully categorized as a dispatch worker, as a way of circumventing employment regulations regarding the maximum length of time (three years) that an employee can be employed as a dispatch worker (*Asahi Shinbun* 2009b). The case was ultimately decided in his favor in 2012.

The organizing efforts of the *Syutoken Seinen* Union highlight the possibility for legal challenges to be made on behalf of dispatch workers. In particular, the absence of more frequent challenges is largely associated with a lack of knowledge on the part of nonunionized workers. With union support, therefore, a number of successful challenges could be made. As Makoto Kawazoe, then an organizer for the *Syutoken Seinen* Union, put it, "as long as workers don't give up and continue to challenge employers, 80 percent of the time we can gain some concession from employers."[21]

The Nissan Diesel Union

On November 29, 2009, the *Haken* Union received a consultation phone call from a dispatch worker who worked at Nissan Diesel in Saitama. The worker had been notified in December 2008 that his contract was terminated and that he would need to leave the company's dormitory within three days of the termination of his contract. This was despite the fact that a one-month notice period was stipulated in his contract. It turned out on investigation that many dispatch workers had been forced to sign statements saying that they agreed with the termination of their contracts, even though those contracts had not expired. This prompted Shuichiro Sekine, the chair of *Haken*, to seek to recruit more workers who would be willing to discuss the actions of the firm, and five dispatch workers agreed to work with the union. As a first attempt to challenge the firm's behavior, Sekine advised the workers to enter into formal union negotiations, and in doing so to rely on Article 28 of the Constitution—which requires companies to respond to requests for negotiations from unions. In a first step toward this aim, three workers formed the Nissan Diesel Union as a branch of the *Haken* Union in December 2008 and entered into union-led negotiations with their employers (three different temp agencies) and their workplace management at Nissan Diesel (Sekine 2009; *Asahi Shinbun* 2008g).

In pursuit of their demand for negotiations, the Nissan Diesel Union adopted a range of methods, including leafleting other dispatch workers who worked at Nissan Diesel, holding a street protest against the dismissal of dispatch workers in front of the MHLW building in December 2008, and calling for the government to do more to protect nonregular workers. Despite these efforts, Nissan Diesel refused to respond to requests for negotiations, and instead the temp agencies were forced to negotiate (due to the legal right to negotiations and Nissan Diesel's refusal to negotiate) (*Asahi Shinbun* 2008d, 2008h, and 2008i). In each case, the three dispatch workers who had formed the Nissan Diesel Union were successful in securing their reinstatement as employees of their temp agencies (despite Nissan Diesel's refusal to reemploy them). Two of the workers were also awarded three months' worth of wages as compensation. Furthermore, the evictions of all three workers from their employer's dormitory were withdrawn, as the evictions had violated the Leased Land and House Lease Law—which requires a six-month notice period when company housing is let at commercial rental rates (Sekine 2009). It was therefore largely due to the legal knowledge of the *Haken* Union that the workers were able to secure these reversals of company decisions, due to the legal requirements for negotiations to be conducted properly, dismissals to be made with proper explanation, and evictions to take place with six months' notice—all requirements that Nissan Diesel and the temp agencies had failed to meet, thus providing the dismissed workers with considerable bargaining leverage (Sekine 2009). As a result, the temp agencies gave in to the majority of the workers' demands at the very first negotiating meeting.[22]

As this chapter has sought to highlight, despite the emergence of an expanded group of precarious nonregular workers in Japan's political economy, a number of new and innovative grassroots organizing efforts have demonstrated the workers' ongoing capacity to act collectively in response to their experience of precarity. As we have seen, this has included precarious workers organizing, including through new independent unions, to combat illegal wage deductions and recover unpaid wages and overtime payments, support precarious female workers, and address the experience of sudden job losses and housing evictions in the wake of the global financial crisis. Thus, the different examples of workplace organizing described in this chapter highlight some of the important ways in which Japanese labor is being recomposed in the context of neoliberalization (Cleaver 1992, 114). Moreover, what is perhaps most notable about these instances is the role of smaller independent unions, which have emerged to support nonregular workers in a way that the more established unions have appeared unable to do. In addition, the cases discussed have shown the way in which a combination of union support and advice—especially legal advice—has been able to improve the position of nonregular workers. This has been complemented by the bargaining leverage that on several occasions has been achieved through publicity campaigns. These have sought to highlight the experience of nonregular workers and gain more widespread public support, while reducing the public reputation of the employing firms or temp agencies involved. As we shall see in the next chapter, similar initiatives have also seen nonregular workers emerge as a significant force in Japan's policymaking process.

PRECARIOUS LABOR AND THE CONTESTATION OF POLICYMAKING IN JAPAN

This chapter explores ways in which precarious workers, including unemployed and homeless workers, have mobilized in ways that have posed a challenge to the political process of neoliberalization. In this sense, the chapter seeks to explore the ways in which Japan's nonregular workers have increasingly become important for policymakers to consider in their efforts to manage Japanese society. In considering the impact of Japan's precarious workers' movement on policymaking in Japan, the chapter highlights three cases through which we can witness the effects of opposition mobilized by Japanese precarious workers on policy outcomes. The cases are opposition to the Worker Dispatch Law (WDL), organized by a network of activists and precarious workers, including the Antipoverty Network and the Committee for the Amendment of the Worker Dispatch Law; a campaign orchestrated by *Moyai* and the unemployed to influence the level of social welfare benefits; and the movement against the sales tax. In each case, we witness political elites being forced to respond to successful mobilizations by precarious workers and organizations that have emerged to represent their interests. These mobilizations have served to attract public attention to the impact that neoliberal government policy has on precarious workers. When faced with criticism and opposition from the public, on each occasion governments were forced either to compromise on policy goals or proposals or to abolish or postpone policies to reduce criticism. While precarious workers were not always able to achieve all of their goals, collectively they have become an important actor that is able to gain concessions or raise significant obstacles to the implementation of neoliberal policy options so that their demands must be accommodated in some way. It is this new capacity for precarious workers to influence policy outcomes in Japan's political economy that this chapter sets out to explore.

Opposing the Worker Dispatch Law

One of the most controversial labor market policies in Japan has been the WDL. The law, first adopted in 1986, determines the level of flexibility that dispatch workers will be exposed to, including the degree to which they can be placed on short-term contracts and the type of work they can be employed to carry out. It defines the employment conditions of nonregular workers and has for many years been a source of controversy, especially since the first proposal for a major amendment in 1997—which was an attempt to enable dispatch workers to work in a broader range of sectors and industries (for a discussion of the various changes and amendments to the WDL over time, see Yun 2016). In the wake of the global financial crisis and the impact that it had—especially on nonregular workers—a network of activists emerged to contest the terms of the WDL and call for its amendment.

A Network of Precarious Dispatch Workers and Activists

The global financial crisis prompted a wave of dismissals and pushed many nonregular workers into homelessness, as their dormitory housing was connected to their employment. In response, an event typically referred to as *Hakenmura* took place, centered on a camp for homeless precarious workers in Tokyo's Hibiya Park (see chapter 3). One of the consequences of this event was the creation of a network of labor, homelessness, and antipoverty activists committed to campaigning against the conditions experienced by Japan's growing population of precarious workers. This network was able to connect with groups such as the Antipoverty Network, which had come into existence in response to the deepening poverty of many people in Japan during the 2000s.[1]

One of the key developments to emerge after the *Hakenmura* events was the creation of the Committee for the Amendment of the Worker Dispatch Law. This sought to challenge the terms of the WDL, whose amendment had already been proposed by the Liberal Democratic Party of Japan (LDP)—although in a form that would make working conditions still worse for dispatch workers. The committee was established by groups of activists, nonprofit organizations (NPOs), and various unions with the specific goal of abolishing zero-hour contracts. This abolition was expected to reduce the number of precarious employees and end the growing practice of employing dispatch workers as the main source of flexible labor in the manufacturing sector (as we saw in our discussion of auto workers in chapter 4). Thus, the initiative represents what Jennifer Jihye Chun and Rina Agarwala (2015) describe as the process of precarious workers developing alternative pathways to build solidarity in an attempt to adjust to their experience of nonregular working.

To advance its agenda, the Committee for the Amendment of the WDL held a number of events in which precarious workers were invited to discuss in public their experience of working as dispatch workers. These public events provided opportunities for precarious workers to talk about and highlight problems surrounding their wages, working conditions, and employment contracts. Politicians and policymakers were also invited, ensuring that political elites were pressured into offering policy solutions to the problems that were described. As a result, all of the opposition parties—including the Democratic Party of Japan (DPJ), the Social Democratic Party, and the Japanese Communist Party—were encouraged to suggest an alternative to the LDP's proposed amendment.[2] This campaign built on initiatives that had already been in place around 2008. For instance, for the annual May Day protests in that year, precarious workers had staged a "May Day for life and existence" demonstration (*Asahi Shinbun* 2008a). Similar events were to occur following 2008 as part of the attempt to promote an alternative amendment to the WDL. A large-scale rally was held in Tokyo in October 2009, involving 2,500 activists and nonregular workers and specifically focused on proposing an alternative amendment. This alternative sought to end the registered dispatch worker system that allowed zero-hour contracts, in which temp agencies paid only for the days that dispatch workers were sent to work for their client firms and that had no provision for monthly salaries or employment insurance (*Asahi Shinbun* 2009c). In addition, the media increasingly ran stories highlighting the experience of dispatch workers and other nonregular workers, further increasing the public awareness of the problems of precarious work.

Growing concern over the experience of precarious workers had led Youichi Masuzoe—the LDP government's minister of health, labor, and welfare—to propose an amendment to the WDL in the summer of 2008 (*Asahi Shinbun* 2008b). However, the government refused to consider the abolition of the registered dispatch worker system, which would have outlawed zero-hour contracts. This decision to keep the registered dispatch worker system was later reversed in 2009, under the DPJ government led by Prime Minister Yukio Hatoyama, with the Ministry of Health, Labor, and Welfare (MHLW) announcing in December 2009 that it would abolish the system and prohibit the dispatching of workers to the manufacturing industry (*Asahi Shinbun* 2009e). This changed government attitude in part reflected growing public unease regarding the poverty associated with the precarious working conditions of dispatch workers—an unease generated largely by the campaigning activities of precarious workers and the network of activists that emerged during the 2000s.

A growing number of legal disputes between precarious workers, on the one hand, and temp agencies and hiring companies, on the other hand, resulted in a context of heightened public concern for, and awareness of, the plight of precarious workers. It was in this context that the Hatoyama administration agreed in March 2010 to ban the registered dispatch worker system and prohibit workers from being hired on dispatch contracts in the manufacturing industry (*Asahi Shinbun* 2010d, 2010e, 2010g, and 2010h). This move, however, was blocked by the opposition LDP, which ensured that the Diet (national parliament) would not pass the amendment. As a result, the DPJ was forced to drop the two key elements of its proposal (banning registered dispatch workers and ending the employment of dispatch workers in manufacturing) and instead included only one of the demands of the Committee for the Amendment of the WDL—the abolition of day labor for employment of less than thirty days. In addition, the revised version promised to review the amended version of the WDL after one year, limit the rate of temp workers in companies to 80 percent of a given workforce, and ban firms from rehiring laid-off regular workers as cheaper dispatch workers. It was this revised version of the amendment that was eventually passed in 2012 (*Asahi Shinbun* 2012a; Yun 2016; MHLW 2015b).

This initial attempt by the committee to significantly revise the WDL therefore had mixed results. On the one hand, labor activists and precarious workers had successfully placed the experience of dispatch workers on the public agenda, resulting in a commitment by both the LDP and the DPJ to revise the WDL. The DPJ, in particular, also sought to adopt a number of the proposed amendments that the committee had been seeking. The difficulties involved in getting the amendments passed by the Diet were such that a number of significant compromises had to be made before the legislation was adopted. Nevertheless, the final outcome did represent an improvement in the degree to which constraints could be placed on the use of dispatch workers as replacements for regular workers, and it therefore represented a partial but important victory for precarious workers in Japan's neoliberalizing political economy. Despite these achievements, the LDP government of Prime Minister Shinzo Abe, which replaced the DPJ government in December 2012, would seek again to amend the WDL, this time in an attempt to make the law more open to employing dispatch workers.

Challenging Abe's Amendment
of the Worker Dispatch Law

The changes to employment regulations that had been introduced under the 2012 amendment of the WDL prompted labor activists to campaign for further reforms. At the same time, unions and lawyer activists set about advising dispatch workers of both the limitations and the improvements that had been secured as a result of the amendment. For instance, Shuichiro Sekine of the *Haken* Union warned that the amendment would not prevent future large-scale job losses for dispatch workers. Furthermore, a lawyers' group, the *Tokai Roudou Bengodan* (Tokai Labor Lawyers Group), issued a statement decrying the amendment as insufficient (*Asahi Shinbun* 2011 and 2012a). At the same time, a range of unions and lawyers' groups began to provide phone advice for precarious workers to ensure that they knew about the new regulations that prohibited the use of short-term contracts (for fewer than thirty days) (*Asahi Shinbun* 2012h and 2012i).

However, this new wave of precarious labor activism prompted the incoming Abe administration to consider further legislative changes to make Japan's labor markets more flexible, especially in the area of dispatch workers. As a result, yet another amendment to the WDL was proposed, with Abe declaring in his 2013 growth strategy that "Japan would become the best country for business to operate" (quoted in *Asahi Shinbun* 2013k, author's translation). Abe instructed the Labor Policy Committee of the Cabinet to consider the possible terms of any amendment, with suggestions that included expanding the range of sectors in which dispatch workers could be sent to work and removing the requirement for firms to make permanent any job that had been filled through dispatch workers for more than three years (instead, firms would simply need to hire a different dispatch worker after three years) (*Asahi Shinbun* 2013l).

Perhaps predictably, unions, NPOs, citizens' groups, and dispatch workers all reacted negatively to the proposed new set of amendments to the WDL. May Day protest events in 2014 attracted thousands of workers who marched and rallied against Abenomics on the ground that it represented a significant shift in favor of business and against workers (*Asahi Shinbun* 2014e, 2014k, 2014m, and 2014n). Thirty thousand members of unions belonging to *Rengo* protested the suggested amendment of the WDL in Kanagawa, and ten thousand in Yamagata and another ten thousand in Yamanashi conducted street demonstrations in opposition to the amendment (*Asahi Shinbun* 2014g, 2014h, 2014j, and 2014r). Seven thousand people demonstrated in Niigata, demanding secure employment and criticizing Abenomics for benefiting only a small section of the Japanese economy, and another thousand people protested in Ehime, demanding an improvement to labor policies (*Asahi Shinbun* 2014i and 2014l). Lawyers' groups and antipoverty activists also protested against the further flexibilization of dispatch work, including staging an "Ibaraki Antipoverty May Day" that was independent of the mainstream unions' May Day events. *Rengo* also announced that, due to its objection to the use of dispatch workers as replacements for permanent employees, it would strongly oppose the suggested amendment (*Rengo* 2012, 2).

As the LDP sought to get the proposed legislation through the Diet, both workers and their unions conducted a range of protest events to seek to build opposition to the proposal. Interestingly both *Rengo*-group unions and *Zenroren*-group unions became more active in the move against nonregular employment (in the past, both mainstream unions had been far more concerned with the conditions of regular workers). The two jointly organized a sit-in involving eight hundred people that was conducted in front of Parliament in October 2014. This was the first time in six years that *Zenroren* had joined a sit-in in front of Parliament. The following month ten unions and *Zenroren*, held a rally around Parliament, also in opposition to the amendment (*Asahi Shinbun* 2014ab).

The bill to amend the WDL created controversy and divisions in the political elite, including in the LDP and the *Koumei* Party (the LDP's junior coalition partner) (*Asahi Shinbun* 2013a). The *Koumei* Party proposed a revision to the bill ahead of its introduction in the Diet, making publicly visible the divisions in the coalition. The opposition party, DPJ, also remained strongly opposed (*Asahi Shinbun* 2014 ad), in part as a result of its strong support from *Rengo* unions—which sought greater protection for dispatch workers and opposed the use of temporary contracts for long-term employment.

The efforts by the government to get the Diet to approve its amendment to the WDL were also impeded by the rising wave of media attention that focused in particular on the behavior of temp agencies. This was especially damaging as the proposed amendment would remove some of the restrictions on those agencies. In an increasing number of cases, the labor standards inspection office and prefectural labor bureaus found that labor-related laws had been violated by many employers, especially by temp agencies. These agencies were subsequently the focus of considerable media scrutiny. For instance, dispatch workers had been unlawfully hired to perform decontamination work in the Fukushima nuclear power plant, which gained widespread media attention (*Asahi Shinbun* 2015ah). In addition, fifty-seven firms were found to have violated the WDL by the Hyogo Labor Bureau (*Asahi Shinbun* 2014d). Another six firms were forced to stop their operations in Mie due to their violation of the law, while over five thousand violations were reported in Saitama City (*Asahi Shinbun* 2015ab).

As a result of the wave of opposition to the WDL amendment, the LDP government was faced with the need on two occasions to withdraw the proposal during 2014 (it was withdrawn once in 2014, reintroduced again that year, and withdrawn a second time). Thus, it was only in March 2015 that Abe was able to announce that the cabinet had again decided on a proposed amendment that it would seek to have the Diet pass. Even with agreement in the cabinet, however, concessions were needed to secure the approval of the legislature. This was especially due to the opposition of the DPJ, which claimed that the amendment would create "life-long dispatch employment" (quoted in *Asahi Shinbun* 2015q, author's translation). The concessions agreed to by the LDP and inserted into the bill that was to be put before the Diet included a new system of regulation for temp agencies. This would require a temp agency to be approved by the MHLW before it could begin operating. The concessions also included a requirement for temp agencies to provide job training to dispatch workers and an appendix to the bill that listed the entitlements of dispatch workers and the requirements placed on temp agencies. Finally, the LDP's concessions also required that the use of a dispatch worker beyond the three-year limit would require prior union consultation (*Yomiuri Shinbun* 2015a).

Despite these concessions, the proposed amendment of the WDL continued to encounter strong opposition. May Day protest events across Japan in April and May 2015 represented another wave of opposition to the amendment. The DPJ and the Communist Party also opposed the amendment. Nevertheless, this opposition proved insufficient: although both parties refused to attend the parliamentary vote, the Diet adopted the amendment in June 2015 (*Toyou Keizai* Online 2015).

Although the amendment was adopted, it continued to be widely criticized. This led Abe to later call on firms to voluntarily increase the wages of low-paid workers ahead of the elections for the upper house of the Diet in summer 2016, in a somewhat futile attempt to reduce ongoing opposition to the precarization of Japan's labor force.

Continuously Contested Policy in the Abe Administration

Rather than signal the defeat of Japan's precarious workers, the adoption of the 2015 amendment to the WDL was met with a further round of organizing and campaigning and new activity by groups and trade unions seeking to represent the interests of nonregular workers. This put pressure on the Abe administration and contributed to a general decline in its popular support. There was also growing unease about the Abe administration over an expanding range of issues. The policies that were the target of criticism included proposed constitutional changes, efforts to restart nuclear power plants, the transfer of the U.S. base to a new location in Okinawa, and agricultural reforms that risked destabilizing local economies. The

Abe government looked increasingly out of touch with public opinion. Its approval rating fell from 67.1 percent in February 2013 to 43.2 percent in February 2016 (TV Asahi Poll n.d.). Partly in an attempt to shore up support, the Abe government announced in 2015 that it would modify its flagship economic program—known as Abenomics—by revising its three arrows (see chapter 1) so it would be more explicitly directed toward dealing with the issue of precarious labor in Japan.

One of the most active groups advocating on behalf of nonregular workers in Japan during the period following the adoption of the 2015 amendment to the WDL was an NPO, the *Haken Roudou* Network (Network for Dispatch Work). This organization held various public events, including both demonstrations and a series of symposiums that took place in the House of Representatives. This was part of a general attempt to generate greater awareness among workers, unions, NPOs, academics, politicians, and civil servants of the problems surrounding the law and precarious workers and to generate collective activity by precarious workers and activists.

The same period saw the creation of the Dispatch Workers' Forum. Consisting predominantly of female dispatch workers, this organization focused its efforts on an attempt to secure equal treatment between dispatch workers and regular workers. It lobbied female members of the Diet in an attempt to highlight the gendered nature of precarious employment in Japan (*Asahi Shinbun* 2015v).

The Dispatch Workers' Forum also joined forces with other precarious workers' organizations, including the *Zenkoku* Union, Tokyo Union, and *Haken* Union, and the *Haken Roudou* Network to launch a campaign in pursuit of equal entitlement to tax exemptions for nonregular workers. This focused on the disparity whereby regular (but not nonregular) workers were able to take a tax deduction for their commuting costs against their tax contributions (*Haken* Union Blog 2017; *Haken* Network 2016). This issue highlighted some of the ways in which nonregular workers were treated unfairly under Japan's employment system, providing labor activists with a grievance around which to mobilize. Thus, negotiations between *Zenkoku* Union and the MHLW resulted in the ministry's issuing an instruction to the Temp Agencies' Association notifying member temp agencies that they were required to apply commuting costs in the same way as regular workers were entitled to (*Haken* Union Blog 2017).

The ongoing publicity surrounding moves toward precarization in Japan's labor force, especially following the adoption of the 2015 amendment, as well as the public discontent following Abe's amendment of the national security bill (and related attempt to remilitarize Japan), contributed to a sense in the remaining months of 2015 that the Abe administration was struggling to secure popular support (*Asahi Shinbun* 2015z). Partly in response, at the end of November 2015 the administration announced a range of policies aimed at addressing the situation of low-paid and nonregular workers. The policies were collectively titled "Urgent Policies to Realize a Society in Which All Citizens Are Dynamically Engaged" (Cabinet Office 2015b). This focused especially on low-paid workers. It was underpinned by a growing concern that domestic consumption remained low in Japan due to stagnating wage growth, which in turn was stifling aggregate demand. The flagship measure of these "urgent policies," therefore, was an announcement that the minimum wage would be increased by 3 percent, to 1,000 yen per hour (ibid.; *Asahi Shinbun* 2015r and 2015w).

It was in this context that the reforms to Abenomics were announced. The reforms centered on the adoption of three new "arrows," referring to the sets of principles or goals that constituted the economic reforms. The new arrows explicitly addressed issues relating to precarious workers and other vulnerable members of society, in an apparent attempt to deal with the government's declining public support on this issue. Therefore, the Abe government included in the new economic reform program a number of reforms designed to improve working conditions and restructure employment relations and how people work. The first arrow included a plan to improve short-term contract workers' status, convert nonregular workers into regular workers, reduce the proportion of involuntary nonregular employment to below 10 percent by 2020, and reduce working hours by revising the Labor Standard Law and enforcing the system that enables workers to take more paid holidays. The Government also sought to devise ways to improve the skills of nonregular workers (Cabinet Office 2016a, 8). The second arrow declared a goal of stabilizing employment and improving working conditions. It also seeks to promote workplace reforms that support employees who have children. Finally, the third arrow promised to improve social security, in particular by guaranteeing the provision of nursing services and support systems for families (Cabinet Office 2015a).

In sum, while the Abe government went ahead with its liberalizing efforts by forcing through the 2015 amendment of the WDL, very shortly afterward it needed to redirect its economic program in an attempt to stabilize popular support. Rather than witnessing the straightforward liberalization of Japan's labor market, the Abe government has been able to introduce liberalizing measures only by simultaneously adopting concessions in response to the demands of precarious workers. Japan's new group of precarious nonregular workers have proven able to challenge, contest, and indirectly shape the nature of the economic reforms adopted as government economic policy in Japan. This capacity to contest and influence policymaking represents an important new development in Japan's political economy, and one that needs to be considered to understand the ongoing direction of economic and social policymaking. Some of the key developments in this area are considered below.

Winning Social Welfare Benefits for the Impoverished: *Moyai*, Lawyers, and the Unemployed

In addition to its direct impact on precarious workers in the workplace, the liberalization of Japan's political economy has also led to rising unemployment and homelessness. This has often had an impact directly on the same group of precarious workers who were affected by the use of short-term and temporary contracts, with those facing unexpected unemployment also suffering from an increased likelihood of homelessness. This growing group of unemployed and homeless precarious workers emerged as a key group with the capacity to challenge the government, especially over its implementation of social welfare benefits, and as a result the MHLW eventually instructed municipal governments that they must adopt the appropriate administrative procedures in overseeing and implementing the provision of social benefits. This was in large part a result of the efforts of *Moyai*, one of the largest NPOs working to support the homeless and the unemployed—both through the provision of temporary accommodation and through helping people secure *seikatsuhogohi* (social welfare benefits) as part of helping the impoverished survive—and end—homelessness. *Moyai* was also one of the first NPOs to politicize the problems of poverty among the homeless, the jobless, and precarious workers (*Asahi Shinbun* 2014c).[3]

Unlawful Bureaucracy and the Struggle for Welfare Rights

Japanese welfare provision under the classic postwar model was largely associated with social security through work and preferential tax treatment for people in vulnerable economic circumstances. One of the outcomes of the restructuring that Japan experienced during the period after 1991 was a move toward a benefits system with a higher level of nonpayments by local municipalities, which are responsible for processing and implementing benefits. Under the Public Assistance Act of 1950, local authorities have a legal responsibility to receive and process all applications for welfare benefits. However, one of the consequences of the rise in benefit claims that municipalities began to experience in the wake of the global financial crisis was an increased frequency of rejected claims, which subsequently turned out to have been declined for inappropriate reasons. For example, some were rejected because the applicants were wrongly considered able to work (and therefore ineligible for disability payments), and others were rejected because applicants were without a permanent address and therefore unable to properly complete the prescribed application form. Many of these bureaucratic obstacles preventing claimants from receiving their welfare entitlements were found by *Moyai* to have been unlawfully constructed by municipalities in an attempt to limit the number of successful applications.[4] These practices, which were subsequently exposed by the media, included measures such as concealing the relevant applications from applicants by failing to put them on display in municipal government offices (*Asahi Shinbun* 2012m).

These unlawful practices were successfully challenged by legal activists and NPOs, especially *Moyai*. They informed potential claimants that there was no legal requirement to use any particular form. Thus, claimants who submitted any written request—including simply by writing the necessary information on any sheet of paper—were entitled to receive the welfare benefits they were eligible for. This knowledge had the clear potential to greatly increase the frequency of successful applications for welfare benefits and was successfully used as a way to challenge local governments over their refusal to pay benefit entitlements over several years (Inaba 2013; *Asahi Shinbun* 2013e). Legal activists helped claimants fill out the relevant paperwork, sometimes using an online form made available by *Moyai* through its website.

This legal activism grew out of an earlier development in 2002. Groups of lawyers who had become active in supporting the homeless used their influence in *Nichibenren* (the Japan Federation of Bar Associations) to encourage it to produce written material that could be distributed to the jobless and homeless. This campaign focused on raising people's awareness of legal entitlements to different elements of social welfare, as well as of how welfare payments could be applied for. These "know your rights" materials were distributed on the streets. The initiative culminated in a meeting in 2006 that was held to coordinate activities focused on the protection of human rights, and in which *Nichibenren* announced its decision to increase its support and advice for the impoverished and homeless (Inaba 2013). This included the creation of a national advice service that could inform potential applicants of their welfare entitlements.[5]

Alongside this rise in the provision of legal advice, various forms of collective action also took place with increasing frequency. One approach was to pursue collective legal cases. Nearly eight hundred social welfare beneficiaries collectively sued several local authorities after their benefits were reduced in violation of Article 25 of the Constitution, which guarantees health and a cultural life for all (*Asahi Shinbun* 2014p, 2014q, and 2015af). Similar cases were successfully brought against the city councils of Kyoto, Hokkaido, Osaka, and Matsuyama in November and December 2014, which secured 10,000 yen ($90) in compensation per person (*Asahi Shinbun* 2014ac, 2014ae, 2014al, 2014am, and 2014an). Other similar cases successfully blocked attempts by municipal governments to reduce the level of welfare provision, with several hundred claimants bringing cases in

Kagoshima, Akita, Ishikawa, Nagano, Saitama, Fukuoka, Tokyo, and Shizuoka (*Asahi Shinbun* 2015l, 2015m, 2015n, 2015o, and 2015ai). Japan's benefit claimant movement also included a number of more public-facing events that sought to draw attention to the government's cost-cutting approach. There were a number of demonstrations and rallies, including a demonstration attended by four thousand protesters in Tokyo in October 2014 and another demonstration in October 2015, both in opposition to the reduction in welfare benefits (*Asahi Shinbun* 2015ae and 2015af).

As can be seen, Japan has witnessed the emergence of a welfare benefit claimant and support movement. This has largely focused on a combination of providing legal advice and pursuing legal claims, in both instances seeking to ensure that welfare entitlements are honored—as well as activities such as demonstrations and rallies that are more focused on attracting publicity. This has also led to a number of developments at the level of public policy in Japan, especially with regard to the implementation of welfare benefit provision.

Changed Attitudes in the Government and Local Authorities

In response to some of the developments and legal challenges mentioned above, in 2006 the MHLW issued a manual aimed at improving the administration and implementation of social welfare benefits and raising awareness of the legal rights of benefits claimants. The manual explicitly encouraged municipal governments to make sure that they honored entitlements (*Asahi Shinbun* 2014ac, 2014ag, and 2014ah).[6] In March 2006 the MHLW issued a notice instructing local authorities to provide appropriate support and counseling and insisting that they should not prevent potential claimants from applying for benefits or prevent applications from being submitted (Inaba 2013). According to the chair of the citizens' group *Kobe no Fuyu wo Sasaeru Kai* (Support People in Winter in Kobe), this directive made it much easier for people to apply for social welfare benefits and contributed directly to a reduction in the number of homeless people in Hyogo Prefecture (*Asahi Shinbun* 2015ak). Thus, the activism outlined above can be considered to have contributed to a significant change in policy implementation, with a resultant improvement in the condition of unemployed and homeless benefit claimants in Japan (Inaba 2013).

The rise in social movements organized around precarious workers, and especially their experience of unemployment and homelessness, eventually led to the landmark *Hakenmura* event in December 2008 (mentioned above). Numerous activists, volunteers, and unionists set up temporary camp for homeless and unemployed people as well as precarious workers with low wages.[7] Many people who gathered in the *Hakenmura* camp were in abject poverty. The most urgent tasks of the event were to provide immediate accommodation, sufficient cash to avoid homelessness, and support in finding jobs or medical care and advice.[8] *Moyai* worked to help camp participants access support from the government. This included submitting the forms of three hundred participants by fax and receiving the necessary money from the government so the claimants could move immediately into housing once their applications had been processed (Inaba 2013).

The *Hakenmura* event also prompted the MHLW to open its assembly hall to the homeless as part of the process of delivering benefits and housing, as well as facilitating job hunting. According to Makoto Kawazoe, then chair of the *Syutoken Seinen* Union, this represented a significant step by the government, which more commonly is slow and bureaucratic in its response to social problems. The change was largely attributed to the public attention that activists had drawn to the experience of precarious workers through events such as *Hakenmura*.[9] Likewise, Inaba, then chair of *Moyai*, considered the greater ease with which the homeless and unemployed could successfully claim welfare benefits to be one of the most significant outcomes of the *Hakenmura* event (Inaba 2013).[10] This included both a significant improvement in the acceptance of benefit claims by the government and the revival in December 2009 of additional benefits for single-parent households (which had been gradually reduced from 2005 onward as a result of a decision taken by the Junichiro Koizumi administration) (Inaba 2013). In addition, the government began to report the rate of relative poverty[11] in Japan. These changes were in part due to the effect of the *Hakenmura* event in terms of raising public awareness of poverty as an issue in Japanese society, ensuring that it was increasingly difficult for political elites to deny the existence of poverty and precarious employment relations for workers in Japan.[12] This, in turn, contributed to a reduction in the social stigma associated with the application for and receipt of social welfare benefits, as well as contributing to a more general politicization of the issue of poverty in Japan.

The Election of the Abe Government: Austerity and Anti-Austerity Initiatives

While some of the more positive developments outlined above were adopted under the DPJ government (2009–2012), the political climate once again became more hostile toward issues of poverty and low pay following the election of the LDP government in December 2012. The LDP returned to power with a manifesto committing it to cut social welfare benefits by 10 percent, and consequently it sought to reduce those benefits. Thus, soon after the second Abe cabinet was established, in January 2013, the government set about reducing a number of the key benefit programs: *seikatsufuzyohi* (livelihood assistance), which is used for food, clothes, and utility costs, was removed from *seikatsuhogohi*, saving 85 billion yen over three years; the year-end temporary assistance payments were reduced by 7 billion yen, or 14,000 yen per person; and the additional winter assistance payments were also reduced. These reductions were implemented in three stages and amounted to a 6.5 percent reduction in social welfare benefits, the largest since the end of the Second World War (*Asai Shinbun* 2014ag, 2014am, and 2015af; Inaba 2013 197).

These austerity measures introduced by the Abe administration were met by a series of protests staged by NPOs, legal activists, and the antipoverty networks that had emerged in response to the global financial crisis (*Asahi Shinbun* 2012k, 2012l, 2012n, 2012o, 2012p, and 2013f). In addition, efforts were made to ensure that people with low incomes were aware of their remaining welfare entitlements. The Antipoverty Network Hokkaido distributed leaflets in an attempt to raise awareness of available support and benefits (*Asahi Shinbun* 2013b). The Antipoverty Network Gifu held a press conference in which it claimed that the government's reduction of benefits would threaten the lives and health of people with low incomes (*Asahi Shinbun* 2013g). Likewise, the Antipoverty Network Aichi issued a statement highlighting the failure of welfare payments to keep up with the rising price of essentials, such as food and heat, light, and water utilities (*Asahi Shinbun* 2013h). In addition, the legal activist group *Ichyo no Kai* (Group Gingko) declared its intention to work with other groups to support single-parent households (*Asahi Shinbun* 2013f). Antipoverty groups in Kohchi formed an antipoverty committee that highlighted its opposition to the reduction in social welfare benefits announced in the 2013 budget (*Asahi Shinbun* 2013i). Some cooperatives, NPOs, and local social welfare councils set up food banks for the impoverished (*Asahi Shinbun* 2016a). Thus, a range of grassroot initiatives—many of a nondisruptive type—emerged in response to and as an attempt to resist the round of austerity measures introduced by the Abe government (see Bailey and Shibata 2017).

In response to this new wave of concern regarding the impact of austerity measures in Japan, a number of new policy responses emerged. In particular, municipal governments sought to address the impact of poverty through a range of educational programs that promised to break the link between low incomes and poor educational achievement. For instance, the Hokkaido Prefectural Government established a new policy that sought to increase the proportion of students from impoverished households advancing to higher levels of education (*Asahi Shinbun* 2015h and 2015ac). Likewise, Kyoto Prefectural Government set aside 176 million yen per year in its budget for the prevention of child poverty (*Asahi Shinbun* 2013j, 2015g, and 2015aa). Some local authorities provided educational services to children in households that received social welfare benefits. Nagoya City announced that it would provide support for supplementary learning opportunities (*Asahi Shinbun* 2014aa). Ōta City in Gunma Prefecture cooperated with citizens' groups and NPOs to provide educational support to children in low-income households, earmarking 2.5 million yen in its 2016 budget to support supplementary lessons (*Asahi Shinbun* 2015ag). In addition, in a measure that would affect over 100,000 children, the national government announced that it would reduce the cost of nursery school, from 59,000 yen (for a public school) and 108,800 yen (private) to 36,000 yen per month for either (*Asahi Shinbun* 2015a). Similarly, as we have seen, Abe routinely called on employers to voluntarily increase pay for low-income workers. And at the same time efforts were made to increase the minimum wage rates set in different prefectural governments, reflecting the MHLW's recommendation in July 2014 to increase the hourly minimum wage (*Asahi Shinbun* 2014t, 2014u, 2014aj, 2014ak, and 2015d).

In sum, therefore, while the Abe government has been determined to reduce social welfare provision, largely in an attempt to decrease government spending, a number of attempts have been made to respond to these reforms. This, in turn, has prompted some important concessions, including reduced child care costs, an increase in the minimum wage, and efforts by local authorities to deal with some of the more damaging effects of low income on educational attainment. As we shall see, the proposed increase in the sales tax would provoke opposition to the Abe administration.

The Anti–Sales Tax Movement

One of the most contentious policies introduced by the Abe government has been that of the sales tax. This was introduced as part of a broad attempt to deal with Japan's high level of public debt, which in turn put considerable pressure on the government to find ways to ensure that spending would move in the direction of fiscal balance. As we shall see, however, the attempt to increase the sales tax (a highly regressive tax) encountered considerable problems that would eventually lead to the sustained delay of its full implementation and at the same time contributed to a significant decline in the popularity of Prime Minister Abe.[13]

Proposed Tax Increases under the DPJ

The initial proposal to increase the sales tax was made by the previous DPJ government. Eventually each of the three DPJ prime ministers (Yukio Hatoyama, Kan Naoto, and Yoshihiko Noda) vacillated on the subject, which destabilized their leadership. Indeed, the DPJ had pledged in the manifesto on which it was elected to office in 2009 that it would not raise sales taxes for four years. This was abandoned by Hatoyama, due to the pressure of Japan's rising public debt and the increased costs of social welfare. Hatoyama announced in 2010 that his government would increase the sales tax by 2 percent (*Asahi Shinbun* 2010i and 2010k). This immediately sparked the opposition of citizens, who focused on the regressive nature of the tax, and many of the 2010 May Day protests focused specifically on the proposed tax reform. The DPJ was divided over the issue, with 34 percent of party members supporting the proposal and 38 percent opposing it (*Yomiuri Shinbun* 2014b). These internal party rifts were exacerbated by disagreement in the business community. The *Kansai Keizai Rengoukai* (Kansai Economic Association) advocated a 15–20 percent tax increase in 2010 (*Asahi Shinbun* 2010j), whereas other business associations advocated not increasing the tax until the economy had recovered. The auto industry was strongly against the sale tax increase, due to its obvious influence on the price of cars and an expected decline in their sales.

In the light of this opposition the Hatoyama administration announced that it would withdraw its proposal to increase the sales tax, replacing it with a proposed rise in income tax rate to 50 percent for high-income earners (*Asahi Shinbun* 2010m). But before this could be implemented, opposition to Hatoyama's leadership—in part over his position on the sales tax, but also related to his handling of the issue of the US army base in Okinawa and an internal party finance scandal—became so great that he abruptly resigned in June 2010.

Prime Minister Kan, Hatoyama's successor, also shifted his position on the sales tax (*Asahi Shinbun* 2010a and 2010b). Initially, the Kan administration avoided introducing a tax hike. The lack of clarity over the government's position on the issue was seen by many members of the DPJ as a reason for the party's poor performance in the July 2010 Upper House election, and it resulted in Kan's resignation the following year (Park and Ide 2014, 692; *Asahi Shinbun* 2010c, 2010l, and 2010n).

Noda, Kan's successor as DPJ leader and prime minister, sought to increase the sales tax. This time the government was successful, securing an agreement with the LDP opposition that led to the adoption of a landmark bill in August 2012 that would increase the sales tax from 5 percent to 8 percent in 2014 and then to 10 percent in 2015 (Park and Ide 2014, 692). However, this prompted severe criticism and public opposition. Oil industry unions held large-scale protests (*Asahi Shinbun* 2012j), and seventy thousand people gathered at a May Day protest in Osaka in May 2012 that was supported by *Rengo* (*Asahi Shinbun* 2012b). In addition, civil groups and trade unions conducted a range of street protests, including one in which a fifty-car parade drove through the center of Kochi City, demanding that the party stick to its manifesto commitments (*Asahi Shinbun* 2012e and 2012g). The issue also further highlighted divisions within the DPJ: for example, Yukio Hatoyama, the former party leader of DPJ and then still a member of DPJ, and Ichiro Ozawa an influential former member of the party, joined a rally against the proposal (*Jiji Tsushin* 2012). In an ultimately unsuccessful attempt to garner public support for the initiative, a number of concessions were offered. These included an increase in welfare benefits for nonregular workers, younger workers, and low-income retirees. Before any increase in sales tax could be implemented, however, the DPJ lost the 2012 general election to the LDP, with many people, including political elites, state elites, and academics, attributing this to the inconsistent approach adopted toward the unpopular sales tax increases (*Asahi Shinbun* 2012c and 2012f).

Tax Hikes and the Abe Administration

In a press conference in October 2013, Prime Minister Abe announced that his government would increase the sales tax in two stages: by 3 percent in April 2014 (from 5 percent to 8 percent), and by an additional 2 percent in October 2015 (to 10 percent). The proposal encountered widespread opposition from within the LDP as well as from business groups, trade unions, precarious workers, citizens' groups, and the public. There were street demonstrations in cities across Japan, including Yamaguchi, Chiba, Tokyo, Fukushima, Tokushima, and Kanazawa (*Asahi Shinbun* 2014k and 2014x; *Zenkoku Hoken Dantai Rengou Kai* 2013), amid claims that the proposal would plunge Japan into a worse recession than the earlier tax hike of 1997 had done. The considerable opposition to this austerity policy made it politically difficult for the Abe cabinet to implement the second stage of tax increase in 2015 (from 8 percent to 10 percent). Attempts to find an acceptable compromise foundered, as members of the political elite tended to view the tax increase as fiscally necessary. Party members were also divided over whether or not the tax increase should be introduced (*Yomiuri Shinbun* 2014b; *Asahi Shinbun* 2012q and 2013c). In addition, this was a key source of conflict between the LDP and its coalition partner, the *Koumei* Party.

The economic effects of the tax rise were particularly dramatic. Consumer spending rose dramatically immediately before the implementation of the tax rise (rising 2 percent from January to March 2014) and then equally dramatically fell after implementation (by over 4 percent from April to June 2014) (*Asahi Shinbun* 2014v and 2015f; Harding 2015b; *Jichiroren* 2014). According to a survey conducted by *Rengo Souken* (2014, 19), nearly 70 percent of households cut their expenses in response to the tax increase, which had a particularly striking effect on low-income households. The retail industry was especially badly hit, in some instances needing to reduce prices in an attempt to offset the effect of the tax rise. Likewise, the auto industry experienced a reduction in the volume of car sales. Gross domestic product growth declined by 1.6 percent from July to September 2014, shocking the Japanese market (*Asahi Shinbun* 2014af).

Largely as a consequence of the economic effects of the sales tax hike, Abe's popularity also declined over the same period, with the rate of people who approved of his performance plummeting from 76 percent in April 2013 to 42 percent in October 2015. Those opposed to the Abe administration increased from 16 percent in April 2013 to 41 percent in October 2015 (*Nihon Keizai Shinbun* 2015). A 2015 public opinion poll found that 56 percent of respondents opposed to the sales tax hike (*Asahi Shinbun* 2015aj).

With protests ongoing against the planned second stage of the sales tax hike (to 10 percent), Abe announced in late 2014 that this increase would be postponed until April 2017 (Cabinet Office 2014a; *Asahi Shinbun* 2013d). In a further attempt to prepare public opinion for the second stage of the tax hike, Abe was forced to offer further concessions. These included a temporary welfare benefit of 6,000 yen each for twenty-four million low-income people and a temporary child benefit of 3,000 yen per child for households with children under eleven (MHLW 2015a and 2016). Also included was a proposal to allow a tax rebate of 2 percent on essential purchases such as food; a payment of 30,000 yen to ten million low-income pensioners; and a promise that 14 trillion yen of the sales tax revenue would be spent on social welfare, including health care and child care (*Yomiuri Shinbun* 2015e; Harding 2015a). The government also announced an increase of 10,000 yen to benefits for people with low incomes, in an attempt to offset the impact on the poorest sections of Japanese society. Despite these efforts to prepare the ground for the second stage of the tax hike, the government later announced that the second stage would be postponed again, this time until October 2019 (*Nikkei* Web 2016). In addition, the government promised that the sales tax would not be increased above 10 percent before 2020 (*Asahi Shinbun* 2015i).

As with earlier contentious policies, the case of the proposed sales tax hike shows the difficulties that Japan's move toward liberalization, and the associated increase in the proportion of the labor force suffering from low pay and insecurity, has faced. Policymakers—in both the DPJ and the LDP—faced considerable opposition and unintended negative consequences in their attempt to push forward a regressive sales tax increase, the negative effects of which would be felt most by low-income people. The capacity for resistance by this new category of workers, alongside the difficulties associated with statecraft and state management created by the public disapproval of the proposed measures, seriously hindered the implementation of significantly regressive tax measures. Together with the increased experience of poverty and precarity in Japan's new political economy, we also therefore see a rise in the capacity for contention, with a subsequent impact on public policymaking.

As this chapter has illustrated, the emergence of a new class of nonregular workers in Japan has led to new incidents of opposition, refusal, and contestation. Through a range of different types of mobilization—by independent unions, through demonstrations and protests, in publicity campaigns aimed at raising awareness and placing the blame on national and local government, and with the assistance of legal activists and NPOs—Japan's new class of nonregular workers is having a significant impact on Japan's public policymaking process, sometimes impeding implementation or prompting the revision of policies, at other times extracting significant concessions, and on still other occasions witnessing the reversal of policy proposals.

As the chapter has shown, these different methods of refusal had a significant impact on a series of prolonged attempts to amend the WDL, witnessing the successful reversal of attempts to amend the law on two occasions—and when the amendment was adopted, witnessing a number of key concessions, the most important of which was the abolition of the practice of day labor. As we saw when we considered the mobilization of the homeless and unemployed in the wake of the global financial crisis, with the support of NPOs and unions it was possible to raise public awareness of, and thereby to politicize, the rising incidence and impact of poverty in Japan. As a result, welfare policies and the way they were implemented were changed at both central and local government levels. In this way, the study confirms the view of Jihye Chun and Agarwala that appeals to "public norms of justice" can advance of workers' interests, even when this is done using the language of "human rights rather than worker rights" (2015, 644). Finally, we considered the way in which the sales tax hikes, proposed by both the DPJ and the LPD, were significantly affected by Japan's precarious nonregular workers. While the first stage of the sales tax hike did go ahead, the second stage was significantly postponed. The emergence of precarity and precarious workers in Japan has therefore had a significant impact on public policymaking. As we shall see in chapter 6, the social tension that this has created has also had an important effect on attempts to steer Japan's political economy back toward a model that seems able to generate growth. It is to these difficulties that we now turn.

JAPAN'S ABSENT MODE OF REGULATION

Impeded Neoliberalization

This book has thus far highlighted the way in which Japan's new political economy has seen a process of neoliberalization throughout the post-1991 period. This was associated with a corresponding growth in the proportion of the labor force who can be considered nonregular workers. As a result, for many in Japan economic insecurity and poverty has increased, as the promise of lifelong regular employment—itself a central pillar on which the postwar class compromise was constructed—has been steadily eroded. At the same time, this has resulted in the emergence of new agents and forms of labor activism, creating a situation whereby both firms and policymakers have faced significant and sustained contestation by Japan's new nonregular working class. This chapter seeks to show that, despite the attempts at neoliberal reform, Japan's political economy has nevertheless been unable to return to sustainable levels of economic growth similar to those experienced before the bursting of the economic bubble in 1991. As figure 6.1 makes clear, if we consider the three-year centered moving average of gross domestic product (GDP) growth in Japan in the period 1961–2018, Japan's economy has consistently struggled to rise above 2 percent annual average growth for any three-year period since 1991. In part, this is a further consequence of the inability to achieve consensus around a new mode of regulation for Japan's national economy throughout this period. Thus, Japan suffers from the absence of a mode of regulation, and its efforts at liberalization have been unsuccessfully implemented—partly as a result of the opposition to efforts at reform. Japan's process of neoliberalization has therefore been impeded, incomplete, somewhat unsuccessful, and

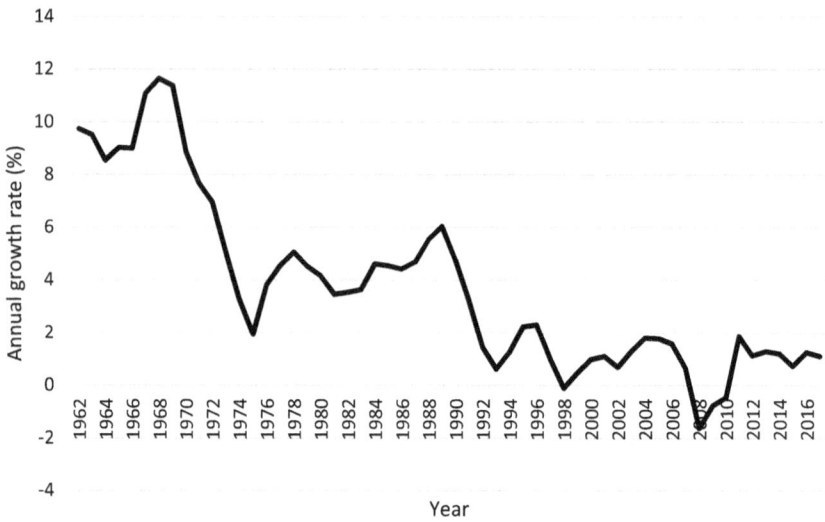

FIGURE 6.1. Real GDP annual growth, 3-year centered moving average, 1961–2018

Source: OECD 2018, Real GDP forecast.

marked more by dissension and a failure to identify an alternative institutional compromise with which to secure a return to economic growth.

Japan's Impeded Neoliberalization

As we have seen throughout this book, the various neoliberalization programs that have been introduced in Japan since 1991 have been designed to lift the economy out of long-lasting deflation, achieve fiscal balance, and generate economic growth by liberalizing the market and making Japan friendlier to business. In the language of regulation theory, this represents an attempt to construct an alternative mode of regulation. That is, it represents an attempt to construct an alternative institutional and social compromise that would oversee a more marketized and liberalized socioeconomic regime in Japan, which would dismantle a number of the forms of social and labor protection, the state-focused mechanisms of economic management, and interfirm coordination—all of which formed part of the pre-1991 classic Japanese model. Yet some of these policies have faced a number of significant obstacles, often as a direct result of the opposition of nonregular workers and labor activists seeking to represent and advance their interests. Contestation of planned reforms of public policies has been common, including policies related to the sales tax hike, the Zero Overtime Payment Bill, and attempts to amend the Worker Dispatch Law. This chapter goes beyond a discussion of individual policy proposals and instead draws on further insights of regulation theory in seeking to understand the apparent failure of Japanese economic policymakers to produce a return to earlier levels of economic growth. Regulation theory understands the management of capitalist economies in terms of the need to identify a way to secure an institutional and social compromise that meets a combination of key requirements for the reduction of the tensions at the core of capitalist economies. Such a compromise includes stabilizing the relationship between firms over the management of labor, the relationship with the world market, and the creation of a functioning monetary regime. All of this must be done in such a way that profitable production can be reconciled with the inevitable social tensions in capitalism, as a result of its inherent reliance on competition and exploitation.

It is the claim of this chapter, therefore, that the emergence of higher levels of social tension in Japan, which we have charted in previous chapters, has thwarted many of the key attempts to neoliberalize Japan's socioeconomic model. This is due in part to the ongoing political and social expectation that policymakers will seek to produce social consensus and avoid excessively exclusionary economic policy outcomes, which is a legacy of the earlier focus on social harmony and inclusion that prevailed in Japan's classic model. In a context still influenced by the earlier prioritization of inclusion and social harmony, Japan's new class of precarious nonregular workers has managed to draw attention to its experience of precarity, insecurity, and poverty, and as a result has been consistently able to highlight the detrimental effect of neoliberalizing measures. The result of such a strategy has been to impede the move toward the neoliberalization of Japan. This failure to fully implement neoliberalization therefore highlights the absence of a coherent mode of regulation in Japan. In such a context, and from the perspective of regulation theory, it is unsurprising that the Japanese economy has failed to return to economic growth. To illustrate these trends, the following discussion highlights the way in which key elements of neoliberalization have been impeded in Japan. The areas discussed are agricultural reform, pension reforms, employment relations, and the disarticulation of coherent class interests. These were chosen as they represent both some of the key pillars of Japan's socioeconomic model during the postwar period and the main areas that have been the focus of reform throughout the post-1991 period. As such, they provide the best lens through which to consider both the attempts to reform and restructure Japan's socioeconomic model, as well as important illustrations of the disagreement, dissent, and contestation that has occurred during this reform process.

Contested Liberalization: Agricultural Reform

Japan's agricultural sector has historically been a key element of the political coalition that formed the near-permanent rule of the Liberal Democratic Party of Japan (LDP) during the postwar period. The Japanese agricultural industry benefited from subsidies, lower taxation, and economic protection throughout the postwar period (Park and Ide 2014, 683). In return, people in Japan's rural areas, and especially farmers, have consistently supported the LDP at the polls. Therefore, the rural sector formed a key pillar in the classic Japanese socioeconomic model. This created a tendency for the rural sector to continue to be supported, and for the LDP's political elite to be wary of introducing any proposals for reform. Japan's agricultural sector grew dependent on government subsidies and preferential tax treatment for farmers. This was complemented by a system of trade protectionism that greatly benefited Japanese agriculture. However, the alliance between Japanese farmers and the LDP has come under consistent and increasingly severe attack as part of the post-1991 period of liberalization. This pressure increased considerably under the government of Prime Minister Shinzō Abe, as part of both a more general attempt to heighten efforts at liberalization that focused especially on an attempt to join the Trans-Pacific Partnership (TPP). These negotiations prompted considerable opposition among some of the LDP's core constituents, creating serious obstacles to the goal of economic liberalization.

The TPP negotiations took place in the period 2008–2015, and while an agreement was reached at the end of these negotiations, the TPP was ultimately unsuccessful when—after Donald Trump became president—the United States withdrew from the partnership. Nevertheless, most of the content of the TPP was subsequently accepted in the successor Comprehensive and Progressive Agreement for Trans-Pacific Partnership, which was adopted without the involvement of the United States. Yet the negotiations over the TPP highlight some of the key difficulties faced by Japanese policymakers in their efforts to liberalize the Japanese agricultural sector.

The attempt to use the TPP as a way to force the liberalization of Japanese agriculture was a key goal of Japan's trading partners in their efforts to eliminate trade barriers on Japan's agricultural products, especially with regard to beef, pork, rice, dairy products, and barley—all of which were subject to high tariffs (Honma 2015, 96). As negotiations proceeded, proliberalization governments saw it as a way to introduce market forces into Japan's rural sector. The administration of Prime Minister Yoshihiko Noda—of the Democratic Party of Japan (DPJ), which had much weaker ties to the agricultural sector than the LDP did—worked hard in 2011–2012 to bring the TPP negotiations to a successful conclusion. Liberalization of the agriculture sector also became a key goal of the Abe administration when it came to power at the end of 2012. Abe viewed liberalization of the agriculture sector as a key element of the wider program of structural reform of the Japanese economy that formed the so-called third arrow of Abenomics (see below and chapter 5). In other words, his ambition was to turn agriculture into a future growth industry (Honma 2015, 94). The TPP negotiations therefore formed part of a wider effort by the Abe government to liberalize the rural sector. In Aurelia Mulgan's words, Abe viewed the TPP as "an external catalyst to implement bold deregulatory reforms" (2015a, 25; see also Harding and Lewis 2015).

One of the key ways in which the Abe administration sought to liberalize the agricultural sector was through an attempt to reform the agricultural cooperative organization, the Japan Agricultural Cooperative (JA). This goal was announced in July 2014 as part of the government's ten-year plan to revitalize agriculture. In taking on the JA, the Abe government sought to challenge one of the most powerful interest groups of postwar Japan. The JA acts to coordinate farmers and as a result has an important influence over Japan's agricultural sector. It is able to lobby for protectionist measures and has had a significant effect in terms of ensuring higher prices for agricultural products than would be the case without government support. The JA also has important lobbying power over the Ministry of Agriculture, Forestry, and Fisheries (Yamashita 2015, 75). In addition, the JA has significant political power as it can influence millions of small rice farmers whose votes can swing elections (Lewis 2015).

The attempt to tackle the JA was therefore an important element of Abe's liberalizing efforts. This included a plan to abolish the role of the JA's national center—the Central Union of Agricultural Cooperatives (JA-*Zenchu*)—in supervising and auditing agricultural cooperatives. The goal of this plan was both to reduce the JA-*Zenchu*'s power as a political entity and to enable the local branches of the JA to run their own businesses with a freer hand, and therefore subject them to greater competitive market pressures (Honma 2015, 110; Pollmann 2015). In addition, the reforms proposed to remove the JA's exemption from Japan's antitrust legislation, which had allowed it to form a monopoly as it had been able to own large swathes of farmland. This monopoly power had enabled the JA-*Zenchu* to control over 650 local JAs. In addition to liberalizing the agricultural market, it was hoped that the break-up of the JA-*Zenchu* would reduce the influence of one of the key opponents of the TPP negotiations (Honma 2015, 111; *Asahi Shinbun* 2015e).

This attempt to reduce the influence of the JA could also be understood in the context of ongoing opposition from across the rural sector to the TPP negotiations. Indeed, the JA was one of the key groups coordinating these protests that a range of participants would attend—including especially farmers, but also members of consumer groups, environmental groups, and housewives' associations. Thus, the JA-*Zenchu* supported several large-scale protest rallies against the TPP, together with other primary industry groups and consumer and other organizations (Mulgan 2015b, 148). These rallies were attended by the members of many interest groups, including the National Representatives' Assembly, which sought the "Protection of Food, Livelihoods and Lives," the National Federation of Fisheries Cooperative Associations, the National Federation of Forest Owners' Cooperative Associations, the Livelihood Club Consumers' Cooperative Union, and the Japan Housewives Association (Mulgan 2015b, 148). In 2013 an anti-TPP rally organized by the JA attracted approximately 3,500 people who were protesting the potential damage that the TPP negotiations could do to agricultural products and food services (Mulgan 2015b, 148). One commentator observed, "The participants demanded that the government not abolish tariffs on sensitive products and adherence to the LDP's and Diet's resolutions" (Mulgan 2015b, 148–49).

In addition to these national events and protests, the JA's local branches organized numerous protest events in big cities and rural areas (*Asahi Shinbun* 2015c). The JA Fukuoka held a rally at which sixty-six groups opposed plans to scrap the import tax on the five so-called sacred products. These groups subsequently formed the Anti-TPP Fukuoka Network and submitted a formal letter to the representatives of Fukuoka in the Diet that set out their key demands (*Asahi Shinbun* 2015t). Other local protests made similar demands, sometimes also focusing on the need to maintain food standards. These were also often coordinated by networks of groups opposed to the adoption of the TPP. For instance, twenty groups with connections to the agricultural sector in Ibaraki Prefecture held a street protest in Mito City opposing the TPP (*Asahi Shinbun* 2015s). In Miyagi, nine hundred people in the agricultural sector joined a street protest, shouting "stop the TPP!" (*Asahi Shinbun* 2015p). Similar types of rallies occurred across Japan, including in Miyazaki in 2014; in Akita in May 2015; and in Yamagata, Kochi, Saga, Niigata, Shimane, Tochigi, Fukuoka, and Fukushima in July 2015 (*Yomiuri Shinbun* 2014b; *Asahi Shinbun* 2015t).

The formation of networks of anti-TPP groups was a common method of organizing opposition. For instance, in June 2012 a group called Stop TPP!! Civil Action—which consisted of forty organizations, including labor unions, consumer cooperatives, and citizens' groups—demonstrated in front of a Tokyo railway station. The activities of this group, agricultural cooperatives, and citizens' groups contributed to the decision of the Noda administration to delay its announcement that Japan would be participating in the TPP negotiations (Mulgan 2015b, 151).

As well as staging demonstrations, the JA also sought to mobilize mass public opinion. In early 2015, the JA gathered over ten million signatures for its petition calling for Japan not to sacrifice the interests of its rice farmers during the TPP talks (Lewis 2015). Alliances were also formed with Japan's trade unions, which opposed the liberalizing measures. In May 2015, a large-scale protest was conducted as part of the May Day protest events in Kyoto, with the participation of twelve thousand members of *Zenroren* (*Asahi Shinbun* 2015k).

As a result of this wave of public opposition, many members of LDP's political elite also expressed concerns over the progress of the TPP talks and agricultural reform. In many cases this was largely due to the close connections of LDP politicians with the rural sector, with many dependent on farmers for their political survival. One hundred and thirty LDP representatives in the Diet explicitly declared their opposition to the agricultural reforms and the proposed reforms of the JA (*Asahi Shinbun* 2015b). In consulting with key interest groups, moreover, the LDP found that a majority of those interest groups were concerned about the proposal (Mulgan 2015b, 129).

Prime Minister Abe also faced legal opposition to the TPP negotiations, with Masahiko Yamada—formerly the DPJ's minister of agriculture, forestry, and fisheries—leading a lawsuit claiming that the TPP negotiations violated the "right to know" defined in Article 21 of the Constitution (*Asahi Shinbun* 2014w and 2014y). This referred to the fact that the TPP negotiations were conducted on the basis of a confidentiality agreement among participant countries, and hence the negotiations had been conducted secretly and their details had not been clarified.

One of the main ways in which Abe sought to handle this opposition was through a series of promises to compromise on the negotiation of tariffs. However, this complicated the negotiations of the TPP, prompting Abe to declare in November 2014 that (for the second time) he would not be able to meet his planned deadline of reaching an agreement by the end of the year. In addition, some concessions were made to those who sought to limit the scale of trade liberalization, with a particular focus on some of the agricultural products that were most important to those lobbying on behalf of the agricultural sector (*Asahi Shinbun* 2014ai).

In June 2014 the Abe administration announced a program of support for vulnerable sectors of the economy—including agriculture, forestry, and the fisheries industry. This program, called "Local Abenomics," sought explicitly to address some of the concerns that had arisen in rural areas as a result of the TPP negotiations and agricultural reforms. This was largely done through the announcement of financial support for the rural economy (*Asahi Shinbun* 2014s). In addition, a new policy was announced—the Immediate Economic Measures for Extending Virtuous Cycles to Local Economies of 2014, which represented a further attempt to provide financial support for the rural economy (Cabinet Office 2014b). These measures involved considerable spending on the rural economy.

Around 2.1 trillion yen were spent boosting regional economies, and another 250 billion yen were allocated to supporting travel in an effort to stimulate consumption in rural areas (Cabinet Office 2015b). Abe also made a number of concessions, including moderating the reforms to the JA, in response to opposition from local JA branches as he sought to steer the Agricultural Reform Bill through the Diet in 2015.

Efforts to liberalize Japan's agricultural sector have clearly been hard fought. The agricultural sector has been a key source of electoral support for the LDP throughout the postwar period. Yet its demands for protection and the maintenance of higher prices have increasingly clashed with the LDP's liberalizing agenda. This became most apparent during the course of the TPP negotiations and included contestation over efforts to decentralize the JA. The response of the JA was considerable, and a sustained opposition movement consistently influenced both the form and the timing of the TPP negotiations. This provides an important insight into the difficulties faced by Japanese policymakers in their attempt to adopt a new and more liberal mode of regulation in Japan. We turn now to consider a second key liberalizing measure in Japan: the attempt to achieve pension reforms.

Contested Pension Reforms

Another area of ongoing neoliberalization in Japan has been a series of attempts to reduce the generosity of public pensions. Faced with rising public debt and an aging population, Japan's government has been seeking to reduce pensions on and off for a number of years. This process began in 2004 when the government of Prime Minister Junichiro Koizumi introduced what came to be known as the "macroeconomic slide." This was an initiative that sought to link pension provision to price levels, including under conditions of price deflation (*Yomiuri Shinbun* 2015c). Until this point public pensions had tended to rise with inflation but not fall when deflation occurred. Given that Japan has routinely suffered from price deflation, this obviously had a significant effect on the country's public spending.

Further attempts to reform the pension system surfaced in 2012 in the Noda government. The Diet passed an amendment to the National Pension Act that would adjust what was referred to as the previous "overpayment" of pension benefits. This amendment also sought to address what was considered to have been the creeping involuntary increase in pension provisions as a result of the failure to account for deflation in Japan's public pension system. Facing political opposition to the move, and experiencing considerable internal division in the DPJ, the Noda administration faltered in its attempt to implement the measure, and it lost the general election in December 2012 before the reforms could take effect (*Asahi Shinbun* 2012d; *Yomiuri Shinbun* 2012).

Following the election of the Abe government, the MHLW again announced that pensions would be reduced. This time the planned reduction was by 1.0 percent in October 2013, with an additional reduction of 1.0 percent to take place in April 2014 and a further reduction of 0.5 percent in April 2015 (MHLW 2014; *Asahi Shinbun* 2014b).

These attempts to reform Japan's public pension system were also affected by an ongoing scandal that had begun in 2007, when the earlier Abe government announced that it had lost over fifty million pension records. As of January 2014, over twenty-one million records had still not been recovered (*Asahi Shinbun* 2014a). This ongoing scandal ensured a general lack of faith in and popular disapproval of the pension system, which made reforms even more difficult.

One of the key forms of opposition to the proposed pension reforms was a series of lawsuits against them, often coordinated by a number of pensioners' groups. These lawsuits were often organized and facilitated by the Japan Pensioners' Union (*Zennihon Nenkinsya Kumiai*). The main objections raised in the lawsuits had to do with a lack of consultation and the claim that the measure violated Article 25 of the Constitution, which guarantees the provision of a healthy and cultural life (*Asahi Shinbun* 2015j and 2016b).

As of February 2014, over 110,000 lawsuits and complaints had been filed, and by July 2015 twenty-seven prefectures had been sued (*Asahi Shinbun* 2014b and 2015u). Examples of the lawsuits could be seen across Japan: 117 pensioners in Chiba Prefecture took the government to court over the pension reduction (*Asahi Shinbun* 2015o); similar lawsuits emerged in Osaka; in Fukushima, 40 pensioners ages 50–80 sued the government, demanding a cancellation of the reduction (*Asahi Shinbun* 2015x); 35 members of the Japan Pensioners' Union submitted an appeal to a branch union of Japan Pensioners' Union, the Kanazawakita branch union, claiming that the measure infringed on their human rights; and in Gifu, 175 people filed lawsuits against the government over their pension reductions (*Asahi Shinbun* 2015 ad).

Alongside this large number of legal cases, a number of vocal public demonstrations also took place, which the media referred to as "pensioners' riots." These occurred, for instance, in Nagasaki, Aomori, and Kumamoto in 2013, and protesters pointed to the way that they were hit by both the pension reduction and the planned sales tax increase (*Asahi Shinbun*, 2013n, 2013o, and 2013p).

There was also an increase in nonparticipation in the pension. This represented an alternative form of opting out, due in part to the ongoing discussion of pensions cuts but also in response to the scandal of the missing pension records. Nonparticipation increased from less than 20 percent in the 1990s to 37 percent in 2014, a trend that was widely viewed as a result of low levels of public trust in the administration of the pension program (MHLW 2014).

The pension reform largely went ahead, but due to the country's poor economic performance—as well as the government's failure to manage the pension system appropriately, political divisions, the continuing problems of nonpayment and nonparticipation of pension contribution, the declining pension premium rate, and public opposition—the Abe administration modified the pension reduction from 1.0 percent to 0.7 percent in April 2014 (MHLW 2014; *Asahi Shinbun* 2014b). In response to ongoing criticism of both the pension reduction and the sales tax hike, in November 2015 the Abe government announced the introduction of temporary benefits amounting to 30,000 yen for low-income pensioners (*Yomiuri Shinbun* 2015e). Perhaps most notably, the proposal to reduce pensions in times of price deflation was ultimately withdrawn in 2015, as a result of excessive opposition (*Asahi Shinbun* 2014z and 2015y).

As this discussion of pensions reforms highlights, attempts to reduce Japan's public pensions experienced ongoing opposition from the early 2000s onward. Through a combination of legal challenges and political opposition, the reforms were either reduced in scale or abandoned altogether. This provides another illustration of the difficulties faced by Japan's policymakers in their declared attempt to liberalize Japan's political economy. We next consider the program of labor market neoliberalization that formed a key part of Abenomics.

The Problematic Reform of Japan's Employment Relations

The program of economic reforms adopted by the Abe administration that came to power in 2012 has come to be known as Abenomics. This was an attempt to combine a number of measures, presented as three arrows: expansionary monetary policy, fiscal stimulus, and structural reforms for long-term growth. However, its implementation has thus far been problematic. with no clear signs of improved economic growth (see Shibata 2017 for a more detailed discussion). Rather than achieve its intended goal of increased investment, the first arrow (expansionary monetary policy) has instead contributed mainly to a reinflation of the equity market, alongside a depreciation of the yen (Ueda 2013, 263). Likewise, the second arrow (fiscal stimulus) has failed to stimulate consumption in the Japanese market, and the sales tax rise has dampened consumption (Shibata 2017, 408). Finally, the third arrow (structural reforms, including agricultural, pension, and labor market reforms), has encountered public opposition, which has hindered its implementation.

In an attempt to revamp Abenomics, in 2016 a set of three new arrows was announced (Cabinet Office 2019; *Nikkei* Web 2015). The first of these incorporated all three original arrows, with a specific focus on reforming working practices and innovation (Cabinet Office 2016b, 4). The second new arrow focused on child care policies and aimed to increase the fertility rate and therefore contribute to addressing the country's labor shortage (ibid.). Finally, the third new arrow was a commitment to social security provisions to ensure that people would not need to leave employment to take care of elderly or sick family members.

In introducing the three new arrows in 2016 the Abe administration explicitly acknowledged the increasing criticism of the rise in the proportion of nonregular employment, including in terms of the way this had increased the prevalence of precarious employment, low wages, and poor working conditions (Cabinet Office 2016b, 7). The government acknowledged and highlighted the fact that nonregular workers were on average paid 40 percent less than regular workers (ibid.). In seeking to address this issue, the government promised to ensure that equal work should receive equal pay and proposed an increase in the minimum wage. The revamped Abenomics also proposed a reduction in the country's long working hours, to be afforded through an increase in labor productivity—which itself was to be achieved in part by encouraging female and elderly people to work (ibid., 8).

Many of the proposals introduced under this attempt to revamp Abenomics faced challenges in their implementation. In many cases this was due to contradictory policy goals or clashes with other aspects of the Abe administration's agenda. In other cases, problems arose as a result of popular opposition.

One key problem resulted from the attempt to reform working practices and the explicit goal of treating regular and nonregular workers equally. While this declared policy ambition might have been welcomed by nonregular workers, it directly clashed with the administration's 2015 amendment to the Worker Dispatch Law, which (as we have seen above) acted to exacerbate the experience of nonregular workers and increase the likelihood that some people would be hired as nonregular workers for extended periods of time (*Yomiuri Shinbun* 2015d). Furthermore, while the government did seek to improve nonregular workers' wages and increased the minimum wage, it was widely considered that this would not close the pay gap between regular and nonregular workers, since only long-term regular workers enjoy seniority pay increases (Harding 2017a).

The revamped Abenomics program also sought to address the problem in Japan of excessively long working hours (Cabinet Office 2016b, 8; Harding 2017b). This led to an agreement between *Rengo* and *Keidanren* (Japan's main business association) to set the country's first overtime limit at a hundred hours per month (*Nikkei* Web, 2017). Immediately after agreeing to this limit, however, the citizens' group Our 8 Working Hours Project publicly warned that any work that exceeded just forty-five hours of overtime per month had the potential to cause significant health problems. The failure to create more restrictive limits on overtime work, it was claimed, would also have a detrimental effect on female labor market participation. In addition, for many large firms the hundred-hour limit represented a minimal reduction in the number of overtime hours worked (Our 8 Working Hours Project 2017). Thus, the attempt to address Japan's culture of long working hours was largely considered to be insufficient and ineffective. The issue of working hours rose in prominence in the public debate in Japan following the much-publicized death of Matsuri Takahashi, who had worked at *Dentsu* (one of the largest advertising agencies in Japan) and whose overtime working hours exceeded a hundred hours per month. The reason for her death was diagnosed as overwork (in Japanese, *karoshi*). This contributed to the public debate that had been taking place in Japan, characterized by public anger at the very long working hours expected of a large proportion of the workforce. Indeed, *Dentsu* had experienced the death of another one of its employees as a result of overwork in 1991. In an attempt to increase awareness of the issue and challenge what were widely viewed as insufficient measures being taken by the government, family members of deceased workers, unions, and citizens' groups opposed the bill legally limiting overtime work to a hundred hours per month on the basis that it was insufficient and therefore harmful.

Furthermore, for many people the goal of reduced overtime work clashed with the more important goal of the Abe administration—to increase consumer spending. While one line of reasoning viewed reduced working time as having the potential to increase consumer spending (as more time would be made available for shopping); others were more skeptical and pointed instead to the effect that it would have on income and therefore effective consumer demand. The latter view seemed to be more generally held, since 80 percent of respondents to an opinion poll reported that the reduced overtime would not cause them to increase consumption (*Nikkei* Web, 2017).

The stated goal of the new third arrow of Abenomics—to reduce the need for workers to leave employment to care for elderly or sick relatives—was directly contradicted by the efforts of the Abe administration to reduce welfare spending, which increased the costs incurred by the elderly and their family members when they were admitted to care services. These higher costs, it was widely noted, would pressure some people to leave work to look after their relatives.

Another neoliberalizing reform whose path has not been smooth in Japan is adjusting the payment and reward systems through which workers are remunerated. There have been attempts since the mid-1990s to reform the system of seniority-based pay that has been prevalent in Japan. According to this system, workers' pay is uniformly increased incrementally based on the length of time that the worker has served the company. This was designed to encourage loyalty to the firm and was largely paid regardless of performance. During the 1990s, however, firms began to view the practice as inefficient and insufficiently motivating on an individual basis. As part of the attempt to introduce neoliberal reforms into Japan's socioeconomic model, a number of attempts were made to reform the payment system. They were largely considered to have failed, in part due to a clash with prevailing working cultures in Japan.

The shift toward performance-based payment was partly the result of the 1995 report of *Nikkeiren* (the Japan Federation of Employers' Association), titled "Japanese Management System in the New Era." This sought the neoliberalization of the labor market and employment relations, not only to reduce wages and labor costs but also to improve international competitiveness (Naruse 2014, 5). Rather than advocate a direct reduction in wages, *Nikkeiren* emphasized the need to review the seniority-based wage system (ibid.). The alternative model that *Nikkeiren* proposed was a new performance evaluation mechanism and wage system that appropriately measured individual ability and performance. Following the lead of *Nikkeiren*, many firms introduced a performance-based payment system—although doing so brought several problems, including a failure to improve labor productivity, demotivation, and the fact that the reform was not well suited to Japan's focus on team working. As a result, many firms have either reconsidered the changes that they adopted or otherwise modified the performance-related pay system so that it is more suited to the Japanese context (Myung 2013, 15). To consider the way in which some of these problems occurred, we will focus on the experience of a number of Japan's large companies in their efforts to reform the payment system.

Fujitsu was the first company to introduce the performance-based payment system in Japan, and in doing so it faced numerous problems. It first introduced the system only for managers, but in 1998 the system was extended to all employees (Myung 2013, 20). The system included a process of evaluation that would reward the achievement of both individual and team goals (ibid.). However, rather than rewarding everyone who performed well or met targets, the system gave improved evaluations to only a fixed proportion of employees. As a result, demotivation quickly set in, resulting in an effect opposite to that which was intended. Ultimately the reforms were so unpopular that employees began to leave their jobs, prompting Fujitsu to adjust the system in response to worker discontent (Myung 2013, 21).

Takeda Pharmaceutical, one of the largest pharmaceutical firms in Japan, also encountered unexpected responses from its employees following its gradual introduction of a performance-based payment system in 1997. This included objections to the removal of allowances, such as the housing allowance and family allowance (Business Labor Trend 2005). The company's proposal in 2003 to replace all allowances, basic wages, and bonuses with a single pay rate faced strong opposition from its union, requiring the company to revise the proposal before it could be adopted (ibid., 22; Takahashi 2006, 90–91). The fact that more than 90 percent of the company's employees were evaluated as performing at the "B" level (satisfactory) had a significant impact on their motivation. Staff surveys indicated that opposition to the program doubled between 1997 and 2000 (Business Labor Trend 2005, 23).

The service company *Daimaru* introduced a new performance-based payment system in which employees who achieved the highest evaluation received an additional 30,000 yen on top of their monthly salary, while who received the lowest evaluation would lose 30,000 yen from their monthly salary (Myung 2013, 23). The system was designed to motivate staff members, but instead it created dissatisfaction and a sense of unfairness and inequality, which ensured that it was difficult to implement. A range of other large firms, including Toyota and Shiseido, experienced similar problems in implementing reforms, often needing to adjust their programs to ensure that they could be implemented (Nakashima 2008, 47).

In sum, while the three new arrows of Abenomics set out a reform agenda that promised to address a number of key issues in Japan's labor market, the measures adopted were each contradictory and often appeared to be implemented only halfheartedly. Furthermore, efforts to introduce a more neoliberal performance-based payment system also encountered a number of serious implementation problems in the Japanese context, frequently requiring firms to reverse or amend the reforms after their implementation, or be reluctant to introduce them in the first place. Performance-based payments are still not the dominant mechanism for determining wages in Japan (*Keidanren* 2016). While many firms use performance-based payment as the main mechanism for determining basic salaries, many other factors are taken into consideration, including the worker's seniority, skill levels, and role (ibid., 4). Therefore, the degree of neoliberalization of Japan's employment relations has been limited, in part due to the difficulties associated with implementation in the Japanese context.

The Disarticulation of Coherent Class Interests in Japan

Japan's socioeconomic model has also seen both business and workers unable to agree on and coordinate a coherent position among themselves. Reflecting the increasingly disorganized socioeconomic context, businesses have been unable to agree with each other, and workers have been unable to coordinate a common position. This disarticulation of coherent class interests represents another problem facing efforts to adopt a new mode of regulation in Japan.

The Incoherence of Japanese Capital

One of the key issues on which businesses have failed to adopt a coherent collective position has been how to deal with the rising prevalence of precarious employment. While the consequences of such employment—including demotivated staff, increased rates of poverty, higher levels of industrial and legal contention, and lower levels of consumption—have all been noted in the public debate, firms have divided over how to respond to this.

This division can be witnessed in a recent divergence of opinion between Toyota and *Keidanren*. Toyota explicitly argued that flexible employment and nonregular workers are an essential part of its employment model. According to Katsuhiko Ogino, in charge of human resources for Toyota, the hiring of nonregular workers allows the firm the flexibility it needs to provide employment stability and security for its regular workers. As a result, Toyota continued to employ staff on nonregular contracts even after the popular outcry that followed the 2008 crisis and the visible effect that precarity had on Japan's nonregular workers. In Ogino's view, the government should be averse to any proposed regulation or reregulation of the labor market that might make it more difficult to hire workers on nonregular contracts. Instead, any policies that the government might consider should, in his view, focus on attempts to improve the skills of nonregular workers so that they can improve their situation (and indirectly that of the Japanese economy) by acquiring a better skill set (Business Labor Trend 2010).

In contrast, *Keidanren* has been much more willing to consider ways in which Japan's nonregular workers can be incorporated into the country's employment model, including by transferring staff onto permanent contracts and therefore converting them into regular workers (*Keidanren* 2016, 18–19). This also reflects the views of many businesses across Japan. Nearly 40 percent of firms surveyed reported that they would change the employment contracts of full-time nonregular workers who have worked at the company more than five years to move those workers onto employment contracts with indefinite terms (up from only 28 percent in 2013). This view reflects a growing desire among employers to improve employee retention. Seventy-two percent of firms that expressed a willingness to transition nonregular workers to indefinite-term employment expected that this shift would retain workers for the long term (Business Labor Trend 2016, 1 and 4). It also appears that businesses in Japan are becoming more likely to consider these options as they seek to deal with labor retention issues. Between 2013 and 2015, firms' opposition to the possibility of transferring nonregular workers to regular work contracts fell from 14 percent to 6 percent, while the share of those who reported that they were considering the option rose from 38 percent to 63 percent (Japan Institute for Labor Policy and Training 2017, 1).

In keeping with *Keidanren*'s endorsement of transitioning nonregular workers to permanent employment, a number of firms (especially those facing staff retention problems) have introduced programs allowing nonregular workers to make the transition to permanent employment. Takeuchi Manufacturing, for instance, has introduced a system that allows nonregular workers to become permanent employees if they pass an exam (Business Labor Trend 2018a, 12). Cainz, a retail chain, has moved to improve the status of nonregular workers by creating a new category of "master staff" (Business Labor Trend 2018b, 4–5). Panasonic AgeFree, a provider of elder care, has established an employment system whereby part-time workers are given permanent status (ibid., 8).

The government has sought to introduce a number of measures to improve the employment conditions of nonregular workers. But these measures have often tended to be weak or have little substantive impact. For instance, an amendment was made to the Labor Contract Law in 2013 that created the entitlement for nonregular workers to have their status changed to regular worker status once they had worked with the same employer for more than five years. While this has made it possible for nonregular workers to acquire permanent employment status, those who have their status changed are not guaranteed better wages or allowances. Further, if a nonregular worker has an employment gap during their employment with that employer, the five-year condition for regular employment status will be broken, leading to a situation in which the worker remains ineligible for regular employment status (Sasaki 2017). The revised Labor Contract Law does not, therefore, necessarily lead to a definitive improvement in the employment status of nonregular workers, and provides considerable leeway to the discretion of employers. Indeed, some employers have been reluctant to grant permanent contract status to employees, and trade unionists have been quick to highlight this discrepancy. Both Tatsuya Sekiguchi of Tokyo Union, and Sekine Shuichiro of *Haken* Union,[1] discussed how April 2018—the key month during which the legislation would take effect—saw unions receive a large number of claims from nonregular workers who had been dismissed by their employers before their renewed contract could exceed the five-year threshold for regular employment status.

In sum, corporate policies related to nonregular workers differ by firm. Toyota views their workers as flexible employees, and continues to use them as substitutes and/or a buffer for regular workers. Many firms have not changed fixed-term contracts to indefinite-term contracts, to prevent labor costs from increasing. Several firms seek to maintain nonregular workers as flexible substitutes and necessary casual employees. In contrast, firms more aligned with the position of *Keidanren* appear to be acknowledging that heightened precarity brings with it some unwelcome consequences, and as a result they have begun to view more positively the prospect of moving greater numbers of nonregular workers onto more permanent and stable contracts. This internal division in the business community has created a situation in which no voice clearly speaks for Japanese business, contributing to the more general difficulty in identifying and constructing a more sustainable mode of regulation.

Divisions in Japan's Labor Movement

Like business, labor has been divided over questions of coordination, representation, and organizational form. Unions have disagreed about how best to support workers and organize and mobilize precarious nonregular workers. Whereas some unions have sought to focus on regular workers, others have welcomed a variety of nonregular workers and the unemployed. The lack of a single national center for unions that represents nonregular workers has also made it difficult to collectively oppose suggested labor market policies such as the Worker Dispatch Law. We have seen in earlier chapters that nonregular workers have used multiple forms of opposition, and questions have been raised over the degree of coordination and unity among these groups and workers.[2] Despite the emergence of labor activism, workers are not always unified in objecting to their working conditions or workplace inequality. Unions have had differing opinions of the problems of nonregular workers. Union activists report that due to the nature of these workers' individualized short-term employment contracts, it can be difficult to unite them and organize acts of contestation. Thus, successes have tended to occur on a case-by-case basis. While workers have become more aware of their work-related problems as social problems,[3] labor activists are well aware of the facts that the majority of nonregular workers are not union members and do not rely on unions, and that many therefore remain unaware of how to tackle workplace problems.[4] For instance, Junichiro Konishi, chair of the *Mukogawa* Union[5] in Hyogo Prefecture and a union activist for over twenty years, explains:

> The problems of non-regular workers have increasingly begun to be recognized as social problems—and this has generated a momentum among some activists and political elites who have started organizing actions that include rallies, demonstrations, and meetings to change the Worker Dispatch Law. However, this momentum has not been sustained. The number of union members remains too small, making it difficult to organize effective actions. It is very difficult to sustain the mobilization

of the labor movement. The number of community unions has increased and attracted public attention, . . . and the potential for the development of the labor movement has also increased. However, no practical achievements have been made yet. . . . People often hesitate to conduct actions against their employers. Managers stratify workers and increase divisions between them, enhancing competition between workers. Those workers who have been stratified and individualized face difficulties in fighting collectively and acting together. This is therefore the challenge we face in terms of mobilizing workers.[6]

While many activists have observed changing attitudes among workers and the public, they are also very aware of the difficulty of organizing workers, maintaining momentum, and strengthening the labor movement. Tatsuya Sekiguchi, the president of *Zenkoku* Union, also points out that the weakening human relations and interactions in the workplace is one of the challenges of organizing workers and increasing solidarity.[7] Thus, Japan's labor movement is not characterized by the mass collective organization of the working class in Japan, but rather by a new movement made up of a relatively small number of workers and unions.

The challenges of organizing is especially acute when it comes to nonregular workers. They are often reluctant to join unions, and when they do, they often face financial difficulties that make it difficult for them to remain as members. Most unions encourage individual workers to form a new branch in their workplace and therefore oversee their own industrial disputes. However, it is hard for workers on short-term contracts to act in this way, especially due to high rates of turnover. While union membership tends to increase when a large number of dismissals are announced, nevertheless the high rate of turnover for nonregular workers remains an ongoing obstacle to union recruitment and organization. As Konishi puts it, "workers are increasingly individualized and stratified by employers, who increasingly rely on non-regular workers as a flexible source of labor."[8]

In addition, many nonregular workers often lack confidence that their working conditions or working lives can be improved as a result of union membership. According to Makoto Kawazoe:

> People used to be able to imagine the practical gains of being involved in a union movement and becoming a union member in the 1960s and 1970s, since their wages were rising and their standard of living had improved significantly in accordance with economic development. Since the 1980s and 1990s, however, the rate of economic growth has slowed down; globalization in the world economy, neoliberalization in the labor market, and related attempts to reduce wage costs have transformed capital-labor relations. It became difficult for people to envision their

future improving and difficult to imagine social and labor movements actually improving life and work. From the unions' perspective, it is not easy to advocate an alternative society that can replace the current model of Japanese capitalism. We may be able to advocate "less aggressive and less exploitative capitalism" among some countries. . . . There has been no consensus between politicians, business and state elites, or within unions.[9]

As Kawazoe notes, unions that recently became active agents in the labor movement have also found it difficult to advocate an alternative to the current model of Japanese capitalism. Without demonstrating practical benefits or advantages for workers (including nonregular workers), the union movement in Japan will—it is feared—remain stagnant, find it difficult to attract members, and therefore also find it difficult to collectively organize workers.

Other problems also face people seeking to organize nonregular workers. Much workplace organizing is left in the hands of the workers themselves, which makes organizing especially difficult for those with temporary or nonpermanent contracts, since they tend to be more vulnerable to reprisals, have higher levels of stress and poor mental health, and be poorer. In addition, the mainstream union movement in Japan remains centered on core regular workers, to the detriment of precarious nonregular workers.[10] While this has meant that smaller, more independent, community unions have often filled the space left by the unenthusiastic support of mainstream unions, it has also meant that relatively poorly resourced unions are faced with more complicated and difficult workplace issues and organizing challenges. This clearly brings with it a number of difficulties.[11]

Another challenge in the current union movement is the lack of a national center for community unions that could improve their ability to negotiate with the government and business associations.[12] This challenge is especially pressing due to the wide varieties of community unions and their different views of unionism, as well as the historical antagonisms between *Rengo* and *Zenroren*.[13] Those unions that do represent precarious and nonregular workers tend to be left out of national negotiations on the ground that they are not part of the established group of "insider" unions with close connections with government, which both excludes representatives of nonregular workers from the discussion and reinforces the division between regular and nonregular workers. *Zenkoku* Union (National Union) represents eleven community unions, most of which have had considerable experience in setting up unions for nonregular workers in workplaces or representing a large number of nonregular workers.[14] However, this community unions' association does not incorporate all of the community unions in Japan and functions only as an association that represents its member community unions. It has not been able to integrate the majority of community unions, in part reflecting the ongoing challenges to unifying nonregular workers and their organizations.

Divisions therefore exist both in the business community and between workers. This further complicates efforts to adopt a new mode of regulation in Japan. Without clear coordination or representation of coherent positions, it becomes difficult to incorporate the views of each sector in policymaking or the contemporary socioeconomic model. This, in part, explains the absence of an alternative, or successful, mode of regulation in contemporary Japan.

The socioeconomic model that has emerged as a result of efforts at neoliberalization by Japan's state managers and firms does not constitute a coherent mode of regulation. Many of the proposals for neoliberalization that have been made—such as agricultural, pension, and labor market reforms—have been thwarted or watered down as a result of the opposition that they have prompted. In other areas, such as the attempt to introduce performance-based pay, the results have been counterproductive. We have seen how the different sectors of Japan's socioeconomic model are internally divided, with businesses disagreeing about the best route to take and workers finding it difficult to organize consistently in a way that unites regular and nonregular workers. Discontent and division prevail, in stark contrast to the claims of regulation theory about the need for mechanisms of cooperation and coordination to (at least partially) manage the social tensions and instabilities inherent in capitalist production. The outcome has been a failure to produce a new mode of regulation, and thus a failure to secure a return to sustainable economic growth in Japan.

Conclusion

The Japanese model of capitalism has often been characterized as a coordinated market economy. As this book has sought to show, those elements of Japan's mode of regulation that served to coordinate, organize, and in part mitigate its potential for socioeconomic tension and instability have undergone a process of transformation and erosion since the bursting of the national economic bubble in 1991. This has led to an attempt to create a new model—one based on neoliberalization, heightened exploitation, and the erosion of the employment security that Japan's workers used to be able to expect. In turn, this has led to the emergence of a growing group of precarious nonregular workers in Japan. The Japanese model of capitalism has shifted from a consensus-based model toward a disorganized model over the past three decades, during which time coordination and consensus building in employment, firm-bank, interfirm, and state-labor relations have weakened and the stability and security that those relations and their coordination created have been undermined. The disorganized model of Japanese capitalism has also resulted in sustained policy contestation, ensuring that the Japanese government has failed to implement its neoliberal agenda in full. In part as a result of this growing social tension, conflict, and the absence of a coherent alternative mode of regulation, Japan continues to experience sluggish growth and social discontent. During the 1980s, Japan enjoyed a certain level of social stability and cohesion, upheld by mutually supporting socioeconomic institutions. The social compromise that was achieved was also able to generate a degree of economic growth. The 1990s, in contrast, were characterized by severe economic crises, including a recession, that prompted the gradual undoing of

Japan's socioeconomic model. State and corporate elites attempted to replace a consensus-based mode of regulation with a more neoliberal model to create a new regime of accumulation.

This continued into the 2000s. In particular, in the early 2000s the government of Prime Minister Junichiro Koizumi accelerated the process of neoliberalization in the labor market. As a result, divisions and inequality in the working class became more visible at that time. The onset of the global financial crisis of 2007–2008 exacerbated these trends and the plight of Japan's nonregular workers became more visible as homelessness and unemployment rapidly increased. The election of December 2012 returned Prime Minister Shinzō Abe to power, and further efforts were made by the government to implement structural reforms that would liberalize a number of key sectors in Japan's economy, including agriculture, pensions, trade, and the labor market.

We have therefore seen the erosion of the coordination and compromise between employers and employees in Japan. The consensus-based mode of regulation in Japan has changed to a neoliberal "disorganized" one, characterized by instability and contradiction. As Wolfgang Streeck observed with regard to similar changes in Germany, capitalist actors are becoming "committed not to any specific national model of capitalism, but only to their own survival and success," and they "take an individualistic and particularistic rather than a collectivistic and universalistic view in selecting their objectives and deploying their resources to attain them" (2009, 260). This tendency resonates with the changes in Japan's model of capitalism. Japan's political economy—which used to consist of leading large corporations and their *keiretsu* groups with subcontracting firms and banks, along with the main bank system—has become a more individualized and less organized economic system.

In response to the changes noted above, there has been an increase in the proportion and number of confrontational acts undertaken by workers, unions, and nonprofit organizations, particularly after the global financial crisis. Furthermore, acts of workers' contestation have become more antagonistic and less institutionalized. Members of Japan's new group of nonregular workers are therefore more likely to mobilize in opposition to the conditions that they face, do so in a more confrontational style, and in the process contribute to the formation of new organizations and institutions that have emerged to challenge the established "insider"-focused approach of Japan's enterprise unions. New unions such as the *Syutoken Seinen* Union, *Freeter Zenpan Rouso*, *Haken* Union, and Union *Bochi Bochi*, established in the early to mid-2000s, have adopted a more flexible approach to solving nonregular workers' problems. They provide opportunities for precarious workers and the unemployed to meet, talk, share experiences, and exchange opinions. This also represents part of the process of redefining class relations. Thus, Japan's model of capitalism has experienced a rising level of class struggle and class antagonism. These new agents (and the antagonistic acts they have undertaken) symbolize the new labor movement in Japan. They have also vocalized opposition to the increasing impoverishment of the Japanese working class. These new organizations have shown a reluctance, unwillingness, or inability to use the strike as a weapon of the new nonregular working class. Instead, they have preferred to rely on lobbying, publicity, using any favorable legislation available, and campaigning to raise awareness of the plight of nonregular workers and the way their growing share of the labor force represents an erosion of Japan's traditional social compromise. As a result, both firms and state managers have been forced to take notice, sometimes reversing and often modifying their attempts to advance neoliberalization.

As we have seen, corporate policies have been resisted, and acts of resistance have affected employment relations. Temp agencies became a target of acts of resistance, which on many occasions successfully challenged the practice of employing dispatch workers on zero-hour contracts. In some cases, temp agencies were forced to go out of business. In other cases, dispatch workers successfully claimed the rights to which they were entitled, as well as improving their working conditions, wages, or working status. These gains would not have been possible without the acts of resistance that were conducted by Japan's growing group of precarious workers and the new organizations that have been created to represent and support them.

In addition to the refusal of neoliberal conditions in the workplace, government policy and efforts to advance neoliberal reforms have also been contested. Austerity measures—in the form of pension reform, sales tax increases, and agricultural liberalization—have each encountered significant public opposition, legal challenges, and criticism from workers and the public. This rise in social tension has also contributed to an ongoing malaise directed at the political elite, which has exacerbated the lack of political leadership and policy direction. Indeed, we have witnessed a broader failure to adopt and implement coherent policy alternatives, with the process of liberalization instead being inchoate, indecisive, and achieving only unimpressive levels of economic growth. Concerns remain regarding the level of effective demand in Japan's economy, especially as a result of the rise in the share of the population earning low incomes. As a result, we have seen calls from the prime minister for firms to increase wages so as to stimulate consumer spending. However, these calls have gone largely unheeded, in part reflecting the failure of both Democratic Party of Japan and the Liberal Democratic Party of Japan governments to put together the sort of stable social coalition that would be necessary for a more coherent mode of regulation to be constructed.

It is important, of course, not to overstate the capacity, power, and influence of Japan's new group of precarious nonregular workers. There remain the problems of discoordination and low levels of involvement by (and the exclusion of) labor in the policymaking process. Unions and nonprofit organizations routinely face obstacles when they seek to intervene and organize in the Japanese labor market. The activists interviewed for this study consistently expressed concerns over the problems facing nonregular workers, including impoverishment and unemployment. The precarious status of the working class in Japan (especially that of nonregular workers) remains largely unchanged. High turnover rates of nonregular workers present a significant challenge to union recruiting and organizing. Divisions remain between the more established *Rengo* unions that represent regular workers and the newer independent unions and organizations that have emerged largely to represent nonregular workers. Policymakers are more willing to consult with the *Rengo* unions and include them in the policymaking process, while they sideline or exclude nonregular workers and their organizations.

The conflict-focused regulation theory approach adopted in this book has therefore underpinned an account of Japan's changing model of capitalism. Regulation theory tends to acknowledge that "social and political struggles matter" (Boyer 2018, 301). The present study, however, is exceptional in that it focuses in much greater detail than many similar studies have done on the frequency, types, and forms of worker-conducted dissent that have been observed as part of Japan's changing mode of regulation. This focus has enabled the present study to examine more directly the shifting pressures for change and the responses that state managers and politicians have needed to adopt (and adapt to) in their efforts to stabilize and reproduce a coherent mode of regulation. It is only through such considerations that we can understand the problems that have been faced by those actors, especially the political elite. Whereas contributions to regulation theory sometimes focus on the different governing options under consideration and those options that proponents of the theory might advocate, the present approach—with its much tighter focus on acts of dissent—is able to contribute to our understanding of the options that are viable (both politically and in terms of policy implementation) and those that might face considerable opposition. The present study, therefore, highlights the way in which regulation theory might be further developed, through a closer consideration of the different forms of contestation and dissent that occur in any particular mode of regulation.

The process of neoliberalization that followed the bursting of Japan's economic bubble in 1991 has resulted in the creation of a new group of precarious nonregular workers. Although other contributors to the literature have noted this trend, this study differs in that it views these precarious workers as active agents contesting Japan's socioeconomic transformation. This allows us to explain the heightened social tension witnessed in Japan, the ongoing failure to produce a coherent or viable mode of regulation, and the continuing instability of Japan's political economy.

This is not to say that if Japan's neoliberal reforms had gone uncontested, they would have resulted in more stable economic growth. Instead, neoliberalization is invariably associated with growing economic inequality, heightened social grievances, and rising patterns of contestation. As regulation theory makes clear, efforts to stabilize national capitalist economies require the search for institutional compromises that are able to regulate and mediate the social conflict that forms a part of capitalism. Yet each institutional compromise, or mode of regulation, brings with it different types of problems and tendencies toward crisis. As Robert Boyer puts it, "each society displays the crises specific to its economic structure" (2018, 17). The most neoliberalized societies have also tended to be associated with the most unstable forms of financialization (Jafee 2018). Likewise, neoliberalism has come increasingly to be associated with authoritarian political developments (Bruff 2014). The problems faced by Japan's contested, and as a result somewhat partial, moves toward neoliberalization have therefore brought with them particular problems. These may be most evident in the ongoing economic stagnation. That does not mean, however, that a more thorough form of neoliberalization would have achieved stable economic growth. Rather, it would have more likely resulted in heightened contestation and destabilization.

We can identify five ongoing problems and challenges that people seeking to construct a more successful mode of regulation in Japan face. First, the economic programs and policies adopted by the Abe administration—Abenomics—appear unable to constitute a series of reforms that both are politically acceptable and result in clear improvements to Japan's record of economic success. There have been no clear signs of improved economic performance throughout the implementation of Abenomics (Hattori 2014, 2017; Ninomiya 2017). This is of considerable concern to those hoping that the liberalization of Japan's economy will increase productivity or improve efficiency. These reforms, it was hoped, would ensure that Japan's economy became more competitive, all of which was intended to prompt a return to growth. The fact that there have been no such obvious improvements thus presents a considerable challenge for Japan's policymakers. Compounding these problems is what appears to be the stubborn refusal of Japan's electorate to support the changes that make up Abenomics. Indeed, while Abe continues to be sufficiently popular to ensure his remaining prime minister, Abenomics has continued to face a lack of popular support. According to a Kyodo News Survey, 84 percent of Japanese have not felt any recovery in the economy (*Mainichi Shinbun* 2019). The support for Abe, therefore, is chiefly due to the lack of an effective political opponent. Abenomics, in contrast, routinely attracts only meager support, and more often opposition, in opinion polls. Policymakers in Japan thus need to identify a progrowth economic program that can also attract the support of the electorate.

Second, and related to the first challenge, Japan faces the ongoing problem of stagnant wage growth and the associated problem of low effective demand. The Abe administration has repeatedly sought to encourage firms to increase wages, in part in an attempt to increase consumption and demand. This, it is believed, would result in an important boost to domestic growth. The inability of the government to successfully encourage firms to increase wages—especially for low-paid and nonregular workers—therefore represents a considerable challenge. To address this problem, we might expect government policy to consider a less voluntary route through which to increase wages, most obviously in the form of further increases to the minimum wage. Opposition to this option remains substantial, however, and there are no obvious signs that this policy will be adopted in the foreseeable future. In addition, it is not clear that increased wages would solve Japan's economic malaise. An increase in wages would have a corresponding detrimental impact on the profit share of capital in Japan, which has the potential to undermine investment and therefore produce its own negative consequences for economic growth. The intractability of these further problems is clear.

Third, alongside the problem of stagnant wage growth, Japan faces an ongoing labor shortage, in part as a result of the combination of low fertility rates, the aging population, and a historic commitment to restrictive immigration policies. With regard to the contribution of illiberal immigration policies to this problem, the issue of labor shortages has in part resulted from the government's policies. In recent years there have been attempts to open up Japan's immigration regime, largely in recognition of the problems created by the labor shortage, yet this threatens to create political problems for Japan's government—which has historically benefited from adopting a restrictive approach to immigration. Finding a balance between the political gains associated with anti-immigrant rhetoric and policy and the economic need to deal with the question of a labor shortage therefore represents another key problem facing Japan's policymakers. Moreover, the consequences of how this problem is resolved have potential further effects on Japan's labor market and the role of nonregular workers in it.

Fourth, Japan continues to maintain an extraordinarily high level of public debt. At 234.3 percent of gross domestic product in 2017 (OECD Data 2019), Japan's public debt is the highest of all countries in the Organisation for Economic Co-operation and Development. Japan has so far been able to maintain this high level of public debt without experiencing excessive financial costs. But the extent to which this can remain the case, for how long, and whether doing so will eventually result in a crisis continue to be questions that vex Japan's political establishment. If it becomes necessary to reduce Japan's public debt to more "normal" levels, further challenges will clearly arise—not the least of which will be how to reduce the public debt in a way that is politically acceptable and also avoids producing recessionary pressures.

Finally, the question of Japan's relationship with China continues to prompt ongoing pressures for change. The trade relationship between the two countries continues to make it necessary for Japan to adjust to China's rapidly ascendant position in the world economy. China is the second largest market for Japanese exports. At the same time, imports from China have a significant impact on Japanese domestic producers. The pressure to compete is unlikely to abate soon. Indeed, the question of Japan's position in the international economy, especially as China moves increasingly into high-tech production, will continue to pose ongoing and considerable questions.

Perhaps the key issues facing Japan, however, are whether and how Japan's new labor movement will develop. It is only in studying this recomposition of Japan's working class that we will be able to understand and explain the trajectory of capitalism as it exists in Japan. It remains to be seen, therefore, whether a new mode of regulation emerges, and what role labor—either regular or nonregular, organized or disorganized—will plays in any new socioeconomic regime. As this book has sought to show, what is certain is that any attempt to undermine, sideline, or eradicate labor will ultimately be futile, as workers in Japan (as they do elsewhere) invariably continue to disrupt and resist—in different ways in different times and contexts—efforts to consolidate a model of global neoliberal capitalism that cannot be stable.

Appendix

Quantitative Method (Event Data Analysis) of the Data Set

The event data analysis used in this study created a new data set on Japan's labor movement. This data set was compiled from reports of labor-related resistance or disputes in *Asahi Shinbun*, one of Japan's major national newspapers. *Asahi Shinbun* is an independent newspaper of public record with a nationwide scope of coverage and readership. Using major newspapers as a source to construct a data set of protests or strikes has become a fairly developed practice in the social sciences (Silver 2003; Franzosi 2004; Koopmans et al. 2005; Koopman and Statham 2012). Paul Burstein claims that "a small but growing group of social scientists has concluded that valid time-series data on many of the more visible aspects of politics could be collected by drawing on an obvious but hitherto untapped data source—major newspapers" (1985, quoted in Silver 2003, 190). This study thus attempted to find articles in *Asahi Shinbun* that contained information about workers during five periods of time, 1986–1988 (to highlight trends before the bursting of the economic bubble), 1995–1998 (to provide an insight into patterns of protest during the initial wave of reforms introduced after the bursting of the bubble), 2000–2003 and 2005–2007 (to update trends as they occurred before the global financial crisis and during the reforming government of Prime Minister Junichiro Koizumi), 2008–2009 (to provide insights into responses to the global crisis), and 2013–2014 and 2016–2017 (to highlight events in the administration of Prime Minister Shinzō Abe). Based on the definitions of Koopmans et al., the articles selected for this study had to include "an instance of claim making as a unit of strategic action in the public sphere that consists of *the purposive and public articulation of political demands, calls to action, proposals, criticism, or physical attacks, which actually or potentially affect the interests of integrity of the claimants and/or other collective actors*" (Koopmans et al. 2005, 24).

However, this study focuses on the actions initiated by workers and workers' organizations. This study will thus limit the selection of claims to those made by individuals, workers, unions, and other labor-related organizations.

The time periods were selected to avoid the possibility of mis-sampling that might arise from the use of single year cases, a problem that is particularly present given the high possibility of "year-to-year fluctuations in the number of each event type" (Oliver and Maney 2000, 474). As explained in chapter 3, these events are a sample taken from key periods in the transformation of Japan's political economy. Each event was coded according to a scheme based on categories of subject-action-object (Franzosi 2009) and time and place (see also Franzosi 2004; Koopman et al. 2005). This original data set was intended to analyze class relations and the labor movement in Japan, and how workers have been resisting or responding to socioeconomic changes over the past four decades.

Objections are sometimes raised regarding the use of newspaper data to report on trends in protest events. Indeed, newspaper coverage is clearly not an undistorted mirror of reality. Only a small proportion of all forms of dissent are reported in the media. However, in accordance with the approach set out by Koopmans et al. (2005, 25), in the present study we are interested in the publicly visible part of protest because this is what has the most impact on the perceptions of both the public and policy makers.

Coding Method and Sampling Rules of the Data Set

The coding method used in this research was formed by applying the methods of Roberto Franzosi (2004), Ruud Koopmans and coauthors (2005), and Beverly Silver (2003) and was based on a pilot run of a hundred articles.

1. Search articles whose title or text includes the word *Rodosha* (workers).
2. Select only articles about events that include the instances of claim making.
3. Select only articles that report on a single worker or group of workers, unions, civil groups, or nonprofit organizations (NPOs) taking some action. Workers include fired and unemployed workers.

4. One article can include several entries to the coding data set, if it includes several events.
5. Include regional events (*Asahi Shinbun*'s data set includes both regional and national news).
6. Include events that happened within one month or less before the published report. Exclude reports on events that happened further back in time (Koopmans et al., 2005, 260).
7. Include an event more than once if it is covered more than once.
8. Code the following elements in an Excel spreadsheet:
   (1) Date of the article.
   (2) Subjects by type—general (for instance, a union, the government, or an NPO), organizational category (national-level unions, community unions, prefectural or central governments, and so on), and individual name (such as the name of the ministry or prefectures)—and number of subjects.
   (3) Action types.
   (4) Objects by type—general (for instance, a company or the government), organizational category (an industry or the government of a village, town, or city), and individual name (such as the name of the company or government).
   (5) Place (prefecture [*Todofuken*]).
   (6) Story grammar (story content, for instance, litigation; the general impression of the story of the event; and the tone of the event, for instance, angry or long-lasting.).
   (7) Title of the article.
   (8) Other (if anything else needs to be recorded).
9. Make each entry in Japanese and then translate it into English.

Interviewees

Unions

Ebana, Arata, chair, *Hiseiki Zenkoku Sentar* (Contingent Workers Action Center), July 13, 2011.

Inoo, Toshinori, chair, *Nara Roren* (Nara labor union), July 19, 2011.

Kamo, Momoyo, president, *Zenkoku* Union (Japan Community Union Federation), July 11, 2011.

Kawazoe, Makoto, chair, *Syutoken Seinen* Union (Metropolitan Young People's Union), July 13, 2011.

Konishi, Junichiro, chair, *Mukogawa* Union (Mukogawa labor union) July 22, 2011.

Minaim, Mamoru, Hashiguchi, Masaharu, and Kimura, Rie, Union *Bochi Bochi*, July 18, 2011.

Ohashi, Naoto, chair, *Kansai Part Kumiai* (part-time workers' union in Kansai region), July 20, 2011.

Sekiguchi, Tatsuya, chair, *Zenkoku* Union, July 15, 2011 and January 11, 2019.

Sekine, Shuichiro, chair, *Haken* Union (Dispatch Workers' Union), July 14, 2011 and January 24, 2019.

Shimizu, Naoko, chair, *Freeter Zenpan Roudou Kumiai* (Part-timer, Arbeiter, Freeter, and Foreign Worker Union), July 14, 2011.

Sugano, Ari, *Tokyo Tohbu Roudou Kumiai* (East Tokyo Labor Union), July 11, 2011.

NPOs

Ibaragi, Satoshi, POSSE, July 15, 2011.

Inaba, Tsuyoshi, chair, *Moyai*, July 16, 2011.

Kawazoe, Makoto, *Han Hinkon* Network, July 13, 2011.

Sasao, Tatsuro, *Attaka* Support, July 22, 2011.

Notes

INTRODUCTION

1. The term "nonregular workers" (*hiseiki rodosya*) has risen in prominence recently in both policy circles and public debate within Japan. The term refers to people without long-term employment security, such as part-time workers (*freeter*), temporary workers (*alubaito*), contract workers (*keiyaku shain, syokutaku,* or *ukeoi*), and dispatch workers (*haken* workers who register at temporary work agencies).

2. For most people in the Global South, the idealized notion of regular employment had never been established, either before or during the neoliberal period.

1. FROM COORDINATED TO DISORGANIZED CAPITALISM IN JAPAN

1. In 1997, the Japanese government had to nationalize the Long-Term Credit Bank to prevent a meltdown in the banking system. This was followed by the bankruptcy of Hokkaido Takushoku, a large city bank, in 1997 (Rosenbluth and Thies 2010, 127–28).

2. Day laborers tend to move from declining rural areas to big cities to find work. They often cannot afford housing and end up spending nights in an internet café or becoming homeless. These workers face a significant level of employment and life insecurity every day.

3. Shuichiro Sekine, "*Haken* Union (Dispatch Workers' Union)." Haken Union, interview by the author, July 14, 2011.

4. Tatsuya Sekiguchi, interview by the author, July 15, 2011; Masaharu Hashiguchi, Rie Kimura, and Mamoru Minami, interview by the author, July 18, 2011. Mamoru Minami, interview by the author, July 18, 2011; Sekine, interview; Toshinori Inoo, interview by the author, July 19, 2011; Satoshi Ibaragi, interview by the author, July 15, 2011.

5. Ibaragi, interview.

2. ORGANIZED LABOR AND SOCIAL CONFLICT IN JAPAN

1. Ari Sugano, interview by the author, July 11 2011.

2. However, thirteen community unions have joined *Rengo* (Fukui 2005, 26).

3. By 2008 nonregular workers had made up 40 percent of *UI Zensen*'s membership (Weathers 2008, 191).

4. This number increased from 307 in 2006 to 1,112 in late March (ibid.).

3. FROM PRECARITY TO CONTESTATION

1. In referring to NPOs, I employ the Japanese usage of the term, meaning a citizens' group that is officially recognized as a nonprofit organization. These are often campaigning or community-facing organizations.

2. Dispatch workers in this book refer to temp agency workers who register with these agencies and are then assigned to work at different workplaces and worksites. These workers are also paid by the temp agencies.

3. Makoto Kawazoe, interview by the author, July 13, 2011; Naoko Shimizu, interview by the author, July 14, 2011.

4. Momoyo Kamo, interview by the author, July 11, 2011, author's translation.

5. Shimizu, interview, author's translation.

6. *Bochi bochi* means little by little, or one step at a time. Since this union does not have any official English name, I have listed this union's name in Japanese.

7. Interview with Mamoru Minami, July 18, 2011, author's translation.

8. Kawazoe, interview.

9. Interview with Tsuyoshi Inaba, July 16, 2011.

10. Kawazoe, interview, author's translation.

11. Ibid.

12. Ibid.

13. Ibid.

14. The term "freeters" is used in Japan to refer to young nonregular workers, sometimes in a pejorative way.

15. Satoshi Ibaragi, interview by the author, July 15, 2011, author's translation.

16. Ibid.

17. Kawazoe, interview.

18. What happened to the other two workers is unknown.

4. PRECARIOUS LABOR POWER AND JAPAN'S NEOLIBERALIZING FIRMS

1. Shuichiro Sekine, interview by the author, July 14, 2011.

2. Ibid., author's translation.

3. Ibid.

4. As Sekine notes, "many day laborers commented on the low wages, harsh working conditions, and long working hours that they experienced. They often worked for twelve hours a day and were sometimes forced to work for a week continuously, without being able to return home" (ibid., author's translation).

5. Ibid.

6. Ibid., author's translation.

7. Ibid.

8. Ibid.

9. Ibid., author's translation.

10. Ari Sugano, interview by the author, July 11, 2011.

11. Ibid.

12. Ibid., author's translation.

13. Ibid.

14. Tsuyoshi Inaba, interview by the author, July 16, 2011, author's translation.

15. Makoto Kawazoe, interview by the author, July 13, 2011.

16. Naoko Shimizu, interview by the author, July 14, 2011, author's translation.

17. Ibid., author's translation.

18. Shimizu, interview, author's translation.

19. Kawazoe, interview.

20. Ibid.

21. Ibid., author's translation.

22. Sekine, interview.

5. PRECARIOUS LABOR AND THE CONTESTATION OF POLICYMAKING IN JAPAN

1. Makoto Kawazoe, interview by the author, July 13, 2011.

2. Ibid.

3. This section draws on Tsuyoshi Inaba, interview by the author, July 16, 2011. At that time, Inaba was chair of *Moyai*.

4. Ibid.
5. Ibid.
6. Ibid.
7. Kawazoe, interview.
8. Ibid.
9. Ibid.
10. Inaba, interview.
11. Relative poverty is "defined as living in a household whose income, when adjusted for family size and composition, is less than 50% of the median income for the country in which they live" (UNICEF Innocenti Research Centre 2012, 3).
12. Ibid.
13. TV Asahi 2017.

6. JAPAN'S ABSENT MODE OF REGULATION

1. Tatsuya Sekiguchi, interview by the author, January 11, 2019. Shuichiro Sekine, interview by the author, January 24, 2019.
2. Makoto Kawazoe, interview by the author, July 13, 2011.
3. Ari Sugano, interview by the author, July 11, 2011; Tatsuya Sekiguchi, interview by the author, July 15, 2011; Shuichiro Sekine, interview by the author, July 14, 2011; Naoto Ohashi, interview by the author, July 20, 2011; Junichiro Konishi, interview by the author, July 22, 2011; Mamoru Minami, interview by the author, July 18, 2011; Satoshi Ibaragi, interview by author, July 15, 2011.
4. Konishi, interview.
5. This is one of the most active unions supporting precarious workers, including foreign workers.
6. Konishi, interview, author's translation.
7. Sekiguchi, interview, author's translation.
8. Ibid., author's translation.
9. Kawazoe, interview, author's translation.
10. Arata Ebana, interview by the author, July 13, 2011; Minami, interview.
11. Konishi, interview.
12. For instance, the chair of *Hiseiki Zenkoku Sentar* (Contingent Workers Action Center) under *Zenroren* noted the lack of coordination among regional branches of *Zenroren* and observed that not all unions have a community-union mechanism (Ebana, interview).
13. Ebana, interview; Kawazoe, interview.
14. Momoyo Kamo, interview by the author, July 11, 2011.

References

PRIMARY SOURCES

Asahi Shinbun. 1998. "Roudou Kijyun Hou no Kaisei Meguri, 2000 nin ga 'Hanntai Syuu-kai' [2,000 people hold 'Opposition Rally' over the amendment of the Labor Standard Law]." September 25.

———. 2008a. "Hinkon/Kakusa, Kaisyou Uttae: 'Dokuritsu Kei Mei Dei' Kakudai [Eliminate poverty and inequality: Expanding 'independent May Day']." May 4.

———. 2008b. "Hiyatoi Haken Kinshi, Hanniha Kourousou, Houkaisei no Ikou, Kakutou no Syutyou ni Hedatari [Abolition of day labor, reflecting the direction of MHLW, division between parties]." June 14.

———. 2008c. Kikan jyuugyouin Kei 700nin sakugen he [700 contracted workers' dismissal: Fuso and Nissan Diesel]." November 26.

———. 2008d. "Haken jyuugyouin atsumarazu: Sanka motome bira kubari Nissan Diizeru yunion ga soudankai [Lacking temp workers: Leafleting, a meeting by the Nissan Diesel Union]." December 13.

———. 2008e. "Kyanon kouzyou kaikosyara ga kenni shidou motomeru [Dismissed Cannon factory workers ask for prefectural government's order]." December 16.

———. 2008f. "Hakensyain futari, Mitsubishi Fusou ni dantai kousyou wo youkyu [Two dispatch workers' lawsuits against Mitsubishi Fuso]." December 18.

———. 2008g. "Haken shain hitorino kaikotekkai de goui: Haken yunion Nissan Diizeru kougyou shibu to Nikken Sougyou [Reaching an agreement on the withdrawal of one temp worker: Haken Union, Nissan Diesel industrial branch and Nikken Sougyou]." December 18.

———. 2008h. "Haken kumiai no sannin, syuugyou wo kotowarareru: Nissan Diizeru kougyou shibu [Three dispatch workers dismissed: Nissan Diesel industrial branch]." December 20.

———. 2008i. "Haken kiruna rouso no kumiaiin raga kourousyou de kougi [Do not dismiss temp workers: Protest at the Ministry of Health, Labor, and Welfare]." December 25.

———. 2009a. "Mitsubishi Fuso trakku basu ga kaiko tsuukoku tekkai [Hakensyain futari, Mitsubishi Fusou ni dantai kousyou wo youkyu [Withdrawal of notice of dismissals by Mitsubishi Fuso truck and bus]." January 28.

———. 2009b. "Aitsugu haken giri sosyou: 'jittai ha seisyain' fukyou ni bareba totsuzen kaiko [Lawsuits against continuing dismissals of temp workers: 'Temp workers work like regular workers' dismissed suddenly during recession]." July 9.

———. 2009c. "Haken kisei kyouka he houkaiseiwo: Hibiyade syuukai, shingikai deno roushi tairitsu ni kikikan ['Amendment toward reregulation of temp work': A rally in Hibiya]." October 30.

———. 2009d. "Kyabakura rouso wo kessei: Tokyou no zyosei ra yonin [The establishment of the *Cabacula* Union: Four women in Tokyo]." December 12.

———. 2009e. "Seizougyou haken to touroku gata, gensoku kinshi ni kkoufubi kara sannen inaino sekou kourousyou shishin [Prohibition of dispatching temp workers to the manufacturing sector and registered temp workers: Implementation within three years, MHLW instruction]." December 16.

———. 2010a. "Shyouhi zouzei '4nenkan nai': Syusyou aratamete meigen [No sales tax increase 'in the next four years': Prime minister declared]." February 16.

———. 2010b. "Kan zaimusou ni kaisan senryaku [Minister of Finance Kan, a strategy of the dissolution of the House of Representatives]." February 17.

———. 2010c. "Chihou syouhizei no kakudai wo meiki: Kodomoteate zengaku genkin dannen [Local sales tax specified: Child benefit cash abolished]." March 7.

———. 2010d. "Tourokugata to seizougyou haken wo Kkinshi: Hakenhou kaiseian wo kakugi kettei [Banning registered dispatch work and dispatching to manufacturing sectors]." March 10.

———. 2010e. "Hakenhou kaisei kakugikettei Hatoyama naikaku [Amendment of the Worker Dispatch Law, decision, Hatoyama cabinet]." March 19.

———. 2010f. "Kyabakura gyuugyouin kabukicyou de demo: Roudoukaizen motome 26 nichi yoru [*Cabacula* workers' demonstration in kabukichyo: Requesting the improvement of working status, evening 26]." March 24.

———. 2010g. "Kakusa kaisyou nado: 800nin tsudoi uttae [Dissolve inequality: 800 people rallied]." May 2.

———. 2010h. "Kenrouren mei dei syuukai: Kakusa kaisyou nado uttaeru [May Day events by *Kenrouren* unions: Dissolve inequality]." May 2.

———. 2010i. "Chihou syouhizei no kakudai wo meiki, kodomo teate zengaku genkin wo dannen, minsyu kouyaku genann [Local sales tax expansion, abandoned child benefit, DPJ manifesto plan]." May 7.

———. 2010j. "Syouhizei 15~20% ni: Kankeiren ga ikensyo [Sales tax rates should be around 15–20%: Opinion from the Kansai Economic Association]." May 13.

———. 2010k. "Meisou no saki: Odoroki tomadoi [After losing his bearing: Surprise and confusion]." June 3.

———. 2010l. "Keiki kaifuku 'Daisan no michi': Kan shin syusyou no jiron [Economic recovery: 'The third way': Kan's strategy]." June 5.

———. 2010m. "Shyamin syouhi zouzeini Hantai [Social Democratic Party opposed to the sales tax hike]." June 16.

———. 2010n. "Kan syusyou hyoukasezu 63% [Prime Minister Kan—63% disapproved]." July 10.

———. 2011. "Haken hou kaisei de moushiire: Haken yunion toukai nado [Appeal on the amendment to the Worker Dispatch Law: *Haken* Union Tokai]." November 23.

———. 2012a. "Hakenhou kaiseiann ni kougi [Protest against the amendment bill of the Worker Dispatch Law]." March 28.

———. 2012b. "Koyou antei: Meidei de uttae [Employment stability: Appeal at May Day events]." May 1.

———. 2012c. "Oshiete: Nenkin 1 [Tell me: Pension:1]." May 10.

———. 2012d. "Shyouhi zei mittsu no ronten, hitsuyousei/keiki heno eikyou, teisyotokusya taisaku, hatsu shingi, yotou wreru syochyou [Three points in sales tax hike, necessity and its impacts upon economy, measures for low-income people, divided opinions between the ruling and opposition parties]." May 12.

———. 2012e. "Syakai hosyouno jyuujitsu ya zaisei saiken heno kadaiha [What are the challenges to the stable social welfare system and fiscal balance?]." June 27.

———. 2012f. "Syouhi zei zouzei hantai: Shimin dantai ga uttae [Opposition to sales tax hike: Citizens' groups' demonstration]." June 27.

———. 2012g. "Zouzei hantai uttae: 50dai pareedo [Opposition to sales tax hike: 50 cars rally]." July 19.

———. 2012h. "Hiyatoi haken kinshi: muikani denwa soudan [Phone consultation, 6 October: Day labor abolishment]." October 4.

———. 2012i. "Hiyatoi haken roudou: Asu denwa soudan [Phone consultation for day laborers tomorrow]." October 5.

———. 2012j. "Sekiyu gyoukai zouzei hantai apiiru [Oil industry opposition to the sales tax hike]." November 15.

———. 2012k. "Hinkon wo kangaeru shimin syuukai [Citizens' meeting to think about poverty]." December 1.

———. 2012l. "Seikatsu hogohi wo motometemo [Even though you apply for social welfare benefits]." December 6.

———. 2012m. "Seikatuhogo kezurudakedeha 'Yowaimono ijime yamete' [Reduction of welfare benefits is insufficient: 'Stop bullying the vulnerable']." December 12.

———. 2012n. "Houmu lesu shien: 23nichi ni mochi tsuki [Support for the homeless: Sticky rice cake making]." December 20.

———. 2012o. "Toshi koshi akaruku atatakaku [Toward a bright and warm new year]." December 23.

———. 2012p. "Seikatsu hogo ya shyakkin nayami 26nichi ni denwa muryou soudan [Free phone consultation, 26 December, for people with social welfare benefits and debt]." December 24.

———. 2012q. "Seisaku Aberyuu kasoku [Accelerating Abe-style policies]." December 27.

———. 2013a. "Keigen zeiritsu: Jikou no mizo senmei [The reduced tax rates: Deep divide between LDP and Koumei]." January 8.

———. 2013b. "Rojou seikatu fusegu syudan, moura Hanhinkon Netto Hokkaidou, sassi wo muryou haifu/Hokkaidou [Measures to prevent homelessness, network, Antipoverty Network Hokkaido, free leaflet/Hokkaido]." January 10.

———. 2013c. "Keigen zeiritsu 'ketsuron isogazu' [The reduced tax rate 'not too rushed to decide']." January 18.

———. 2013d. "Shyouhizei 8% hikiageji, keigen zeiritsu miokuri [The reduced tax rates postponed at the time of 8% sales tax rate]." January 20.

———. 2013e. "Seikatsu hogohi 850oku en gengaku [Social welfare benefits, 85 billion yen reduction]." January 25.

———. 2013f. "Hanhinkon he renkei uttae [Solidarity for antipoverty]." February 10.

———. 2013g. "Seikatsu hogo sakugen houshin ni kaiken [Press conference against the reduction of social welfare benefits]." February 14.

———. 2013h. "Seikatsu hogo iji syukyuusya kyuuzyou uttae [Appeal for the sustaining of social welfare benefits]." February 19.

———. 2013i. "Seikatsu hogohi sakugen hantai no kinkyuu seimei [An urgent declaration against the reduction of social welfare benefits]." March 1.

———. 2013j. "Hinkon, gyakutai, kodomo sasaeru [Poverty, abuse . . . support for children']." March 22.

———. 2013k. "Haken roudou kakudai he tenkan [A shift to an expansion of dispatch work]." August 21.

———. 2013l. "Hakenhou kaisei dou miru [How to interpret the amendment to the Worker Dispatch Law]." August 30.

———. 2013m. "Moto hakenroudousya chinjyutsu, Matsuda ha arasou shisei, chi kakunin meguru kousoshin [The former temp workers' statements: Mazda intends to fight: The court case for the status of temp workers]." September 10.

———. 2013n. "Nenkin hikisage hantai demo: Kumamoto/Chyuouku [Rally against the pension reduction: Kumamoto]." October 23.

———. 2013o. "'Nennkinsya Ikki', Nagasaki de 70nin sanka, shyuukai ya demokoushin ['Pensioners riot': 70 pensioners demonstrate in Nagasaki]." October 19.

——. 2013p. "Hikisageni kougi, 'Nenkinsya Ikki' shuukai, Aomori demomo [Opposition against the pension reduction: 'Pensioners' riot' rally, Aomori, demonstration]." October 18.

——. 2014a. "Nenkin kiroku, kaimei kugiri, 2112manken, 'kanzen na kaifuku fukanou,' Yuushikisya Kaigi [Pension record, ending the investigation, 21.12 million unrecovered records, 'it is impossible to recover all missing recors,' expert committee]." January 18.

——. 2014b. "Syouhizei maeni "kakekomigai" suru? ['Rush shopping' before sales tax hike?]." February 1.

——. 2014c. "Houmu resu heritsutsumo [Although the number of homeless is declining]." February 9.

——. 2014d. "Sinn nendo staarto, ippo ippo: Syouhizei zouzei kennai demo [A new year, one step at a time: The sales tax hike in Ishikawa]." April 2.

——. 2014e. "Hakengyou 57 sya ni jigyou teishi meirei: Hyougo roudoukyoku/ Hyougoken [An order of suspension of 57 temp agencies' operations: Hyogo labor office]." April 12.

——. 2014f. "Mei Dei 'Kakusa No,' Kendnai jyukkaijyou de rengou Fukuoka ['No to inequality,' Rengo Fukuoka, 10 rallies]." April 27.

——. 2014g. "Rengo kei mei dei, nana kasyo ni 2.9 mannin [*Rengo*-led May Day, 29,000 in 7 places]" April 27.

——. 2014h. "Mei dei ichi manning a koushin [May Day, 10,000 marching]." April 27.

——. 2014i. "Chyuou mei dei ni issennin, kakusa no zesei ya antei koyou uttae [1,000 rallied in the central May Day, Appeal for equality and stable employment]." April 27.

——. 2014j. "Meidei ni 3000nin [3,000 rallied on May Day]." April 27.

——. 2014k. "Kenrorenkei meidei: zouzei hantai nado uttae/shigaken [Kenroren-group May Day events: Opposing the sales tax hike]." May 2.

——. 2014l. "Antei motomeru koe keshyuu: Abenomikusu ni gimon [Collective voice for safety: Questioning Abenomics]." May 2.

——. 2014m. "Seiken he hihan issyoku: Naganoshi de meidei syuukai [A unified criticism against the administration: May Day rallies in Nagano City]." May 2.

——. 2014n. "Meidei atsuku, Tokushima shinai de syuukai ya demokoushin [Hot May Day, demonstrations and street protests in Tokushima City]." May 2.

——. 2014o. "Anshin motomeru koe keshyuu: Abenomikusu ni gimon [Collective voice for safety: Questioning Abenomics]." May 2.

——. 2014p. "Seikatu hogohi gengaku fufuku wo moushitate [Appeal for an examination for the reduction of social welfare benefits: 534 households in Tokyo]." May 20.

——. 2014q. "Seikatu hogohi sage fufuku no shinsa seikyuu: 145 ninbun chiji he teisyutu [Appeal for an examination for the reduction of social welfare benefits: 145 claims to the prefectural governor]." May 24.

——. 2014r. "Mei dei ni 7,000 nin, rengou kei kennai yon kaijyou de/niigataken [May Day, 2000, *Rengo* group, 4 places]." May 27.

——. 2014s. "Chihou nerau Abenomikusu [Abenomics targeting rural economy]." July 10.

——. 2014t. "Saitei chingin: hatarakite nao fuman [Minimum wages: Discontented workers']." July 30.

——. 2014u. "Saitei chingin, jyu yo en hikiage 748 en ni [Minimum wage increase by 14–748 yen]." August 13.

——. 2014v. "Shiren no Abenomikusu [Challenge Abenomics faces]." August 14.

——. 2014w. "Kousyou sashitome motomete teiso [Filing a suit: Appeal for a cancellation of TPP negotiations]." September 25.

——. 2014x. "Shyouhi zouzeini hantai: Yamaguchi de gaitou syomei [Opposing the sales tax hike: Street demonstration and petition in Yamaguchi]." September 25.

——. 2014y. "Shinbunya kiso syokuhin eno keigen zeiritsu motomete gaitou shyomei [Claim for a reduced tax rate for food and basic goods Street demonstration and petition]." September 25.

——. 2014z. "Datsu defure vs. kakusa kakudai kokkai ronsen, Abenomikusu [Getting out of deflation vs. expanding inequality: Debates in the Diet, Abenomics]." October 4.

——. 2014aa. "Hinkon no rennsa idomu jichitai [Local governments challenge the poverty chain']." November 3.

——. 2014ab. "Hakenhou shingi, yatouga kyohi, daizin touben to kourousyou kuichigai, hanpatsu [Discussions of the Worker Dispatch Law, opposition parties refused to accept, ministry and the Ministry of Heath Labor and Welfare differ, opposition]." November 8.

——. 2014ac. "Seikatsu Hogohi Sakugen 'Iken,' Jyukyuusya 51 Nin ga Syuudan Sosyou [The reduction of social welfare benefits, 'illegal,' 51 beneficiaries' collective lawsuit]." November 8.

——. 2014ad. "Kaisei haken hou, seiritsu konnan ni, syuunai, shingi okonawarezu, konn kokkai [Amendment to the Worker Dispatch Law, difficult to be passed, no deliberation in the Diet]." November 12.

——. 2014ae. "Seikatsu hogohi no gengaku iken: shikoku hatsu, 42nin, ken to Matsuyamashi wo teiso [The reduction of social welfare benefits: illegal: 42 collective lawsuits against the Ehime Prefectural Government and Matsuyama City Council]." November 12.

——. 2014af. "-1.6%, GDP shyokku: 'Souteigai' kojin shyouhi jyuutaku teimei [-1/6% GDP shock: 'Unexpectedly' staggering consumption and housing investment]." November 18.

——. 2014ag. "Seikatsu hogohi no toki kasan gengaku [The reduction of winter allowance from social welfare benefits]." November 19.

——. 2014ah. "Seikatsu hogohi no torikeshi motome teiso [Appeal for cancellation of the reduction of social welfare benefits]." November 29.

——. 2014ai. "Semeno nougyou kaikaku: genbano noukato zure [Aggressive agricultural reforms: Gap with rural farmers]." November 30.

——. 2014aj. "Chingin hikiage seikatu suijyunn koujyou wo mokuhyou ni [Wage increase With an aim to improve the standard of life]." December 17.

——. 2014ak. "Chinage he futatabi kansei syuntou seiroushi saidaigen doryoku: Syouhi kaifukuhe seiken ga shyudou [Wage increase, public collective wage bargaining, state, labor, and business maximum efforts: Toward the recovery of consumption with the leadership from the administration]." December 17.

——. 2014al. "Seikatsu hogohi gen 'iken': jyukyuusya 51nin ga syuudan teiso [The reduction of social welfare benefits is 'illegal': 51 collective lawsuits]." December 19.

——. 2014am. "Seikatsu hogo gengaku ihou: Funai no jyukyuusya 40nin [Lawsuits against the reduction of social welfare benefits: 40 beneficiaries in Kyoto]." December 26.

——. 2014an. "Seikatsu hogo gengaku ihou: Funai no jyukyuusya 40nin [Lawsuits against the reduction of social welfare benefits: 40 beneficiaries in Kyoto]." December 27.

——. 2015a. "Hoikuryou ichibu hikisage [A partial reduction of nursery costs]." January 12.

——. 2015b. "Noukyou Kaikaku Koubou Honkakuka [Agricultural reform: offensive and defensive battle get real]." January 21.

——. 2015c. "Ken nouseiren ga 400nin shyuukai [Ken Nouseiren 400 rally]." January 28.

——. 2015d. "Chinage 'Tsuki 10,500yen': Rengo Aomori, syuntou de mousiire [Wage increase 'monthly 10,500-yen' increase: *Rengo Aomori* appeal at the spring wage offensive]." January 29.

——. 2015e. "Zenchu no kansaken chyuushi he [*Zenchu's* inspection right cancelled]." February 4.

——. 2015f. "Suupar uriagedaka gensyou tsuduku [Supermarket sales decline continues]." February 24.

——. 2015g. "Kodomono hinkon taisakuni hongoshi [More realistic measures to solve child poverty']." March 4.

——. 2015h. "Hinkon rennsa tachikire [Cut the poverty chain]." March 6.

——. 2015i. "20nendo made zouzei sezu [No further tax hike until 2020']." March 14.

——. 2015j. "Kouteki nennkin gengaku, "iken" jyukyuusya 16nin, kuni wo teiso/Tokushima [Public pension reduction, 'illegal,' 16 pensioners suing the government]." April 11.

——. 2015k. "Zenrouren kei mei dei ichiman nisennin [Zenrouren Group May Day Event: 12,000 Rally']." May 2.

——. 2015l. "Syakai hosyouhi gengaku ni kigyouga hantai [Complaint against the reduction of social welfare benefits]." May 16.

——. 2015m. "Seikatu hogohi gengaku fufuku no shinnsa seikyuu [Appeal for an examination for the reduction of social welfare benefits]." May 20.

——. 2015n. "Seikatu hogohi sagenaide [Please do not reduce social welfare benefits']." May 20.

——. 2015o. "Seikatsu hogo hikisage 300nin fufuku [300 people show their discontent with the reduction of social welfare benefits']." May 27.

——. 2015p. "TPP hantaino kenmin syukai [Rally against TPP]." June 16.

——. 2015q. "Haken hou kaisei an, syuuinn kaketu, minsyu nado saiketsu kesseki [The suggested amendment of the Worker Dispatch Law, passed in the Diet, DPJ abstained]." June 20.

——. 2015r. "Saitei hingin hikiage seiken ga iyoku [The cabinet is interested in the increase of minimum wages]." July 18.

——. 2015s. "TPP kokkai ketsugi jyunsyu motome demo [Appeal for the implementation of the parliamentary decision on TPP']." July 21.

——. 2015t. "TPP Hantai ketsugi: JA Fukuoka chyuuoukai nado [Opposing TPP rally: JA Fukuoka]." July 22.

——. 2015u. "'Nenkin gengaku ha iken' to teiso, kennai no 53nin, torikeshi motomeru [Pension reduction is illegal, 53 pensioners' lawsuits, calling for cancellation]." July 28.

——. 2015v. "Haken roudousya ga fooramu kessei [A forum established by temp workers]." August 2.

——. 2015w. "Chingin nobi nibuku, syouhi teimei [Stagnating wages, stagnating consumption]." August 15.

——. 2015x. "Nenkin gengaku 'Iken,' 40nin teiso: kennai genkoku jisedai no anshin no tame ['Illegal' pension reduction: Toward safety for the next generation]." August 19.

——. 2015y. "Nenkin Yokusei Kyouka, Sakiokuri, Akiikou no Teian Mexasu [Pension reduction plan postponed: To be proposed after this fall]." September 4.

——. 2015z. "Annpo shingi tsukusarezu [Insufficient discussions on Japan-US security treaty]." September 15.

——. 2015aa. "Kodomono hinkon taisaku suishin keikaku: 8tsuno suichi mokuhyou [A plan for the prevention of child poverty: 8 numerical goals]." October 19.

——. 2015ab. "Kaisei haken hou syunai nimo seiritsu [Arrest of the president of the second layer subcontractor, the amended Worker Dispatch Law will pass in a week]." September 9.

——. 2015ac. "Seikatu hogohi gengaku ni hantai 4000nin [4,000 people rallied against the reduction of social welfare benefits]." October 19.

——. 2015ad. "Nennkin gengaku 'iken,' kennnai 175nin ga teiso, zenkoku de 37banmen/Gifu [Pension reduction is 'illegal,' 175 pensioners' lawsuit, 37th in the country]." October 22.

——. 2015ae. "Seikatu hogohi gengaku ni hantai 4000nin [4,000 people rallied against the reduction of social welfare benefits]." October 29.

——. 2015af. "Seikatsu hogo gengaku: kakuchi de iken sosyou [Reduction of social welfare benefits: Lawsuits across the country]." November 3.

——. 2015ag. "Niji sitauke syatyou ra taiho 'nijyuu haken' ukeire yougi Fukushimano jyosen sagyou meguru jiken [Arrest of the president of the second layer subcontractor, 'double dispatch work' over decontamination work]." November 12.

——. 2015ah. "Hinkon kateino jyuku gayoi shien [Extra school support for impoverished households]." November 17.

——. 2015ai. "'Touki kasan' gengaku torikeshite [Abolish the reduction of 'winter allowance']." November 21.

——. 2015aj. "Honsya scron chyousa: Shitsumon to kaitou [Head office's opinion survey: Questions and answers']." December 22.

——. 2015ak. "Nojyukusya shien: 21kaimeno fuyu [Support for homeless: 21st winter]." December 30.

——. 2016a. "Fuudo banku de konkyuusya sukue [Support the impoverished with a food bank]." January 22.

——. 2016b. "Nenkin gengaku iken: 40nin teiso [Reduction of pension is violation of constitution: 40 people filed suits]." August 19.

Business Labor Trend. 2005. "Syokumukyuu no tetteiniyoru Seikasyugi [The performance-based payment system by thoroughly completing the job-based evaluation mechanism]." 2005.3. http://www.jil.go.jp/kokunai/blt/bn/2005-3/p22-25.pdf.

——. 2010. "Roushi kankeino saikouritsu: shudanseiwo kijikuni kangaeru[Restructuring of capital-labor relations: Thinking based on collectiveness]." http://www.jil.go.jp/kokunai/blt/backnumber/2010/01/002-015.pdf.

——. 2016. "Tayouka suru shyain to hatarakiyasui syokuba [Diversifying workers and improved workplace]." http://www.jil.go.jp/kokunai/blt/backnumber/2016/01/003-012.pdf.

——. 2018a. "Kaisei roudou keiyaku hou to kigyou no taiou [Amendment to labor contract law and corporations' response]." May. https://www.jil.go.jp/kokunai/blt/backnumber/2018/05/index.html.

——. 2018b. "Tayou na koyou ni taiou shita syoguu kaizen [Improvement of treatment for diversifying employment]." March. https://www.jil.go.jp/kokunai/blt/backnumber/2018/03/002-010.pdf.

Cabacula Union. 2015. "Katsudou houkokui [Report on activity]." December 13. http://ameblo.jp/cabaunion/entry-12102148863.html.

Cabinet Office. 2009. Nenji keizai zaisei houkoku [*Annual Report on Economy and Finance 2009*]. http://www5.cao.go.jp/j-j/wp/wp-je09/09p00000.html.

——. 2014a. "Abe naikaku souri daijin kisya kaikei [Prime minister press conference]." http://www.kantei.go.jp/jp/96_abe/statement/2014/1118kaiken.html.

——. 2014b. "Immediate Economic Measures for Extending Virtuous Cycles to Local Economies." http://www5.cao.go.jp/keizai1/keizaitaisaku/2014/141227_economic_measures.pdf.

——. 2015a. "Chihouheno koujyunnkan kakudaini muketa kinkyuu keizai taisaku [Immediate economic measures for extending virtuous cycles to local economies]." http://www5.cao.go.jp/keizai-shimon/kaigi/minutes/2015/1104/sankou_01.pdf.

——. 2015b. "Urgent Policies to Realize a Society in Which All Citizens Are Dynamically Engaged—Toward a Positive Cycle of Growth and Distribution." http://www.kantei.go.jp/jp/topics/2015/ichiokusoukatsuyaku/kinkyujisshitaisaku_en.pdf.

——. 2016a. "Keizai zaisei unei to kaikaku no kihon keikaku 2016 [2016 basic policies of economic and financial management and reform]." http://www5.cao.go.jp/keizai-shimon/kaigi/cabinet/2016/2016_basicpolicies_ja.pdf.

——. 2016b. "Nippon ichioku soukatsuyaku pulan. [Plan for promoting Dynamic Engagement of All Citizens]" http://www.kantei.go.jp/jp/singi/ichiokusoukatsuyaku/pdf/plan3.pdf.

——. 2019. Abenaikaku no keizaizaisei seisaku [*Abe Cabinet Economic Policies*]. https://www5.cao.go.jp/keizai1/abenomics/abenomics.html.

CGS Online. 2007. "ACW2 daihyou Itou Midori shi heno intabyuu [Interview with Ito Midori, the chair of ACW2]." *CGS Newsletter*, Gyendaa Kenkyuu Sentaa (Center for Gender Studies). September 15. http://web.icu.ac.jp/cgs/2007/09/nl008_010.html.

Fackler, Martin. 2008. "Standing Up for Workers' Rights in Japan," *New York Times*, June 11.

Keidanren. 2016. Douitsuroudou douitsu chinginno jitsugen ni mukete [Towards the Achievement of Same Work for Same Pay, Keidanren, Policy and Action]. http://www.keidanren.or.jp/policy/2016/053_honbun.pdf.

Haken Network. 2016. "Hakenroudousyano tsuukinkoutsuuhi shikyuu kyanpeen[Campaign for equal payment of transportation fees]." December 8. http://haken-net.or.jp/?p=448.

Haken Union Blog. 2017. "Kourousyou tsuutatsu: Haken roudousya heno tsuukin teate no sikyuu ni tsuite [Instruction from the MHLW: Provision of Transportation Fees with Temp Workers]." http://hakenunion.blog105.fc2.com/blog-entry-365.html.

Harding, Robin. 2015a. "Japan Falls Back into Recession." *Financial Times*, November 1. https://www.ft.com/content/9be8bb08-8bf9-11e5-8be4-3506bf20cc2b.

——. 2015b. "Political Storm Rages in Japan over Sales Tax Relief Plan." *Financial Times*, September 17.

——. 2017a. "Abenomics Hit by Japan's Meagre Wage Rises." *Financial Times*, March 15.

——. 2017b. "Shinzo Abe Fears Wrath of the Salaryman on Labour Reform." *Financial Times*, October 12. https://www.ft.com/content/5e3114be-902a-11e6-8df8-d3778b55a923.

Harding, Robin, and Lewis, Leo. 2015. "The Third Arrow of Abenomics: A Scorecard." *Financial Times*, September 9. https://www.ft.com/content/ee40a73c-521d-11e5-8642-453585f2cfcd?mhq5j=e1.

Hataraku Joseino Akushon Sentaa [Action Center for Working Women]. 2016. "Kessan/yosan, 2016 katsudou keikaku/yakuin, 2015 Katsudou houkoku [Final account/budget, 2016 plan/board members, 2015 report]." March 6. http://wwt.acw2.org/?p=3558.

Hikita, Sawaaki. 2015. "Kyabakura Ihan Oukou Kyouyo Mibarai Uttae, Dantai Kousyou, Kachitotta Sanjyu Go Manen [*Cabacula*, rampant illegal infringements: Lawsuits against unpaid wages, gained 350,000 yen]." *Asahi Digital*, September 25. https://www.asahi.com/articles/DA3S11981326.html.

Inaba, Tsuyoshi. 2013. *Seikatsu hogo kara kangaeru* [Think from public assistance]. Tokyo: Iwanami Shinsyo.

Japan Institute for Labor Policy and Training. 2017. "Kaisei roudou keiyakuho heno taiou jyoukyo ni kansuru intavyu kekka [Result on the survey on the revised labor contract act]." https://www.jil.go.jp/institute/siryo/2017/documents/195.pdf.

Jichiroren. 2014. "[Opposition to the sales tax hike to 8%]." *Nihon Jichitai Roudou Kumiai Sourengou*, April 1. https://www.jichiroren.jp/dd/.

Jiji Tsushin. 2012. "Ittai kaikaku/syouhizei hanntai syuukai no hatoyamashi to Ozawashi [At the opposition rally against the comprehensive reform and sales tax hike: Hatoyama and Ozawa]." June 14. https://www.jijiphoto.jp/dpscripts/DpFeature.dll?DpFeatureResult&L_URL_ID=qbFfbeFijWrjkSqs.

Kihachi Logu. 2010. "'Kyabakura yunion' kabuki chyou demo. Tokyo/Shinjyuku ['*Cabacula* Union' demonstration in Kabuki Chyo. Tokyo/Shinjyuku, 03/26/2010]." http://kihachin.net/klog/archives/2010/03/cabauni_demo.html.

Lewis, Leo. 2015. "Japan: End of the Rice Age." *Financial Times*, September 21.

Mainichi Shinbun. 2019. "Kyodo Tsushin Seron Chyosa: Keikino Kaifuku wo Jikkan Sezu 84% [Kyodo News Opinion Poll: Not feeling the recovery of the economy 84%]." 11 March. https://mainichi.jp/articles/20190311/ddm/002/010/088000c.

Ministry of Economy, Trade, and Industry. 2011. Sekaito wagakunino tsusyokosyo no hensen [Transformation of trade between the world and Japan]. In *Tsusho Hakusyo* [*White Paper on International Economy and Trade 2011*]. Chapter 2. 86–104. https://www.meti.go.jp/report/tsuhaku2011/2011honbun_p/2011_02-1.pdf.

——. 2018. *Summary of the White Paper on International Economy and Trade 2018*. https://www.meti.go.jp/english/press/2018/pdf/0710_001a.pdf

Ministry of Finance. 2017. Zaiseikinyuu toukei geppo dai 798 [*2017 Financial Statements Statistics of Corporations by Industry, no.798*]. https://www.mof.go.jp/pri/publication/zaikin_geppo/hyou/g798/798.htm.

——. 2019. "Yushyutsu aitekoku jyoui 10 kakoku no Suii (nen beesu) [Transformation in the top 10 exporting countries (annual)]." Trade Statistics Japan. http://www.customs.go.jp/toukei/suii/html/data/y4.pdf.

Ministry of Health, Labor, and Welfare [MHLW]. 2001. "Haken roudousyasuu 139 mannin ni zouka [The number of dispatch workers has reached 1.38 million]." December 28. http://www.mhlw.go.jp/houdou/0112/h1228-3.html.

——. 2008. Heisei 20 nen ban roudoukeizai hakusyo [*White Paper on Labor and Economy 2008*]. http://www.mhlw.go.jp/wp/hakusyo/roudou/08/.

——. 2009. Heisei 21 nen ban roudoukeizai hakusyo [*White Paper on Labor and Economy 2009*]. http://www.mhlw.go.jp/wp/hakusyo/roudou/09/.

——. 2010. Heisei 22 nen ban roudoukeizai hakusyo [*White Paper on Labor and Economy 2010*]. http://www.mhlw.go.jp/wp/hakusyo/kousei/10/.

——. 2014. "2014 Pension Reduction by 0.7%." January 31. https://www.mhlw.go.jp/stf/houdou/0000035972.html.

——. 2015a. "Kosodate Setai Rinji Tokurei Kyuufukin [Temporary allowances for households with children]." http://www.mhlw.go.jp/stf/seisakunitsuite/bunya/kodomo/kodomo_kosodate/rinjitokurei/index.html.

——. 2015b. "Roudou Haken Hou ga Haken Roudousya no Hogo to Koyou no Antei wo Hakaru tame Kaisei Saremashita [The amendment to the Worker Dispatch Law has been made to protect workers and stable employment relations]." http://www

.mhlw.go.jp/seisakunitsuite/bunya/koyou_roudou/koyou/haken-shoukai/kaisei
/02.html.

——. 2016. "Kanso na kyuufu sochi (rinji fukusi kyuufukin) [Basic allowance measure (temporary welfare allowances)." https://www.mhlw.go.jp/stf/seisakunitsuite /bunya/0000196510.html.

——. n.d. Roudou Kumiai Kisochousa: Jikeiretsu deita (Labor Union Basic Survey: historical data) https://www.mhlw.go.jp/toukei/list/13-23c.html.

Ministry of Internal Affairs and Communications. 2019. Roudouryoku Chyousa [*Labour Force Survey*]. Statistics Bureau of Japan. "Hyou 9(1): Chyouki jikeiretsu deita [Figure 9(1): Long-term time-series data]." http://www.stat.go.jp/data/roudou/longtime /03roudou.html.

National Tax Agency. 2016. "2016 Minkan kyuuyo jittai toukei chousa [Salary survey in the private sector]." https://www.nta.go.jp/publication/statistics/kokuzeicho/minkan /gaiyou/2016.htm#a-01.

Nihon Keizai Shinbun. 2015. "Keigen Zeiritsu Hitsuyou 74%, Honsya Yoron Chyousa, Naikaku Shijiritsu 41% [Those saying the reduced tax rate is necessary, 74% Nikkei survey, cabinet approval rate 41%]." October 25. http://www.nikkei.com /article/DGXLASFS25H1E_V21C15A0MM8000/.

Nikkei Web. 2015. "Abenomikusu 'shin sanbon no ya' wo yomi toku [Interpret Abenomics three new arrows]." September 25. http://www.nikkei.com/article/DGXZZO9 2034300U5A920C1000000/.

——. 2016. "Syouhizei Zouzei Saienki no Kaiseihou ga Seiritsu [The revised tax law on sales tax postponement passed]." November 18. http://www.nikkei.com/article /DGXLASFS17H65_Y6A111C1EAF000/.

——. 2017. "Hatarakikata kaikaku: Jittai chyousa de hanmei sita syouhigentai no wake [Work reform: The reason of staggering consumption, revealed from the survey]." April 4. http://www.nikkei.com/article/DGXMZO14659350Z20C17A3000000/?df=3.

NPO Houjin Rodo Soudan Center. 2007a. "Dai sankai dantai kousyou houkoku [The report on the third negotiation]." April 18. http://blog.goo.ne.jp/19681226_001/e/b b57e5bd6b1e7590dd72fcc4b558877f.

——. 2007b. "Hankyu traberu sapooto Tokyo shiten no tenjoyuin ga nengan no roudou kumiai wo kessei shimashita! [Hankyu Travel Support Tokyo branch workers established a union (HTS Branch)!]." February 21. http://blog.goo.ne.jp/19681226 _001/e/349a3f78970968a70f4053b0df99eeb5.

——. 2007c. "Hankyu traberu tenjoyuin tachiagaru! Roudou kumiai kessei! [Hankyu tour conductors rise up: The establishment of a union]." February 21. http://blog .goo.ne.jp/19681226_001/e/349a3f78970968a70f4053b0df99eeb5.

——. 2007d. "Kousei syo heno mousiire to kishya kaiken HTS ahibu [An appeal to the Ministry of Health, Labor and Welfare and press conference: HTS Branch]." March 12. http://blog.goo.ne.jp/19681226_001/e/ece0d81367a8e5fe79421be6b066a 92ae.

——. 2007e. "Koyou hoken kanyuu ga jitsugen ahimashita: Hankyu Travel Sapooto sai 11kai dantai koushyou houkoku [Realizing employment insurance scheme for tour conductors: Hankyu Travel Support, 11th negotiation]." November 30. http://blog.goo.ne.jp/19681226_001/e/a07ac93bbc27b96931e4e730700e40d0.

——. 2007f. "Minashi jikan wo iiharu ryokou kyoukai to sabisu sengou kumiai [Labor Standard Office and travel association insist on unreal working hours]." April 27. http://blog.goo.ne.jp/19681226_001/e/4feaccc1653884efc6934b64e28bb25f.

——. 2007g. "Tenjou in ni jinken wo [Human rights for tour conductors! 9.1 demonstration in Ueno Station]." April 18. http://blog.goo.ne.jp/19681226_001/e/5e8dd2e79 60a7e2ab4cf2524df1de40e.

———. 2007h. "Tsui ni lokkai demo toriagerareta tenjouin heno futou na 'minashi roudou jikansei' [Unreasonable 'unreal working hour system' for tour conductors discussed in the Diet]." October 31. http://blog.goo.ne.jp/19681226_001/e/3c43c8cc1 066f4a9847718b9e7d592bd.

———. 2008a. "Hankyu travel sapooto dai 14kai dantai koushyou houkoku [Hankyu Travel Support, fourteenth negotiation]." February 29. http://blog.goo.ne.jp/19681226 _001/e/9e128d9485fb99e0464de7e06ff2aef7.

———. 2008b. "Hankyu travel sapooto dai 17kai dantai koushyou houkoku & minashi futou no roudou shinpan/syuudan sosyou he [Hankyu Travel Support, seventeenth negotiation and labor tribunal and collective suits against unreal working hours.]" May 23. http://blog.goo.ne.jp/19681226_001/e/1fdb5516baa183e5717021c54e59d e35.

———. 2008c. "Kakki teki roudou shinpan kudaru! 'jigyou gai minashi roudou' no tekiyou ha mitomenai [Epoch-making labor tribunal: 'unreal working hour system' is not allowed]." July 19. http://blog.goo.ne.jp/19681226_001/e/d2e1ae6cb57471ecbffe1 0f54a0873c5.

———. 2010a. "HTS shibu 'gisou minashi roudou' saiban no kanzen syouri ni Hankyou [HTS Branch Union's victory on 'disguised unreal working' suit]." May 12. http://blog.goo.ne.jp/19681226_001/e/074916ee3679b2133a08417594a90d42.

———. 2010b. "Sokuhou: HTS shibu, 1/2 jin saiban hanketsu [Breaking news: HTS Branch Union, order of the first and second lawsuits]." September 29. http://blog.goo.ne .jp/19681226_001/e/7e7392ff0868619fe0b27f15356a4f11.

———. 2011. "'Gisou minashi roudou' zangyou dai seikyuu saiban nishin mo HTS shibu ni syouri hanketsu! [Lawsuits on 'unreal working' over unpaid overtime, HTS won at the second trial!]." September 15. http://blog.goo.ne.jp/19681226_001/e/ad93242e 93b899f7f96a265a0761d474.

———. 2014. "Sokuhou: 'gisou minashi roudou' zangyou dai seikyuu saiban nokori 2jiken mo saikousai de syouri! [Breaking news: 'Disguised work' lawsuits on unpaid overtime, the two other cases won at the Supreme Cour]." January 27. http://blog.goo .ne.jp/19681226_001/e/f9173ca0d13f17aa4fb2e7b7dedc8180.

———. 2018. "Tenjyouinno chyoujikan roudouwo onzon saseru futouhannketsu kyuudann [Opposition to the decision that worsens the long-working hours of travel workers]." November16. https://blog.goo.ne.jp/19681226_001/e/ea97bab1bae956 0d1f93c1eebce623dc.

OECD (2019), Real GDP forecast (indicator). doi: 10.1787/1f84150b-en (Accessed on 27 September 2019). http://www.nikkei.com/article/DGXZZO03556450S0A300C100 0000/.

Pollmann, Mina. 2015. "Agricultural Reforms in Japan Pave the Way for TPP." *Diplomat*, February 12. http://thediplomat.com/2015/02/agricultural-reforms-in-japan-pave -the-way-for-tpp/.

Project for My Work for 8 Hours. 2017. "'Watashitachino shigoto hachijikan projekuto syomei teisyutuno gohoukoku', syomeiteisyutuno gohoukoku [A report from Project for My Work for 8 Hours, submission of petition]." http://union.fem.jp/?p =346.

Rengo Souken. 2014. *Rengo Souken Report*, July–August, no. 295. https://www.rengo -soken.or.jp/dio/dio295.pdf.

Sasaki, Yukiko. 2017. "'Seisyain ha gonen hatarakeba seisyainnka' ha daigokai [Big Mistake: 'Nonregular workers can become regular workers']." *Toyo Keizai Online*. September 17. https://toyokeizai.net/articles/-/189202?page=2.

Sekine, Shuichiro. 2009. *Haken no gyakusyuu* [Counterattacks by temp workers]. Tokyo: Asahi Shinbun.

Social Democratic Party. 2014. April 1. http://www5.sdp.or.jp/comment/2014/04/01.

Syutoken Seinen Union. 2011. "Mitsubishi Fuso haken giri saiban no wakai seiritsu ni atatte no seimei [Declaration on resolution of dismissals of temp workers at Mitsubishi Fuso]." July 28. https://blog.goo.ne.jp/harumi-s_2005/e/31373c8d1ad629c 83d8a89f7956e6c68.

Tokyo Metropolitan Government Labor Relations Commission. 2017. "Overview of System to Remedy Unfair Labor Practices." http://www.toroui.metro.tokyo.jp/lang /en/futougaiyou.html.

Toyou Keizai Online. 2015. "'Haken hou kaisei ann' no ittai naniga mondai nanoka [What is the problem with the 'amendment bill of Worker Dispatch Law'?]." June 17. http://toyokeizai.net/articles/-/73553.

TV Asahi Yoron Chousa [TV Asahi Poll]. n.d. "Naikaku Siziritsu no Suii [Change in approval rates of cabinets]." http://www.tv-asahi.co.jp/hst/poll/graph_naikaku.html.

Josei Yunion Tokyo [Women's Union Tokyo]. N.d. "Kaiketsu jirei: Kaikowo kyouseisareta Y san no jirei [Solved Cases: In the Case of Miss Y, who was pressured to resign.]." Accessed 01/02/2017. http://w-union.org/jirei.html.*Yomiuri Shinbun*. 2012. "Kisokara wakaru nenin [Basic knowledge on pension: Dissolving overpayment]." December 21.

——. 2014a. "TPP hantai 2600nin kinkyuu shyuukai JA guruupu Miyazaki nichibei shyunou kaidan maeni [Opposition to TPP: 2,600 rally, JA Miyazaki before Japan-US conference]."<6>

——. 2014b. "Syouhizei 10% sakiokuri: minsyu nibun [Sales tax hike 10% postponed: DPJ divided]. December 6.

——. 2015a. "2015nen, kou kawaru, susumu koureika: kaikaku mejirooshi [How things will change in 2015: Accelerating aging population, numerous reforms]." January 11.

——. 2015c. "Kisokara wakaru makuro keizzai sulaido [Macroeconomic slide basics]. March 25.

——. 2015d. "Haken hou de kou kawaru [The amendment passed, how dispatch work will change, three points]." September 9.

——. 2015e. "Teisyotoku nenkinsya ni sanmanen: taisyou 1000mannin seifukyuufu he [30,000 yen for the low-income pensioners: State allowances for 10 million people]." November 25.

Zenkoku Hoken Dantai Rengou Kai. 2013. "14nen Shigatsu yori no syouhizei no souzei sisshi no syosyou hyoumeini kougi suru [Opposition to the prime minister's sales tax hike from April 2014]." October 1. http://hodanren.doc-net.or.jp/news/teigen /131001syouhizei.html.

SECONDARY SOURCES

Aglietta, Michel. 1998. "Capitalism at the Turn of the Century: Regulation Theory and the Challenge of Social Change." *New Left Review* 232 (November–December): 41–90.

Aglietta, Michel, and Antoine Rebérioux. 2006. "Corporate Governance Adrift: A Critique of Shareholder Value." *Journal of Economics* 88 (3): 307–11.

Aguilera, Ruth V., and Gregory Jackson. 2010. "Comparative and International Corporate Governance." *Academy of Management Annals* 4 (1): 485–556.

Ahmadjian, Christina L. 2012. "Corporate Governance Convergence in Japan." In *The Convergence of Corporate Governance: Promise and Prospects*, edited by Abdul Rasheed and Yoshikawa, Toru. 117–136. Basingstoke, UK: Palgrave MacMillan.

Amable, Bruno. 2003. *The Diversity of Modern Capitalism*. Oxford: Oxford University Press.

Anchordoguy, Marie. 2005. *Reprogramming Japan: The High Tech Crisis under Communitarian Capitalism.* Ithaca, NY: Cornell University Press.

Arrighi, Giovanni. 1994. *The Long Twentieth Century: Money, Power, and the Origins of Our Times.* London: Verso.

Baccaro, Lucio, and Chris Howell. 2011. "A Common Neoliberal Trajectory: The Transformation of Industrial Relations in Advanced Capitalism." *Politics and Society* 39 (4): 521–63.

Baccaro, Lucio, and Jonas Pontusson. 2016. "Rethinking Comparative Political Economy: The Growth Model Perspective." *Politics and Society* 44 (2): 175–207.

Bailey, David, and Saori Shibata. 2014. "Varieties of Contestation: The Comparative and Critical Political Economy of 'Excessive' Demand." *Capital and Class* 38 (1): 239–51.

——. 2017. "Austerity and Anti-Austerity: The Political Economy of Refusal in 'Low-Resistance' Models of Capitalism." *British Journal of Political Science* 49 (2): 683–709.

Bailey, David J., Monica Clua-Losada, Niko Huke, and Oltaz Ribera-Almandoz. 2018. *Beyond Defeat and Austerity: Disrupting (the Critical Political Economy of) Neoliberal Europe.* London: Routledge.

Bailey, David, and Roger Sugden. 2007. "*Kúdóka*, Restructuring and Possibilities for Industrial Policy in Japan." In *Crisis or Recovery in Japan: State and Industrial Economy*, edited by David Bailey, Dan Coffey, and Philip Tomlinson, 133–56. Cheltenham, UK: Edward Elgar.

Belfrage, Claes, and Magnus Ryner. 2009. "Renegotiating the Swedish Social Democratic Settlement: From Pension Fund Socialism to Neoliberalization." *Politics and Society* 37 (2): 257–88.

Bohle, Dorothee, and Béla Greskovits. 2009. "Varieties of Capitalism and Capitalism." *Archives européennes de sociologie* 3: 355–86.

Bonefeld, Werner, and John, Holloway. 1991. *Post-Fordism & Social Form: A Marxist Debate on the Post-Fordist State.* London: Palgrave.

Botman, Denis P., Stephan Danninger, and Jerald Schiff, eds. 2015. *Can Abenomics Succeed? Overcoming the Legacy of Japan's Lost Decades.* Washington: International Monetary Fund.

Boyer, Robert. 2018. "Marx's Legacy, *Régulation* Theory and Contemporary Capitalism." *Review of Political Economy* 30 (3): 284–316.

Boyer, Robert, and Yves Saillard. 2002. "A Summary of *Régulation* Theory." In *Régulation Theory: The State of the Art*, edited by Robert Boyer and Yves Saillard, 36–44. London: Routledge.

Boyer, Robert, Hiroyasu Uemura, and Akinori Isogai, eds. 2012a. *Diversity and Transformations of Asian Capitalism.* Oxford: Routledge.

——. 2012b. "Asia: a social laboratory of contemporary capitalisms?" In *Diversity and Transformations of Asian Capitalism*, edited by Robert Boyer, Hiroyasu Uemura, and Akira Isogai, 1–11. Oxford: Routledge.

Boyer, Robert, and Toshio Yamada. 2000. "Conclusion: An Epochal Change . . . but Uncertain Future." In *Japanese Capitalism in Crisis: A Regulationist Interpretation*, edited by Robert Boyer and Toshio Yamada, 192–214. New York: Routledge.

Brinton, Mary C. 2011. *Lost in Transition: Youth, Work, and Instability in Postindustrial Japan.* Cambridge: Cambridge University Press.

Bruff, Ian. 2011. "What about the Elephant in the Room? Varieties of Capitalism, Varieties in Capitalism." *New Political Economy* 16 (4): 481–500.

——. 2014. "The Rise of Authoritarian Neoliberalism." *Rethinking Marxism* 26 (1): 113–29.

Bruff, Ian, and Laura Horn. 2012. "Varieties of Capitalism in Crisis?" *Competition and Change* 16 (3): 161–68.

Buchanan, John, Dominic H.Chai, and Simon Deakin. 2018. "Unexpected Corporate Outcomes from Hedge Fund Activism in Japan." *Socio-Economic Review*. doi: 10.1093/ser/mwy007.

Burnham, Peter. 2001. "Marx, International Political Economy and Globalization." *Capital and Class* 25(3): 103–12.

———. 2006. "Marx, Neo-Gramscianism and Globalization." In *Global Restructuring, State, Capital and Labour: Contesting Neo-Gramscian Perspectives*, edited by Andreas Bieler, Werner Boneveld, Peter Burnham, and Adam David Morton, 187–94. Basingstoke, UK: Palgrave Macmillan.

Calder, Kent. E. 2003. "Japan as a Post- Reactive State?" *Orbis* 47(4), 605–616.

Cassegård, Carl. 2014. *Youth Movements, Trauma and Alternative Space in Contemporary Japan*. Leiden, the Netherlands: Global Oriental.

Chiavacci, David, and Carola Hommerich, eds. 2017. *Social Inequality in Post-Growth Japan: Transformation during Economic and Demographic Stagnation*. London: Routledge.

Choi, Byung-il, and Jennifer Sejin Oh. 2017. "Reversed Asymmetry in Japan's and Korea's FTAs: TPP and Beyond." *Pacific Focus* 32 (2): 232–58.

Clarke, Simon. 1988. *Keynesianism, Monetarism, and the Crisis of the State*. Aldershot, UK: Edward Elgar.

Cleaver, Harry. 1992. "The Inversion of Class Perspective in Marxian Theory: From Valorization to Self-Valorization." In *Open Marxism volume 2: theory and practice*, edited by Bonefeld, Werner, Richard Gunn, and Psychopedis, Kosmas. 106-144. London: Pluto.

Clift, Ben. 2014. *Comparative Political Economy: States, Markets and Global Capitalism*. Basingstoke, UK: Palgrave Macmillan.

Coates, David. 2005. "Paradigms of Explanation." In *Varieties of Capitalism and Varieties of Approaches*, edited by David Coates. London: Palgrave Macmillan.

Crouch, Colin. 2001. "Welfare Regimes and Industrial Relations System: The Questionable Role of Path Dependency Theory." In *Comparing Welfare Capitalism*, edited by Bernhard Ebbinghaus and Philip Manow. 105–124. London: Routledge.

Culpepper, Pepper D. 2011. *Quiet Politics and Business Power: Corporate Control in Europe and Japan*. Cambridge: Cambridge University Press.

Cumbers, Andy, Corinne Nativel, and Paul Routledge. 2008. "Labour Agency and Union Positionalities in Global Production Networks." *Journal of Economic Geography* 8 (3): 369–87.

Daniels, Gary, and John McIlroy, eds. 2009. *Trade Unions in a Neoliberal World: British Trade Unions under New Labour*. London: Routledge.

Davies, Matt, and Ryner, Magnus, eds. 2006. *Poverty and the Production of World Politics: Unprotected Workers in the Global Political Economy*. London: Palgrave Macmillan.

De Ville, Ferdi, and Jan Orbie. 2014. "The European Commission's Neoliberal Trade Discourse since the Crisis: Legitimizing Continuity through Subtle Discursive Change." *British Journal of Politics and International Relations* 16 (1): 149–67.

Dönmez, Pinar E. 2019. "Politicisation as Governing Strategy versus Resistance: Demystifying Capitalist Social Relations and the State in Turkey." In *Comparing Strategies of (De)Politicisation in Europe: Governance, Resistance and Anti-Politics*, edited by Jim Buller, Pinar E. Dönmez, Adam Standring, and Matt Wood, 155–88. Basingstoke, UK: Palgrave Macmillan.

Dore, Ronald. 2000. *Stock Market Capitalism: Welfare Capitalism: Japan and Germany versus the Anglo-Saxons*. Oxford: Oxford University Press.

Durand, Cédric, and Phillippe Légé. 2013. "Regulation beyond Growth." *Capital and Class* 37 (1): 111–26.

Engeman, Cassandra. 2015. "Social Movement Unionism in Practice: Organizational Dimensions of Union Mobilization in the Los Angeles Immigrant Rights Marches." *Work, Employment and Society* 29 (3): 444–61.

Estévez-Abe, Margarita. 2008. *Welfare and Capitalism in Postwar Japan*. New York: Cambridge University Press.

Flesher Fominaya, Cristina, and Laurence Cox, eds. 2013. *Understanding European Movements: New Social Movements, Global Justice Struggles, Anti-Austerity Protest*. London: Routledge.

Franzosi, Roberto. 2004. *From Words to Numbers: A Journey in the Methodology of Social Science*. Cambridge: Cambridge University Press.

——. 2009. *Quantitative Narrative Analysis*. London: Sage.

Friedman, David. 1988. *The Misunderstood Miracle: Industrial Development and Political Change in Japan*. Ithaca, NY: Cornell University Press.

Fu, Huiyan. 2012. *An Emerging Non-regular Labor Force in Japan: The Dignity of Dispatched Workers*. London: Routledge.

Fukui, Yusuke. 2005. "Nihon ni keru syakai undo teki rodo undo to shiteno comyunitii union: kyoeki to koeki no aida [Community unions as social movement–type labor movements in Japan: Between common benefit and public wealth]." *Journal of Ohara Institute for Social Research*. No. 562/563–63: 17–28.

Funabashi, Harutoshi. 2011. "The Duality of Social Systems and the Environmental Movement in Japan." In *East Asian Social Movements: Power, Protest, and Change in a Dynamic Region*, edited by Jeffrey Broadbent and Vicky Brockman. 37–62. New York: Springer.

Gerbaudo, Paolo. 2017. *The Mask and the Flag: Populism, Citizenism and Global Protest*. London: Hurst.

Gordon, Andrew. 1985. *The Evolution of Labor Relations in Japan: Heavy Industry, 1853–1955*. Massachusetts: Harvard University Asia Center.

Gotoh, Fumio, and Sinclair Timothy. 2017. "Social norms strike back: why American financial practices failed in Japan," *Review of International Political Economy* 24 (6). 1030–1051.

Goto, Michio. 2011. *Waakingu pua genron* [Theory on the working poor]. Tokyo: Kadensya.

Gumbrell-McCormick, Rebecca, and Richard Hyman. 2013. *Trade Unions in Western Europe: Hard Times, Hard Choices*. Oxford: Oxford University Press.

Guttmann, Robert. 2002. "Money and Credit in Regulation Theory." In *Regulation Theory: The State of the Art*, edited by Robert Boyer and Yves Saillard. 57–63. London: Routledge.

Hall, Peter A., and David Soskice. 2001. "An Introduction to Varieties of Capitalism." In *Varieties of Capitalism: The Institutional Foundations of Comparative Advantage*, edited by Peter A. Hall and David Soskice. Oxford: Oxford University Press.

Harrod, Jeffrey. 2006. "The Global Poor and Global Politics: Neomaterialism and the Sources of Political Action." In *Poverty and the Production of World Politics: Unprotected Workers in the Global Political Economy*, edited by Matt Davies and Magnus Ryner, 38–61. London: Palgrave Macmillan.

Harvey, David. 2006. *Limits to Capital*. London: Verso.

Hasegawa, Miki. 2006. *We Are Not Garbage! The Homeless Movement in Tokyo, 1994–2002*. London: Routledge.

Hatch, Walter F. 2010. *Asia's Flying Geese: How Regionalization Shapes Japan*. Ithaca, NY: Cornell University Press.

Hathaway, Terry. 2018. "Corporate Power beyond the Political Arena: The Case of the 'Big Three' and CAFE Standards." *Business and Politics* 20 (1): 1–37.

Hattori, Shigeyuki. 2014. *Abenomics no Syuen* [The end of Abenomics]. Tokyo: Iwanami Sinsyo.

——. 2017. *Itsuwari no keizai seisaku: Kakusa to teitaino Abenomics* [False economic policies: Abenomics of inequality and stagnation]. Tokyo: Iwanami Shinsyo.

Hayashi, Sharon, and Anne McKnight. 2005. "Good-Bye Kitty, Hello War: The Tactics of Spectacle and New Youth Movements in Urban Japan." *East Asia Cultures Critique* 13 (1): 87–113.

Henk, Vinken, Yuko Nishimura, Bruce L. J. White, and Masayuki Deguchi. 2010. "Introduction." In *Civic Engagement in Contemporary Japan: Established and Emerging Repertoires*, edited by Henk, Vinken, Yuko Nishimura, Bruce L. J. White, and Masayuki Deguchi. New York: Springer.

Herod, Andrew. 2011. "What Does the 2011 Japanese Tsunami Tell Us about the Nature of the Global Economy?" *Social and Cultural Geography* 12 (8): 829–37.

Hirakawa, Hitoshi, Nobuhiro Takahashi, Ferdinand.C. Maquito, and Norio Tokumaru. 2016. "Preface." In *Innovative ICT Industrial Architecture in East Asia*, edited by Hirakawa, Hitoshi, Nobuhiro Takahashi, Ferdinand, C. Maquito, and Norio Tokumaru. Tokyo: Springer Japan.

Hirano, Yasuo, and Toshio Yamada. 2018. "Multinationalization of Japanese Firms and Dysfunction of Companyist *Régulation*." In *Evolving Diversity and Interdependence of Capitalisms: Transformations of Regional Integration in EU and Asia*, edited by Robert Boyer, Hiroyasu Uemura, Toshio Yamada, and Lei Song. 431–458. Tokyo: Springer Japan.

Hofäker, Dirk, Heike Schröder, Yuxin Li, and Matthew Flynn. 2016. "Trends and Determinants of Work-Retirement Transitions under Changing Institutional Conditions: Germany, England and Japan Compared." *Journal of Social Policy* 45 (1): 39–64.

Hollard, Michel. 2002. "Forms of Competition." In *Regulation Theory: The State of the Art*, edited by Robert Boyer and Yves Saillard, 101–7. London: Routledge.

Holloway, John. 1987. "The Red Rose of Nissan." *Capital and Class* 32 (2): 142–64.

Hongo, Akashi. 2010. "Effects of Foreign Shareholders on Corporate Governance: Empirical Analysis of Executive Compensation and Stock Options." *Japanese Journal of Administrative Science* 23 (2): 93–106.

Honma, Masayoshi. 2015. "The TPP and Agricultural Reform in Japan." In *The Political Economy of Japanese Trade Policy*, edited by Aurelia George Mulgan and Masayoshi Honma, 94–122. London: Palgrave Macmillan.

Hope, David, and David Soskice. 2016. "Growth Models, Varieties of Capitalism, and Macroeconomics." *Politics and Society* 44 (2): 209–26.

Hoshi, Takeo, and Anil K. Kashyap. 2010. "Will the US Bank Recapitalization Succeed? Eight Lessons from Japan." *Journal of Financial Economics* 97 (3): 398–417.

Huke, Nikolai, David, J. Bailey, and Mònica Clua-Losada. 2015. "Disrupting the European Crisis: a Critical Political Economy of Contestation, Subversion and Escape." *New Political Economy* 20(5): 725–51.

Ibsen, Christian Lyhne, and Maite Tapia. 2017. "Trade Union Revitalisation: Where Are We Now? Where to Next?" *Journal of Industrial Relations* 59 (2): 170–91.

Ikeler, Peter. 2018. "Precarity's Prospect: Contingent Control and Union Renewal in the Retail Sector." *Critical Sociology* 45 (4–5): 501–16.

Imai, Jun. 2011. *Transformation of Japanese Employment Relations: Reform without Labour*. Basingstoke, UK: Palgrave Macmillan.

——. 2017. "Are Labour Union Movements Capable of Solving the Problems of the 'Gap Society'?" In *Social Inequality in Post-Growth Japan: Transformation during Eco-*

nomic and Demographic Stagnation, edited by David Chiavacci and Carola Hommerich. 89–104. London: Routledge.

Inglehart, Ronald. F. 1997. *Modernization and Postmodernization: Cultural, Economic, and Political Change in 43 Countries*. Princeton, NJ: Princeton University Press.

Isogai, Akinori, Akira Ebizuka, and Hiroyasu Uemura. 2000. "The Hierarchical Market-Firm Nexus as the Japanese Mode of Regulation." In *Japanese Capitalism in Crisis: A Regulationist Interpretation*, edited by Robert Boyer and Toshio Yamada, 32–53. New York: Routledge.

Jackson, Ben. 2016. "Neoliberalism, Labour and Trade Unionism." In *The Handbook of Neoliberalism*, edited by Simon Springer, Kean Birch, and Julie MacLeavy. 262–270. London: Routledge.

Jeong, Dae Yong, and Ruth V. Aguilera. 2008. "The Evolution of Enterprise Unionism in Japan: Socio-Political Perspective," *British Journal of Industrial Relations*, 46 (1). 98–132.

Jaffee, David. 2018. "Disarticulation and the Crisis of Neoliberalism in the United States," *Critical Sociology*, doi: 10.1177/0896920518798122.

Jessop, Bob, and Ngai-Ling Sum. 2006. *Beyond the Regulation Approach: Putting Capitalist Economies in Their Place*. Cheltenham, UK: Edward Elgar.

Jihye Chun, Jennifer, and Rina Agarwala. 2015. "Global Labor Politics in Informal and Precarious Jobs." In *The Sage Handbook of the Sociology of Work and Employment*, edited by Stephen Edgell, Heid Gottfried, and Edward Granter, 634–50. London: Sage.

Johnson, Chalmers. 1982. *MITI and the Japanese Miracle: The Growth of Industrial Policy, 1925–1975*. Stanford, CA: Stanford University Press.

Johnston, Paul. 1994. *Success while others fail: Social movement unionism and the public workplace*. New York: Cornell University Press.

Juego, Bonno. 2011. "Wither Regulationism: Reflection on the Regulation Approach." *Interdisciplinary Journal of International Studies* 7 (1): 55–66.

Kalleberg, Arne. L., and Kevin Hewison. 2015. "Confronting Precarious Work in Asia: Politics and Policies." In *Policy Responses to Precarious Work in Asia*, edited by Hsiao, Hsin-Huang Michael, Arne L. Kalleberg, and Kevin Hewison. Taipei, Taiwan: Academia Sinica.

Kang, Myung-koo. 2010. "Is Japan Facing a Public Debt Crisis? Debt Financing and the Development of the JGB Market." *Asian Politics and Policy* 2 (4): 557–82.

Katz, Richard. 2003. *Japanese Phoenix: The Long Road to Economic Revival*. New York: M. E. Sharpe.

Kazama, Naoki. 2007. *Koyo Yukai: Korega Atarashi* [Dissolution of employment: Is this the new 'Japanese-Style Employment'?]. Tokyo: Toyo Keizai Shinpo Sya.

Keizer, Arjan B. 2019. "Inclusion of 'Outsiders' by Japanese Unions? The Organizing of Non-Regular Workers in Retail." *Work, Employment and Society* 33 (2): 226–43.

Kiersey, Nicholas J. 2009. "Neoliberal Political Economy and the Subjectivity of Crisis: Why Governmentality Is Not Hollow." *Global Society* 23 (4): 363–86.

Kinoshita, Takeo. 2007. *Kakusa syakai ni idomu yunion: Nijyu isseiki rodo undo genron* [Unions that challenge unequal society: Labor movement theory in the twenty-first century]. Tokyo: Kadensya.

Koopmans, Ruud, and Paul Statham, eds. 2012. *The Making of a European Public Sphere: Media Discourse and Political Contention*. Cambridge: Cambridge University Press.

Koopmans, Ruud, Paul Statham, Marco Giugni, and Florence Passy. 2005. *Contested Citizenship: Immigration and Cultural Diversity in Europe*. Minneapolis: University of Minnesota Press.

Kriesi, Hanspeter, Ruud Koopmans, Jan W. Duyvendak, and Marco G. Giugni, 1995. *New Social Movements in Western Europe: A Comparative Analysis*. New York: Routledge.

Laraña, Enrique, Hank Johnston, and Joseph R. Gusfield. 1994. *New Social Movements: From Ideology to Identity*. Philadelphia: Temple University Press.

Lebowitz, Michael A. 2003. *Beyond Capital: Marx's Political Economy of the Working Class*. Basingstoke, UK: Palgrave Macmillan.

Lechevalier, Sébastien. 2014a. "Conclusion: Capitalisms and Neo-Liberalism—Lessons from Japan." In *The Great Transformation of Japanese Capitalism*, edited by Sébastien Lechevalier and translated by Stockwin, James. A. A. 157–61. London: Routledge.

——, ed. 2014b. *The Great Transformation of Japanese Capitalism*. Translated by Stockwin, James. A. A. London: Routledge.

——. 2014c. "Is Japanese Capitalism Still Co-Ordinated?" In *The Great Transformation of Japanese Capitalism*, edited by Sébastien Lechevalier and translated by Stockwin, James. A. A. 73–84. London: Routledge.

——. 2014d. "Is This the End of the J-Model of the Firm?" In *The Great Transformation of Japanese Capitalism*, edited by Sébastien Lechevalier and translated by Stockwin, James. A. A. 56–72. London: Routledge.

——. 2014e. "What Is the Nature of the Japanese Social Compromise Today?" In *The Great Transformation of Japanese Capitalism*, edited by Sébastien Lechevalier and translated by James, A. A. Stockwin. 85–105. London: Routledge.

MacDonald, Ian Thomas. 2014. "Towards Neoliberal Trade Unionism: Decline, Renewal and Transformation in North American Labour Movements." *British Journal of Industrial Relations* 52 (4): 725–52.

Mathers, Andy, Martin Upchurch, and Graham Taylor. 2018. "Social Movement Theory and Trade Union Organising." In *Social Movements and Organized Labour: Passions and Interests*, edited by Jürgen R. Grote and Claudius Wagemann, 22–42. London: Routledge.

Miura, Mari. 2008. "Labour Politics in Japan during 'the Lost Fifteen Years': From the Politics of Productivity to the Politics of Consumption." *Labour History* 49 (2): 161–76.

——. 2012. *Welfare through Work: Conservative Ideas, Partisan Dynamics, and Social Protection in Japan*. New York: Cornell University Press.

Moody, Kim. 2017. *On New Terrain: How Capital Is Reshaping the Battleground of Class War*. Chicago: Haymarket.

Moore, Phoebe V. 2018. "E(a)ffective Control and Resistance in the Digitalised Workplace." In *Austerity and Working-Class Resistance: Survival, Disruption and Creation in Hard Times*, edited by Adam Fishwick and Heather Connolly, 181–200. London: Rowman and Littlefield International.

Mōri, Yoshitaka. 2005. "Culture = Politics: The Emergence of New Cultural Forms of Protest in the Age of Freeter." *Inter-Asia Cultural Studies* 6 (1): 17–29.

Mouer, Ross, and Hirosuke Kawanishi. 2005. *A Sociology of Work in Japan*. Cambridge: Cambridge University Press.

Mulgan, Aurelia George. 2015a. "Understanding Japanese Trade Policy: A Political Economy Perspective." In *The Political Economy of Japanese Trade Policy*, edited by Aurelia George Mulgan and Masayoshi Honma, 1–40. London: Palgrave Macmillan.

——. 2015b. "To TPP or Not TPP: Interest Groups and Trade Policy." In *The Political Economy of Japanese Trade Policy*, edited by Aurelia George Mulgan and Masayoshi Honma, 123–156. London: Palgrave Macmillan.

Munck, Ronaldo. 2018. *Rethinking Global Labour: After Neoliberalism*. Newcastle upon Tyne (UK): Agenda Publishing.

Myung, Taesook. 2013. "Nihon kigyouno seikasyugi jinjiseido no genjyou to kadai [The Current Status and Challenges of Japanese Performance Wage System]." Sankenronshu 44/45 (2013.3).

Nabeshima, Naoki. 2000. "The Financial Mode of *Régulation* in Japan and Its Demise." In *Japanese Capitalism in Crisis: A Regulationist Interpretation*, edited by Robert Boyer and Toshio Yamada, 104–16. New York: Routledge.

Nadel, Henri. 2002. "Regulation and Marx." In *Régulation Theory: The State of the Art*, edited by Robert Boyer and Yves Saillard, 28–35. London: Routledge.

Nakashima, Tetsuo. "Seikasyugiha Nihonno Chinginseido wo Kaetaka [Whether Performance Wage System Has Changed the Japanese Wage System]." Tsusetu wo Kenshousuru. *Nihon Roudou Kenkyuu Zasshi*. No. 573. April 2008.

Narisada, Yoko. 2010. "Negotiating Gender Equality in Daily Work: An Ethnography of a Public Women's Organisation in Okinawa, Japan." PhD diss., University of Edinburgh. https://www.era.lib.ed.ac.uk/bitstream/handle/1842/15829/Narisada2011.pdf.

Naruse, Takeo. 2014. "Koyou porto folio teigen to korekara no koyou mondai [Employment portfolio suggestion and future employment problem]." *Rengou Souken Report*, no. 295 (July–August): 5–8.

Neilson, David. 2012. "Remaking the Connections: Marxism and the French Regulation School." *Review of Radical Political Economics* 44 (2): 161–77.

Ninomiya, Atsumi. 2012. *Sin jiyu syugi karano dassyutu: Guloobal ka no naka no shin jiyuusyugi vs. shin fukusi kokka* [Escape from neoliberalism: Neoliberalism vs. the new welfare state]. Tokyo: Shin Nihon Syuppan Sya.

——. 2017. *Syukatuki no Abe seiken: Post-Abe seiji he no preryudo* [End of life of the Abe administration: Prelude to post-Abe politics]. Tokyo: Sinnihon Syuppansya.

Obashi, Ayako, and Fukunari Kimura. 2016. "The Role of China, Japan, and Korea in Machinery Production Networks." ERIA Discussion Paper Series ERIA-DP-2016-10 http://www.eria.org/ERIA-DP-2016-10.pdf.

Nishinarita, Yutaka. 1998. "Japanese-style industrial relations in historical perspective." In *Japanese business management: Restructuring for low growth and globalization*, edited by Hasegawa Harukiyo and Glenn D. Hook. 195–216. London: Routledge.

Odaka, Konosuke. 1999. "'Japanese-Style' Labour Relations." In *The Japanese Economic System and Its Historical Origins*, edited by Tetsuji Okazaki and Masahiro Okuno-Fujiwara. 135–155. Oxford: Clarendon Press of Oxford University Press.

Ōhki, Kazunori. 1998. New trends in enterprise unions and the labour movement. In *Japanese business management: restructuring for low growth and globalization*, edited by Hasegawa, Harukiyo and Hook, Glenn. D. London: Routledge.

Oliver, Pamela E., and Gregory M. Maney. 2000. "Political Processes and Local Newspaper Coverage of Protest Events: From Selection Bias to Triadic Interactions." *American Journal of Sociology* 106 (2): 463–505.

Park, Gene, and Eisaku Ide. 2014. "The Tax-Welfare Mix: Explaining Japan's Weak Extractive Capacity." *Pacific Review* 27 (5): 675–702.

Preminger, Jonathan. 2018. *Labor in Israel: Beyond Nationalism and Neoliberalism*. Ithaca, NY: Cornell University Press.

Rebick, Marcus. 2005. *The Changing Japanese Employment System*. Oxford: Oxford University Press.

Reed, Steven R., Kenneth Mori McElwain, and Kay Shimizu. 2011. *Political Change in Japan: Electoral Behaviour, Party Realignment, and the Koizumi Reforms*. Wellington, New Zealand: Asia Pacific Research Institute.

Rosenbluth, Frances McCall, and Michael F. Thies. 2010. *Japan Transformed: Political Change and Economic Restructuring*. Princeton, NJ: Princeton University Press.

Sako, Mari. 2006. *Shifting Boundaries of the Firm: Japanese Company—Japanese Labour.* Oxford: Oxford University Press.

Schaede, Ulrike. 2007. "Globalization and the Japanese Subcontractor System." In *Crisis or Recovery in Japan: State and Industrial Economy*, edited by David Bailey, Dan Coffey, and Philip Tomlinson, 82–105. Cheltenham, UK: Edward Elgar.

Schaede, Ulrike, and William W. Grimes. 2003. "Introduction: The Emergence of Permeable Insulation." In *Japan's Managed Globalization: Adapting to the Twenty-First Century*, edited by Ulrike Shaede and William W. Grimes, 3–16. New York: M. E. Sharpe.

Schoppa, Leonard. J. 2011. *The Evolution of Japan's Party System: Politics and Policy in an Era of Institutional Change.* Toronto: University of Toronto Press.

Shaikh, Anwar. 2016. *Capitalism: Competition, Conflict, Crises.* Oxford: Oxford University Press.

Shibata, Saori. 2016. "Resisting Japan's Neoliberal Model of Capitalism: Intensification and Change in Contemporary Patterns of Class Struggle." *British Journal of Industrial Relations* 54 (3): 496–521.

——. 2017. "Re-Packaging Old Policies? 'Abenomics' and the Lack of an Alternative Growth Model for Japan's Political Economy." *Japan Forum* 29 (3): 399–422.

Shinoda, Toru. 2008. "The Return of Japanese Labor? The Mainstreaming of the Labor Question in Japanese Politics." *Labor History* 49 (2): 145–59.

Silver, Beverly J. 2003. *Forces of Labor: Workers' Movements and Globalization since 1870.* Cambridge: Cambridge University Press.

Song, Jiyeoun. 2014. *Inequality in the Workplace: Labour Market Reform in Japan and Korea.* New York: Cornell University Press.

Standing, Guy. 2011. *The Precariat: The New Dangerous Class.* London: Bloomsbury. http://pubman.mpdl.mpg.de/pubman/item/escidoc:2117030/component/escidoc:2123448/JP_12_2014_Bayram.pdf.

Streeck, Wolfgang. 2009. *Reforming Capitalism: Institutional Change in the German Political Economy.* Oxford: Oxford University Press.

Suzuki, Akira. 2008. "Community Unions in Japan: Similarities and Differences of Region-Based Labour Movements between Japan and Other Industrialized Countries." *Economic and Industrial Democracy* 29 (4): 492–520.

Suzuki, Munenori, Midori Ito, Mitsunori Ishida, Norihiro Nihei, and Masao Maruyama. 2010. "Individualizing Japan: Searching for Its Origin in First Modernity." *British Journal of Sociology* 61 (3): 513–38.

Tabata, Hirokuni. 1997. "Industrial Relations and the union Movement." In *The Political Economy of Japanese Society, Volume 1: The State or the Market?*, edited by Banno, Junji. New York: Oxford University Press.

Tachibanaki, Toshiaki. 2006. "Inequality and Poverty in Japan." *Japanese Economic Review* 57 (1): 1–27.

Takahashi, Toshiyuki. 2006. "Takedano seikasyugi to sono kadai [Performance-based pay system at Takeda Pharmaceutical and its challenge]." *Nihon Roudou Kenkyuu Zasshi* [Japan Labor Research Journal], no. 554. https://www.jil.go.jp/institute/zassi/backnumber/2006/09/pdf/084-093.pdf.

Tansel, Cemel Burak. 2018. "Authoritarian Neoliberalism and Democratic Backsliding in Turkey: Beyond the Narratives of Progress." *South European Society and Politics* 23 (2): 197–217.

Tarrow, Sidney. 2010. "Dynamics of Diffusion: Mechanisms, Institutions, and Scale Shift." In *The Diffusion of Social Movements: Actors, Mechanisms, and Political Effects*, edited by Rebecca Kolins Givan, Sarah. A. Soule, and Kenneth M. Roberts, 204–20. Cambridge: Cambridge University Press.

Tejerina, Benjamin, Ignacia Perugorría, Tova Benski, and Lauren Langman. 2013. "From Indignation to Occupation: A New Wave of Global Mobilization." *Current Sociology* 61 (4): 377–92.

Thelen, Kathleen, and Ikuo Kume. 2003. "The Rise of Nonliberal Training Regimes: Germany and Japan Compared." In *The Origins of Nonliberal Capitalism*, edited by Wolfgang Streeck and Kozo Yamamura, 200–28. Ithaca, NY: Cornell University Press.

Thelen, Kathleen, and Ikuo Kume. 2006. "Coordination as a Political Problem in Coordinated Market Economies." *Governance* 19 (1): 11–42.

Tohyama, Hironori. 2000. "The capital-labour compromise and the financial system: a changing hierarchy" In *Japanese Capitalism in Crisis: A Regulationist Interpretation*, edited by Robert Boyer and Toshio Yamada, 73–86. London: Routledge.

Tronti, Mario. 1964. "Lenin in England," *Class Operaia*, Issue no.1.

Ueda, Kazuo. 2013. "Response of Asset Prices to Monetary Policy under Abenomics." *Asian Economic Policy Review* 8 (2): 252–69.

Uemura, Hiroyasu. 2000. "Growth, Distribution and Structural Change in the Post-War Japanese Economy." In *Japanese Capitalism in Crisis: A Regulationist Interpretation*, edited by Robert Boyer and Toshio Yamada, 138–61. New York: Routledge.

Uni, Hiroyuki. 2000. "Disproportionate Productivity Growth and Accumulation Regimes." In *Japanese Capitalism in Crisis: A Regulationist Interpretation*, edited by Robert Boyer and Toshio Yamada, 54–70. New York: Routledge.

UNICEF Innocenti Research Centre. 2012. "Measuring Child Poverty: New League Tables of Child Poverty in the World's Rich Countries." *Report Card 10*. Florence, Italy: UNICEF.

Upchurch, Martin, Graham Taylor, and Andrew Mathers. 2009. *The Crisis of Social Democratic Trade Unionism in Western Europe: The Search for Alternatives*. Surrey, UK: Ashgate.

Van Bas, Heur. 2010. "Beyond Regulation: Towards a Cultural Political Economy of Complexity and Emergence." *New Political Economy* 15 (3): 421–44.

Vidal, Matt. 2012. "On the Persistence of Labour Market Insecurity and Slow Growth in the US: Reckoning with the Waltonist Growth Regime." *New Political Economy* 17 (5): 534–64.

Vogel, Steven K. 2006. *Japan Remodeled: How Government and Industry Are Reforming Japanese Capitalism*. Ithaca, NY: Cornell University Press.

Vosko, Leah. F. 2010. *Managing the Margins: Gender, Citizenship and the International Regulation of Precarious Employment*. Oxford: Oxford University Press.

Walter, Andrew. 2005. "From Developmental to Regulatory State? Japan's New Financial Regulatory System." *Pacific Review* 19 (4): 405–28.

Watanabe, Richard Hiroaki. 2012. "Why and How Did Japan Finally Change Its Ways? The Politics of Japanese Labour-Market Deregulation since the 1990s." *Japan Forum* 24 (1): 23–50.

——. 2014. *Labor market deregulation in Japan and Italy: Worker protection under neoliberal globalization*. London, Routledge.

——. 2015. "The Struggle for Revitalisation by Japanese Labour Unions: Worker Organising after Labour-Market Deregulation." *Journal of Contemporary Asia* 45 (3): 510–30.

——. 2018. "Labour Market Dualism and Diversification in Japan." *British Journal of Industrial Relations*. 56(3): 579–602.

Waterman, Peter. 1993. "Social-Movement Unionism: A New Union Model for a New World Order?" *Review (Fernand Braudel Center)* 16 (3): 245–78.

Watson, Matthew. 2018. *The Market*. New York: Columbia University Press. Weathers, Charles. 2008. "Shuntō and the Shackles of Competitiveness." *Labor History* 49 (2): 177–97.

———. 2010. "The Rising Voice of Japan's Community Unions." In *Civic Engagement in Contemporary Japan: Established and Emerging Repertoires*, edited by Henk Vinken, Yuko.

Nishimura, Bruce L. J. White, and Masayuki Deguchi, 67–83. New York: Springer.

Witt, Michael A., Luiz Ricardo Kabbach de Castro, Kenneth Amaeshi, Sami Mahroum, Dorothee Bohle, and Lawrence Saez. 2018. "Mapping the Business Systems of 61 Major Economies: A Taxonomy and Implications for Varieties of Capitalism and Business Systems Research." *Socio-Economic Review* 16 (1): 5–38.

Witt, Michael A., and Gordon Redding. 2009. "Culture, Meaning, and Institutions: Executive Rationale in Germany and Japan." *Journal of International Business Studies* 40 (5): 859–85.

Woodcock, Jamie. 2017. *Working the Phones: Control and Resistance in the Call Centres.* London: Pluto.

Wright, Steve. 2002. *Storming Heaven: Class Composition and Struggle in Italian Autonomist Marxism.* London: Pluto.

Yamada, Toshio, and Yasuo Hirano. 2012. "How has the Japanese mode of *régulation* changed?" In *Diversity and Transformation of Asian Capitalisms*, edited by Boyer, Robert, Hiroyasu Uemura, and Akinori Isogai. Oxon: Routledge.

———. 2015. "Multinationalization of Japanese Firms and Dysfunction of Companyist Régulation." Paper presented at the Theory of Régulation in Times of Crisis International Conference, Paris, June 9–12.

Yamashita, Kazuhito. 2015. "The Political Economy of Japanese Agricultural Trade Negotiations." In *The Political Economy of Japanese Trade Policy*, edited by Aurelia George Mulgan and Masayoshi Honma, 71–93. London: Palgrave Macmillan.

Yun, Ji-Whan. 2010. "Unequal Japan: Conservative Corporatism and Labour Market." *British Journal of Industrial Relations* 48 (1): 1–25.

Yun, Ji-Whan. 2016. "The Setback in Political Entrepreneurship and Employment Dualization in Japan, 1998–2012." *British Journal of Industrial Relations* 54 (3): 473–95.

Zacharias-Walsh, Anne. 2016. *Our Unions, Our Selves: The Rise of Feminist Labor Unions in Japan.* Ithaca: Cornell University Press.

Index

Page references in italics indicate a table.

www.ingramcontent.com/pod-product-compliance
Lightning Source LLC
Chambersburg PA
CBHW031136270326
41929CB00011B/1645